Jazz Matters

Jazz Matters

SOUND, PLACE, AND TIME SINCE BEBOP

David Ake

UNIVERSITY OF CALIFORNIA PRESS

BERKELEY   LOS ANGELES   LONDON

The publisher gratefully acknowledges the generous
contribution to this book provided by the University of
Nevada, Reno.

University of California Press, one of the most distinguished
university presses in the United States, enriches lives around
the world by advancing scholarship in the humanities, social
sciences, and natural sciences. Its activities are supported
by the UC Press Foundation and by philanthropic
contributions from individuals and institutions.
For more information, visit www.ucpress.edu.

University of California Press
Berkeley and Los Angeles, California

University of California Press, Ltd.
London, England

Library of Congress Cataloging-in-Publication Data

Ake, David Andrew, 1961–.
    Jazz matters : sound, place, and time since bebop / David
Ake.
        p.   cm.
    Includes bibliographical references and index.
    ISBN 978-0-520-26688-9 (cloth : alk. paper)
    ISBN 978-0-520-26689-6 (pbk. : alk. paper)
    1. Jazz — History and criticism.   2. Jazz — Social
aspects.   I. Title.
    ML3506.A444   2010
    781.65'5—dc22

                                        2010008919

Manufactured in the United States of America

19   18   17   16   15   14   13   12   11   10
10   9   8   7   6   5   4   3   2   1

This book is printed on Cascades Enviro 100, a 100% post
consumer waste, recycled, de-inked fiber. FSC recycled
certified and processed chlorine free. It is acid free, Ecologo
certified, and manufactured by BioGas energy.

IN MEMORY OF HILLARY CASE

CONTENTS

ILLUSTRATIONS

INTRODUCTION

IN A STUDY ON THE FUNCTIONS of literature and literary criticism, Milan Kundera wrote, "As a novelist, I have always felt myself to be within history, that is to say, partway along a road, in dialogue with those who preceded me and even perhaps (but less so) with those still to come."[1] Kundera was describing his own sense of belonging and purpose, but he also unintentionally provided a spot-on summary of the scholar's life and, in doing so, gave me a handy way of characterizing my goals with this book. More than other nonfiction authors, the scholar moves between past and present, responding to those who have come before—building on, or spinning off, or challenging a predecessor's point—always with an awareness of and gesture toward subsequent scholars.

Yet while I identify with Kundera's historical awareness, I also recognize that what matters to him as a novelist and what matters to me as a scholar could not differ more. Kundera claims, "Of course, I am speaking of the history of the novel, not of some other history . . . because the history of humanity and the history of the novel are two very different things."[2] In Kundera's view artists create by working on and through the technical problems and aesthetic precepts handed down by their forebears. My scholarly response is, well, yes and no. One can readily trace the joys, anxieties, and other markers of one artist's influence on another and acknowledge that works are, to some extent, "born within the history of their art and

I

as *participants* in that history," as Kundera asserts.[3] But the fact remains that all artists live within the "history of humanity," as do their audiences, contemporary and future. And as Howard Becker showed so convincingly in his indispensable book, *Art Worlds,* this in-the-world reality unavoidably shapes what those artists create, as well as how their creations will be understood, evaluated, and put to use by others (including other artists who imagine themselves as working outside of that larger history).[4]

There is no real danger in Kundera's position. If visualizing himself thusly helps him to write his novels, more power to him. And given that he has lived as an expatriate in France for more than thirty years after coming of age in a Czech homeland occupied first by the Nazis and then by the Soviets, who can blame him for taking refuge within a transhistorical, transcultural community of seemingly like-minded individuals? But the conscientious scholar today does not have the luxury, if one wants to call it that, of such a viewpoint. It suits the jazz scholar least of all. Jazz music is almost never produced by a lone artist sequestered, hermitlike, from the public. For the most part, groups of people make jazz, usually in front of other people who show their appreciation (or not) right on the spot. Those seeking to understand this music's past and present, and also to ponder its possible futures, must take these intersections and relationships into account. The musicologist's job, then, is to locate and examine the history of music *within* the history of humanity, and vice versa. And what I aim to show in this book is how the actions, interactions, and interests of a wide range of participants—musicians, naturally, but also journalists, scholars, listeners, teachers, record company executives, politicians, recording engineers, and others—result in an ongoing process of reclaiming and reshaping the practices and values of the art form called jazz.

As I have suggested, I am not alone in this venture. This study represents just one addition to a rapidly growing list of publications that address jazz and its people. The recent upswing of jazz research marks a striking shift from only two decades ago, when few scholars were confident enough to risk their academic careers on this music and, not coincidentally, few academic publishers encouraged authors to write on it. What does it mean that more and more graduate students and faculty members devote their time and energy to producing conference papers, articles, dissertations, and book-length manuscripts about jazz? Or that every year university presses commit significant resources in an increasingly cost-conscious market toward transforming those manuscripts into books? What does it mean that the issues raised and confronted by these studies resonate beyond college classrooms, as scholars find their names and ideas cited on the pages of major newspapers, Web sites, and other mass media? What does all this mean? It means, of course, that jazz matters.

Such a vibrant collective scholarly effort can only be in motion because the diverse activities that occur under the jazz umbrella remain so compelling to so many people. True, few major jazz record labels remain. True, jazz receives minimal coverage on traditional radio and television stations. True, jazz-only performance spaces are not as plentiful as they once were. But as the saxophonist Joshua Redman noted in 2006, "One of the problems with how people view jazz today is that people are still trying to view today's jazz through the same lens that viewed an earlier time in jazz history."[5] And if we broaden our perspective to look at what is available and happening now, we can recognize that jazz people currently enjoy an enormous range of venues, media outlets, funding sources, and educational programs to accommodate and assist an unprecedented number of inventive performers and composers. In fact, it would not be off base to suggest that historians and fans will someday regard the early twenty-first century as one of the music's golden ages.

THIS IS OUR MUSIC (OR NOT)

Ornette Coleman recently opined, "The word *jazz* basically is a freedom of expression that has no prejudice for race, creed, color, which is very healthy."[6] Although Coleman's belief in an all-embracing jazz *esprit de corps* does indeed seem healthy (or at least generous), it strikes me as somewhat facile, for it does not acknowledge or account for the multiplicity of understandings that continually float around and bump into one another. Whether or not we want to admit it, the jazz world is not now, nor was it ever, an artistic or social utopia. Like all music (and every other human activity), jazz always relates to individual and cultural senses of "you" or "them" as much as it helps to express and celebrate notions of "me" or "us." Indeed, one reason that jazz continues to fascinate and to make for such a rich area of study is that it so often serves as a crowded, even contentious, forum for what are widely called issues of *identity*.

Take the matter of race. As Coleman's quote intimates, jazz is played (and played well) by people from widely diverse places and backgrounds. Even so, because many of jazz's most influential and well-known performers have been African Americans, racial identity often factors into how people will understand and appraise the music. Accordingly, the dozens of world-renowned African American jazz musicians, from Louis Armstrong, Duke Ellington, and Nat Cole, through Ella Fitzgerald, John Lewis, Max Roach, Miles Davis, and Wynton Marsalis, have played significant roles in shaping how people understand blackness (and so also how those people understand whiteness, Asian-ness, Latin-ness, and so on) in this country and beyond. The ways in which jazz has influenced and been influenced by gender, sexuality, class, nationality, and other identity markers are sometimes less apparent. But they are all there as well, in manners and circumstances large and small, reflecting and affecting our everyday thoughts and actions. One could go so far as to say that such markers make us who we are, though rarely in any stable or quantifiable way. Among my aims in *Jazz Matters* is to show how these notions have worked in and on various jazz communities.

Big-ticket identity politics are not my only concern, however. For instance, I also explore in various ways the topic of cultural hierarchy. Specifically, I address the fact that some people view jazz as inherently superior to other music genres, a stance manifested most often through a variation of the "America's classical music" premise. There are very compelling reasons why jazz aficionados would latch on to a European-style classical narrative, especially in the early and middle decades of the twentieth century. Race enters here once again, for, given the considerable presence in and contributions to jazz by black Americans during a period of Jim Crow segregation and other atrocities, such a stance made sense in order to gain overdue respect, attention, and economic rewards. Still, it is time to ask whether the elevating rhetoric is warranted anymore, particularly among scholars. Despite the racism that continues to haunt the United States, jazz has established an irrevocable presence in this country as what the National Endowment for the Arts (NEA) calls a "benchmark arts activity." Witness the recent NEA awards, MacArthur Fellowships, Doris Duke Foundation grants, Pulitzer Prizes, and other accolades bestowed on jazz musicians. Or consider that Scott DeVeaux's 1991 declaration, "The goals of the [jazz] neoclassicists will have been admirably fulfilled if and when busts of Armstrong and Parker stand alongside busts of Beethoven and Bach in practice rooms and music studios across America," has come to pass throughout much of the nation.[7] I am not suggesting that we need a "color-blind" or otherwise "unmarked" jazz discourse. I mean, simply, that celebrating the creators, or raising public awareness, or seeking to improve the economic viability of one genre (in this case, jazz) need not come at the expense of another.

Truth be told, pushing the high-art dogma may actually be counter-productive at this point. While the "classical" moniker has helped generate greater capital, both symbolic and real, for a number of jazz people (including scholar-performers such as myself), it has also estranged a segment of the public that wants something more from its music than to feel edified. Jazz can be immensely powerful in many ways, but when it takes itself too seriously, it can be a bore. One commentator employed the useful phrase "esthetic name-dropping" to describe the practice of musicians or business interests associated with one genre attempting to "piggyback" on the achievements of those from a genre perceived to be higher than their own. This is just what jazz people do when they embrace the classical label. (Of course, there is no shortage of irony in the fact that it was Wynton Marsalis who coined "esthetic name-dropping" to disparage those performers and producers from the world of pop music who piggyback on jazz's supposed sophistication in the very same article that he plugged his newly minted Classical Jazz series at Lincoln Center.)[8] Besides, conferring art-music status on the entirety of jazz is simply not accurate. Some jazz idioms do aspire to the grand and noble, but some do not, and this is not a qualitative assessment of either variety. Musicologists and everyone else should recognize these distinctions.

Put another way, although Bach, Beethoven, and Brahms produced some great music, their greatness is only different from, not better than, that of the many incredible jazz musicians of the past century. But by that same token, jazz is not intrinsically better than any other genre, and that includes country, disco, hip-hop, polka, or other supposedly lowbrow styles. Consider a couple of points. First, one has to admit that there is a lot of bad jazz in the world. I'm not referring only to the stuff that's poorly played or conceived, though there is plenty of that, even from some of the music's biggest names. (Check Bud Powell's 1963 recording of "Like Someone in Love." Ouch.)[9] Just as regrettable are the countless rote performances churned out by entirely competent professionals (including, once again, myself on far too many occasions over the years). Audience members who are unlucky enough to experience their first jazz through yet another warm-toned guitar rendition of "The Shadow of Your Smile," or pseudosultry vocalist's take on "Lover Man," or a purportedly hip, odd-meter reworking of "Cherokee" may rightly wonder what all the jazz-greatness fuss is about. The banality of performances like these gets easily overlooked or forgiven when we cloak them in words like *classic* or *sophisticated*. No doubt, the Smithsonian Institution means well when it celebrates Jazz Appreciation Month each April by depicting the genre as "Spontaneous. Never Ordinary. Completely Genuine." But jazz *isn't* always spontaneous, including some of the best performances (see my discussion in chapter 2 of Buster Bailey's "St. Louis Blues" solo). And sometimes it *is* ordinary—or worse. (For that matter, what does it mean for something to be "completely genuine"? Can music be *partially* genuine?) We do everyone a disservice when we pretend that "it's all good," as that hackneyed expression goes.

Second, jazz's staunchest advocates must also grant that there are a great many musicians in fields other than their own (or that other classical music) who have produced deeply inspired, inspiring, thought-provoking, or just irresistible sounds. Think of it: since the middle 1940s, when jazz officially became "modern," we've been privileged to hear and see such distinctive performers as Muddy Waters, Mahalia Jackson, Bill Monroe, Professor Longhair, Sister Rosetta Tharpe, Ray Charles, Hank Williams, Howlin' Wolf, Fats Domino, Chuck Berry, Jerry Lee Lewis, Johnny Cash, Clifton Chenier, The Beach Boys, Bob Dylan, James Brown, Willie Nelson, Gladys Knight and the Pips, the Jackson 5, Dolly Parton, Aretha Franklin, Stevie Wonder, the Grateful Dead, Sly and the Family Stone, Jimi Hendrix, War, Randy Newman, George Clinton, the Allman Brothers Band, Steely Dan, the Ramones, Little Feat, Prince, Beastie Boys, Public Enemy, Beck, Wilco, and on and on. Admittedly, this collection of artists betrays my own personal favorites, but what a range of creativity! Still more impressive: that list represents only U.S.-born musicians, so it excludes all the amazing performers and composers from Brazil, Bulgaria, Canada, Cuba, England, Egypt, Ethiopia, India, Indonesia, Ireland, Jamaica, Senegal, South Africa. On and on, and on and on. Until jazz's proselytizers accept that their favorite style is created, distributed, evaluated, influenced by, and its history narrated within a field of these and other valid musics, and that it competes for many of the same dollars, ears, minds, and bodies, their pronouncements will (and should) be taken with a grain of salt by the rest of the musical and academic world.

Justifications for cultural hierarchies are typically founded on shaky aesthetic grounds, anyway. Promoters of jazz superiority tend to argue in various guises that their genre is somehow better than the rest because of its relatively greater harmonic complexity, technical demands, degrees of dissonance, or other markers of "difficult music."[10] No doubt, some jazz styles do evince complex chord progressions or rhythmic schemes, and some demand tremendous facility to play. But it's a slippery slope to suggest that the degree of difficulty determines the value of a performance or composition. Do we really want to say that Thelonious Monk's structurally treacherous "Brilliant Corners" is better than his almost naively simple "Misterioso"? That is the conclusion one must draw if one follows the logic of the complexity, virtuosity, and/or dissonance argument. Wouldn't it make more sense to say that those two jazz compositions serve different purposes, and each fulfills its own purposes remarkably well? This same truth holds across genre borders. Musicians create and listeners are drawn to certain sounds, forms, and grooves because of the identities they celebrate or the ideas or emotions they convey or evoke *at a particular place and time.* A performance that speaks to us in youth (or in winter, or in Berlin, or in the morning, or in a barroom) may not speak to us in old age (or in summer, or in Memphis, or at night, or in a concert hall). Moreover, denigrating popular nonjazz genres or less-challenging styles of jazz as "mere entertainment" means engaging in the same sort of reflex elitism that proponents of European classical music used against jazz for decades and, in some ways and places, still try to do.[11]

To be sure, certain musics and uses of music are never acceptable, as when governments or other entities employ sounds to incite prejudice or provoke violence. We should condemn such actions when they occur.[12] Yet these rare and extreme examples aside, the musicologist has a duty to assess compositions and performances with an ear and eye toward the historical milieus and aesthetic values within which they were created and heard. I recognize that significant differences mark the attention and backing that the various genres receive. Record labels, print media, concert producers, and other business interests have put vastly greater amounts of energy and money toward promoting pop, hip-hop, rock, and country than toward promoting jazz. High- and mid-level jazz gigs may be more difficult to land and generally pay less than high- and mid-level gigs from these other realms.[13] But don't blame nonjazz performers for their successes. Musicians are supposed to speak to, for, and about people. Why should we hold it against certain musicians if their work resonates with a lot of people?

In a related matter, I am sympathetic to the progressive politics espoused by a number of jazz writers, and I commend those writers' efforts toward increasing the visibility and audibility of their favorite artists, many of whom belong to the avant-garde.[14] Still, the explicit connection commentators sometimes make between the political left and "freer" forms of jazz oversimplifies the situation. One such writer has even acknowledged the problems of his own position. In an admirably honest and self-questioning essay exploring "the ethicopolitical authority of jazz," Ajay Heble conceded that not all artists whose work ventures outside the mainstream are as welcoming of people whose lifestyles some may consider to be outside the mainstream.[15] Conversely, just because someone plays "inside" does not mean that that person lacks a strong political conscience. Ingrid Monson's recent work has shown how Count Basie, Tony Bennett, Dave Brubeck, and a number of other "straight-ahead" performers took active roles in the civil rights battles of the 1960s. Even Louis Armstrong, a jazz figure largely viewed as apolitical, if not derided as explicitly counterproductive to the struggle, entered the fray, though not without receiving hostile responses from many sides.[16] The scholar Eric Drott rightly pointed out that such circumstances should "dispel the simplistic homology that converts an artist's rupture with musical convention into an indexical sign of political commitment."[17] In other words, a libratory jazz affect does not necessarily denote a libratory social ethic in the musician(s) who created those sounds.

This notion applies on a broader level, too. The choices performers make about what and how to play are based on a variety of factors, including not only their own personal preferences (which are shaped by their cultural, historical, and geographical situations; educational backgrounds; state of health; time of day; and so on) but also the demands placed on them by club owners, fellow musicians, teachers, listeners, and industry executives. Thus, the structure, timbre, or style of music does not automatically correlate directly to the personality, mood, or biography of the person(s) who performed or composed that music. This would seem to be an obvious fact, yet listeners often take for granted that such a correspondence always exists. Take, for example, one writer's declaration: "In jazz more than any other way of music, a man's music will reflect the man, his thoughts, his emotions."[18] Or John Szwed's assessment: "Beyond anything else he might have been, Miles Davis was the sound of his trumpet."[19] With all due respect to Szwed, who is a very discerning jazz writer, Miles Davis was *not* the sound of his trumpet. He was an immensely creative, skillful, and shrewd professional musician who crafted his sound—actually a range of sounds—based on the situation(s) at hand. I take up this crucial distinction in various ways throughout the book.

The preceding paragraphs may have left the impression that I have come to bury jazz's devotees. Rest assured that I have not. I allotted a significant amount of print space to this discussion of cultural hierarchy only because

I foresee that this will rank among the most consequential, most pressing, and, I suspect, the least-queried matters in jazz over the coming years. No, far from disparaging jazz, I come mostly to praise its many practices and practitioners. Which brings me back to another area featured prominently in these chapters: musicians.

It has been an inescapable fact of life for some time that the music experienced by those of us in the Western world (and most everywhere else now, I imagine) typically emanates not from live performances but from places unseen. Music fills our automobiles, homes, ear pods, and public spaces, yet we rarely witness its creation. Even our loudspeakers are often hidden from sight, recessed in restaurant ceilings or car doors or disguised as rock formations in backyard gardens. So while an ever-greater variety of technologies enables a multifaceted entertainment industry and the computer-savvy consumer to access, replicate, and distribute a previously unthinkable amount of music, it has also happened that the very individuals who make those tunes we care so much about have seemed to vanish from our sight. (And, as they say, out of sight, out of mind.) These diligent folks deserve a better fate.

Earning a living as a jazz musician is a tough row to hoe. Beyond the formidable chops required to cover the many contingencies faced when playing a gig, success in the profession demands uncommon levels of determination, resilience, energy, self-confidence, and all too often the ability to live with a minimum of creature comforts. (One NEA-sponsored study reveals that in 2000 almost 66 percent of the San Francisco Bay Area's estimated 18,700 self-identified jazz musicians earned less than $7,000 per year for their jazz gigs.)[20] Given the challenges and demands of the field, it comes as no surprise, nor is it a sign of failure, that some individuals opt for a less-taxing lifestyle. What never ceases to amaze me is the number of people for whom jazz matters so much that they continue to compose and play it despite the uncertainties. And one of my primary goals here is to remind everyone how and why jazz musicians work so hard for whatever money may come their way. I would add, too, that since jazz is made by and for people, I have sought to place all discussions of "music theory"—the nuts-and-bolts aspects of chords, grooves, melodies, timbres, forms, etc.—in the context of the experiences, understandings, and identities surrounding those people.

Ultimately, then, *Jazz Matters* is about meanings. It focuses, specifically, on how some of the meanings people have taken to and from jazz get reflected in and configured through aspects of performance, location, and temporality. The three chapters that form part 1 concentrate on sounds (or in one case, *a* sound). Chapter 1 offers an interpretation of "musical subjectivities" to help account for the widely varying understandings that have accrued around John Coltrane and his music. In chapter 2 I point to some of the values and assumptions of jazz revealed through one brief sonority on a Miles Davis recording. Chapter 3 shows how the timbres and other musical elements deployed by the group Sex Mob exemplify a largely overlooked carnivalesque aesthetic in jazz. Part 2 of the book explores a handful of the settings, real and imagined, that jazz people have called home. Chapter 4 describes an American pastoral style that emerged in the 1970s, countering the prevalent understandings of jazz as city music. Chapter 5 traces the rise of college-level jazz programs in the United States, as well as the general reluctance by jazz writers to address jazz's move from "the street" to the conservatory. I travel to Paris in chapter 6 to see how the notion of jazz as "America's music" is represented (or not) among the latest group of U.S.-born musicians living and working overseas.

Bridging these twin pillars of sound and place is the issue of time. Jed Rasula offers an intriguing way of thinking about temporality in and as jazz when he asserts that the genre "is—musically, conceptually, historically—an exploration of the plasticity of time."[21] There is no question that music affects how we experience ourselves chronologically. Ahmad Jamal's spacious *Live at the Pershing* covers roughly the same amount of "clock time" as Ornette Coleman's densely polyphonic *Free Jazz,* but I don't imagine that many listeners would feel those two forty-odd-minute episodes in the same way. And, as Rasula suggests, jazz always refers in some way to the past: as memory, document, nostalgia, or allusion. The truth is, all facets of music exist in, work on, and change over time (including our notion of what gets lauded as "timeless").[22] For the jazz scholar this requires paying attention not only to which stylistic details emerge or recede to mark a given generation (for example, acoustic bass players in the 1970s and 1980s tended to have brighter sounds than their counterparts in the decades before and since) but also to the ways in which different listeners from different eras, places, and backgrounds have understood and regarded jazz's sounds and musicians. Each chapter addresses some aspect of these fundamental distinctions.

It seems appropriate during this discussion of time to note that *Jazz Matters* concentrates almost exclusively on music since World War II. A spate of recent studies demonstrates that we still have much to learn from and about styles before the middle 1940s.[23] Nevertheless, I chose to focus on the postwar era here, both because so many of the meanings surrounding jazz today emerged with bebop's ascendance at midcentury and also because it is widely regarded as the moment when any (supposedly) easily traceable stylistic evolution in jazz breaks down.[24] To my mind the current untidy profusion and diffusion of jazz models renders it all the more important and illuminating to study how various factions have tried to hold together—or resist—a unified conception of the genre. In other words, it means keeping an eye on *historiography*. Scholars, journalists, and documentarians are no mere innocent bystanders, objectively chronicling jazz history as it moves along. These commentators participate directly in that history, affecting the music's who, what, how, why, and where. (I am aware that by exploring such issues, I, too, participate in that ever-revolving cycle of meanings and practices.)

I built *Jazz Matters* around case studies. This approach offers the handiest way I have found to address a small number of fundamental ideas in depth while maintaining the flexibility to move among a variety of historical periods, musical styles, and geographical regions. Because there is always more than one way to see and hear music, each chapter introduces or adopts its own analytical strategies to help describe and interpret the musical practices, discourses, and institutions discussed there. And while every chapter can stand on its own as a self-contained essay, I mean the book to be taken as a cohesive whole, a multifaceted take on jazz sounds, times, and places.

In hindsight I can see that the study's themes, tone, and perspective were shaped to a great extent by where it was written. Reno, Nevada, my home since 1999, bills itself as The Biggest Little City in the World. In reality, though, it's a fairly unassuming place, tucked away in the high desert just east of the Sierra Nevada Mountains. This relative isolation from jazz's traditional centers has forced me to rethink a number of the conceptions I held about the geographical and metaphorical location of the music when I lived in Los Angeles, Brooklyn, Munich, Miami, or the suburban Chicago of my youth.

The book also bears the marks of my multidimensional position at the University of Nevada, where, on top of teaching music history classes and engaging in academic research, I give jazz piano lessons, coach jazz ensembles, play gigs, compose tunes, and assist with various other aspects of the Program in Jazz and Improvisational Music. Most obviously, my role as a jazz educator molded the chapter on music in schools, but it also affected the study in more subtle ways (for example, the initial impetus for the Coltrane chapter came to me while working through an improvisation exercise with one of my student groups). I am hardly the first musician to bring together the practical side of making jazz, the pedagogical side of teaching it, and the academic side of writing about it, but this is still a relatively rare combination in this country.[25] Despite the fact that more and more active musicians are returning to school, whether to teach or to study, the boundary between scholars and performers in college-level music programs remains fairly distinct. Too often such divisions devolve into sites of professional squabbles: applied music instructors feel the need to "protect" their students from supposedly overly taxing history courses, while scholars argue that those students (and teachers!) need more than ever to consider notions of meaning, identity, and context in the face of rapidly changing circumstances within and beyond the academy's walls. I hope that more faculty members will choose to defy this unfortunate split. All sides have important contributions to offer, and nothing but good can come if we increase the number of scholars who can play, players who can cite music's sociocultural history, and instructors who can do both.

A word about names: There are dozens of studies with two-word titles that play on the flexible use of *matters* as both a noun synonymous with *topics* and a verb highlighting the significance of one specific topic. Books covering such diverse themes as food, mathematics, reading, religion, and sex have all adopted this strategy. There's one called *Music Matters* and even a *Jazz Matters,* a fine collection of reviews and essays by the journalist Doug Ramsey.[26] Of course, any work labeled in this fashion and published in the past two decades is also bound to call to mind Cornel West's *Race Matters.*[27] But while the text you hold addresses a wide range of topics (and does cite West's now-classic volume), it is not an extension of or commentary on any of these previous *Matters.* I just happen to like that verb/noun ambiguity, however unoriginal the concept, and also how it seems to pair nicely with the title of my earlier book, *Jazz Cultures.*

Finally, I do not pretend or intend that these chapters amount to a comprehensive overview of postwar jazz. Quite the contrary. I aim to show that one of the great wonders of the music today is that the scope of its reach—geographically, culturally, stylistically—is too wide to contain within any single, supposedly all-encompassing, narrative. And in any event, the sounds and meanings of jazz continue to evolve, so no one has the final say on any jazz matter. I do trust, however, that the book offers some new ways to think about, listen to, teach, and perhaps even create this amazingly resilient and adaptable genre—not just the music's overlooked or undervalued areas but the full range of styles and identities, from the purportedly safe mainstream to the furthest reaches of "out there." Above all, I hope readers find here a useful contribution to those ongoing dialogues, suggested at the outset, among scholars (as well as journalists, fans, and musicians) from the past and those still to come.

PART ONE

Sound and Time

ONE

Being (and Becoming) John Coltrane

Listening for Jazz "Subjectivity"

MUCH HAS BEEN WRITTEN ABOUT John Coltrane's dramatic rise from humble beginnings to exalted status in the jazz world. Journalists and scholars alike have described the path of Coltrane's performing career, one that saw him starting out as a workmanlike hard-bop tenor saxophonist to emerge in quick succession as a master of difficult harmonic progressions, an early proponent of modal jazz, and a leading voice in the avantgarde. Writers have remarked, too, on the unprecedented, and thus far unrepeated, trajectory of Coltrane's reputation as a public figure, from pitiable heroin addict to clean and respected spiritual seeker, mentor, and (for some) saint. Book titles such as *Ascension: John Coltrane and His Quest* and *Chasin' the Trane* suggest how closely understandings of this musician are tied to notions of change, search, and journey.[1]

I touch on similar understandings in this chapter, but I approach them from a somewhat atypical angle. Identifying three predominant performance models favored by John Coltrane and his groups from the late 1950s until the saxophonist's death in 1967, I posit three subjectivities—which I call *being, becoming,* and *transcendent,* respectively—that correlate to musical "personas" configured by these models. I suggest that listeners have heard in and imagined through these personas their own notions of who Coltrane was as a person and what his performances mean. My aim here, then, is not about trying to descry John Coltrane's thoughts, beliefs, personality, or what some might call his musical "voice."[2] Rather, it more closely resembles the project musicologist Carolyn Abbate sets forth in *Unsung Voices* when she "endow[s] certain isolated musical moments with faces, and so with tongues and a special sonorous presence."[3] Such a methodology is far from exact or quantifiable, of course, but in this case it may help to account for how and why audiences have long heard in Coltrane's performances, as Ingrid Monson put it, "an analogy for their own experience, their own passions, and their own desires for self-transformation."[4]

Those of us involved in what some (still?) call the "new musicology" are not the only ones who practice these sorts of interpretive strategies. It is safe to say that almost every listener has engaged at one time or another in a kind of musical anthropomorphizing, if you will, in which they ascribe human qualities—emotions, moods, (im)moral characteristics—to music.[5] Furthermore, they often turn around and ascribe those qualities to the musician who performs or composes that music. To wit: the artist "equals" the art (and vice versa). Thus, it is not just that Chet Baker's singing voice or trumpet playing sounds sensitive and introspective. Many people assume that Chet Baker himself was a sensitive and introspective individual, even though they never had the chance to know him personally, nor can they have known his frame of mind when making music. (Even if it were once possible to ask the late Mr. Baker what he was thinking while performing this or that tune, he might not have recalled considering or sensing anything at all and may have responded that he was "just playing.")[6] To be sure, parallels sometimes exist between the style of a musical performance and the biographical circumstances, attitude, or personality of the artist who created that performance. But such parallels are not requisite to the creative process; it is just as likely that listeners project onto the musician a sense of the kind of person they feel he or she "must" be. Such assumptions are always based in part on the sound of the music but also on the listener's own background and myriad other factors. Instead of dismissing this sort of transference as mere fantasy, however, I want to explore its implications, for this common phenomenon is a crucial component in shaping deep-seated musical and cultural meanings in and of jazz.

"BEING" JAZZ

The first type of subjectivity to be discussed here—*being*—equates to a snapshot of the musical persona in one metaphorical state of mind or body in one particular time. To configure this sense of self (or *a* self) requires, above all, a relatively stable or consistent musical presentation. That is, parameters such as dynamics, dissonance, and tempo remain more or less fixed from beginning to end, even to the point that one could swap formally equivalent portions of a performance without fundamentally altering how we hear the music. A typical example of this approach is Charlie Parker's "KoKo." Widely considered one of the great jazz recordings of all time, "KoKo" would remain essentially as it is if one were to flip-flop the order of Parker's two solo choruses. For that matter, one could swap just the B sections of his two choruses (that is, replace the bridge from the first chorus with the bridge of the second chorus, and vice versa), and Bird's playing and also that of his bandmates would be just as intelligible and effective as it is in the original.[7]

This same musical consistency can be heard in hundreds, perhaps thousands, of other jazz recordings, as it is almost certainly the most common approach jazz performers have taken to their material. A variety of factors contributes to this situation and helps to explain why consistent performances and *being* subjectivities have predominated for so long. For instance, the vast majority of jazz musicians, even to this day, find their aesthetic roots in swing- and bebop-based practices. Both bop and swing emerged when technology limited the length of records to around four minutes, a constraint that encouraged performers to sustain one predominant mood.[8] In addition, many jazz professionals in the middle decades of the last century had honed their skills playing for dancers, which generally requires a steady pulse and tempo. Moreover, the repertoire favored by swing- and bop-oriented players derives in large measure from cyclical forms based on twelve-bar blues or Tin Pan Alley popular songs. When working with these types of tunes, musicians have tended to emphasize to greater or lesser degrees the "top" of the form and the downbeat of every four-bar or eight-bar section thereafter. These regular accentuations often serve as welcome touchstones for both performers and their audiences, but they can also delimit fluctuations in dynamics and other musical elements. And there is at least one other vital reason why so many musicians (and not just jazz musicians) choose to uphold a consistent tempo, mood, and time feel: establishing and maintaining a solid groove energizes body and soul. The ethnomusicologist Charles Keil went so far as to describe it as "the ultimate thing."[9] If something feels that good, there's often little reason to leave it behind.

Many other writers have outlined and analyzed traditional jazz practices on standard cyclical forms.[10] But my goal here is not just to recount how musicians play most frequently. Instead, I want to show how this approach can represent a certain kind of musical persona and why listening for subjectivity might offer insight into some of the meanings that have accrued around at least one jazz performer.

BEING JOHN COLTRANE: "GIANT STEPS"

One can hear a *being* persona on dozens of John Coltrane's recorded performances, as Coltrane opted for a bop-infused, consistent approach almost exclusively throughout the 1950s. Rather than cataloging these instances, it will suffice to point to his most famous example of this performance model, "Giant Steps."

Lewis Porter, whose 1998 biography of Coltrane ranks as the most erudite of many such studies, has noted how the unusual harmonic progression and fast tempo of "Giant Steps" led Coltrane "to construct his solo largely out of four-note patterns that could be transposed to fit each chord."[11] The jazz historian and theorist Ekkehard Jost praises Coltrane's "Giant Steps" solo as "a masterfully presented, well-planned etude," in which "some melodic patterns in the first chorus . . . also appear note for note in the following choruses."[12] Bill Cole, another Coltrane biographer, uses similar terms to describe the saxophonist's approach on "Giant Steps" (and also "Countdown," another harmonic minefield): "There is a recurrence of melodic material, mainly to remind the listener of where the piece is harmonically." Cole adds, "These pieces are exercises by a master musician, containing modulating material moving in both arpeggios and scalar lines."[13]

The point of these writers' assessments is clear: John Coltrane's "Giant Steps" solo demonstrates his ability to improvise compelling lines over an unusual chord progression at a brisk tempo while using a fairly limited amount of melodic and rhythmic material. Even after his initial elevenchorus statement, and taking a breather during Tommy Flanagan's piano solo, Coltrane comes back for two more choruses built of the very same devices he used in his opening gambit before proceeding headlong to the closing melodies. There are no dynamic contrasts here, no attenuations of energy. In jazz parlance he's just "burning"—which is precisely what marks his "Giant Steps" performance as consistent. And given the unobtrusive accompaniment the saxophonist receives from drummer Art Taylor, bassist Paul Chambers, and pianist Tommy Flanagan, we can see that

Coltrane's playing on "Giant Steps" carries that same degree of stability and interchangeability displayed in Charlie Parker's "KoKo." Just as on Bird's masterpiece, Coltrane's blistering solo would suffer no damage to its comprehensibility or jaw-dropping bravura if we shuffled the order of his choruses.[14]

This sort of approach is not exclusive to jazz. It remains the hallmark of any number of popular genres, especially, as I have suggested, those geared for dancing. We can recognize it, too, in some European classical repertoires. Writing in the early seventeenth century, the music theorist Michael Praetorius advised, "In constructing a good fugue one must with special diligence and careful thought seek to bring together as many ways as possible in which the same [material] can be combined with itself, interwoven, duplicated, [used] in direct and contrary motion; [in short,] brought together in an orderly, artistic, and graceful way and carried to the end."[15] In our own day, musicologist Karol Berger has observed that idea at work in J.S. Bach's polyphonic writing, even suggesting that *The Well-Tempered Clavier* be heard as a "temporally unordered set." Berger acknowledges that all musical ideas have to be presented in some temporal arrangement, but he argues that in the *WTC* and similar works "the order [of Bach's fugal demonstrations] is not of much interest. What matters are the [fugal] subject and the demonstrations."[16] Fugues proceed, then, by displaying or spinning out melodic lines that can come in almost any sequence so long as they correspond to the basic harmonic progression (or what jazz people would call the "changes"). Certainly, we can imagine Bach extending portions of his fugues for dozens of measures, just as we can envision Coltrane, Parker, or any other great bop-based improviser taking a half-dozen more choruses without changing the established character of the performance.

These musics also share strategies and concerns regarding musical endings. Namely, how does one conclude a piece that does not seem to be "about" the move toward closure? Berger explains: "Because one never knows in advance how many demonstrations there will be . . . or in what order they will be introduced, the end is in danger of seeming arbitrary and abrupt." He shows how Bach solved this problem in *The Well-Tempered Clavier*'s C-major fugue by using "emphatic" cadential gestures.[17] On "Giant Steps" the musicians announce the conclusion through their own emphatic, if quite conventional, touch: they restate the melody twice and, to further arrest the momentum, Coltrane plays a high-to-low flurry of a cadenza on the final E-flat-major chord over Art Taylor's press roll on the snare drum. Neither Bach's fugue nor Coltrane's "Giant Steps" comes to an earth-shattering climax in the manner of, say, Tchaikovsky's *1812 Overture,* the Who's "Won't Get Fooled Again," or, as I show below, some of Coltrane's other performances. But then "consistent" works such as these don't really call for the big finish. They just have to "be carried to the end," as Praetorius put it.[18]

As similar as eighteenth-century fugues and bop-type playing are in these ways, we need to recognize that they come from very different cultures and historical eras, so how people have heard and understood them will differ, too. One fundamental distinction between the John Coltrane of "Giant Steps" and Bach's C-major fugue concerns how each shapes or reflects different notions of temporality and place. Karol Berger contends that Bach's work represents a premodern European subjectivity in which time is cyclical, eternal, and, above all, holy. Berger even titles one of his Bach-related chapters, "There Is No Time Like God's Time." Now, John Coltrane certainly explores a sense of "God's time" in some of his music. But "Giant Steps" does not figure into that sacred realm. Nor, as we will see, do Coltrane's spiritually tinged performances typically involve a stable, *being* subjectivity. With "Giant Steps" there is no time like the present, and a very earthly present at that. The musical persona related to Coltrane's performance on that song addresses the listener: "I *am*—creative, intelligent, fearless, and in-charge—right here and now." It speaks to an ethic of individual know-how or "can-do . . . and better than you."

"Giant Steps" stands as just one of seemingly countless jazz performances that suggest some version of *being* subjectivity. And while the range of such personas is wide, there is no question that *being* subjectivities have continued to speak to generations of performers for whom consistent approaches virtually define the jazz genre. With few exceptions, the hallmark of jazz discourse has been to revere the (ostensibly) lone soloist while paying little or no attention to the rest of the ensemble. It is not much of a stretch to say that this presentation/subjectivity gave rise to the prevalent jazz narrative of the "great man" (and I do mean "man," since so few women have entered the canon).[19] Musicians, journalists, scholars, and fans must like these kinds of performances. Apparently we—I can't exclude myself from this throng—identify with the steadfast "characters" inhabiting those musical worlds, which helps to explain the continued production and popularity of transcriptions, music-minus-one recordings, and other pedagogical tools designed to highlight the individual player.[20] Coltrane's well-known reputation as an indefatigable practicer only serves to reinforce such meanings and aesthetics.

There are important social and cultural implications of Coltrane's "Giant Steps" persona, as well. John Coltrane is not generally recognized as one of the most politically outspoken jazz musicians of his day, certainly not to the same extent as Max Roach, Archie Shepp, Charles Mingus, or Abbey Lincoln. On those occasions when writers do link Coltrane to the civil rights movement, it is usually in the context of his later performances.[21] But whether or not John Coltrane himself had anything in mind during the "Giant Steps" sessions beyond "making the changes," the bold persona configured on that record seems to manifest aurally the values of discipline and excellence that have long been championed in African American communities as a means to combat feelings of despair.[22] In this way Coltrane's recording both reflected and gave voice to the resolute attitude of many human rights advocates as the debates about social inequality heated up. It follows that if the composition "Giant Steps" represents the "logical culmination" of bebop, as some have argued, historians might also want to locate Coltrane's fierce performance of that tune within the discourse that marks bebop as a music of mindful black intelligence, assertion, and resistance and not simply recommend it as a textbook example of how to play over difficult chord changes.[23]

Before proceeding, I want to reiterate that the musical personas I discuss here should not be understood as directly equating to any musician's actual history, beliefs, or experiences. They are, instead, fictions—quasi personalities suggested by a performance—that, I argue, affect listeners' understanding of both that performance and the artist(s) who created it. To help avoid confusion from here on, I use Coltrane's nickname—Trane—to distinguish the musical persona from the actual performer. Hence, John Coltrane plays saxophone on "Giant Steps." Trane is the musical persona configured and represented by the saxophone in that performance. As a public figure John Coltrane was known to be self-effacing, introspective, even shy.[24] The Trane of "Giant Steps" is determined, confident, and relentless.

While Coltrane's playing on "Giant Steps" serves as an object lesson in the formation of one kind of *being* subjectivity in jazz, not all aspects of that recording are as consistent as the saxophonist's contributions. Something happens during Tommy Flanagan's piano solo that suggests a degree of variability. In the original liner notes to the *Giant Steps* album Nat Hentoff writes of the title track: "Tommy Flanagan's relatively spare solo and the way it uses space as part of its structure is an effective contrast to Coltrane's intensely crowded choruses."[25] Contrast? No doubt about it. Effective? Well, I have to believe that Hentoff was being kind to the pianist. Tommy Flanagan was an outstanding musician who enjoyed a long and productive career, but his playing on "Giant Steps" is shaky at best. His four-chorus solo begins in typical bebop-piano style, with single-note lines in the right hand while the left hand "comps" underneath. Yet it becomes apparent very quickly that Flanagan is struggling with the tune's brisk tempo and unfamiliar harmonic progression. This is no knock on Tommy Flanagan's skills, by the way. Few but Coltrane had even seen that chord sequence, much less played on it . . . at that tempo . . . with the tape machine rolling! The pianist does regain his footing in spots, but by the fourth chorus he has pretty much given up on the take, resorting to quiet, sustained, two-handed chords. As noted, Coltrane follows the piano solo with two more energized saxophone choruses.

Put in terms of subjectivity, the Flanagan persona starts off vigorously but falters in short order. By the third chorus he has begun to lose confidence. By the fourth he has become disheartened, if not entirely broken, clearly not the "man" he was at the start. It is a marked contrast, indeed, to Trane here. In the recording studio the pianist Tommy Flanagan might have laughed off the take or just mentally "moved on" the way a relief pitcher in baseball must do after blowing a lead. The Flanagan persona of "Giant Steps" can never move on. He will always stumble and gradually weaken before our ears.

BECOMING JAZZ: THE CHANGING PERSONA

Tommy Flanagan's uneven performance brings us to the second type of subjectivity: *becoming*. Here the musical persona moves from one metaphorical state of mind, body, or attitude toward another. Unlike the consistent music representative of the *being* persona, *becoming* personas can form only when musical events seem to emerge out of (rather than merely follow) the previous material. These sorts of subjectivities do not typically involve the sort of deterioration heard in Tommy Flanagan's "Giant Steps" solo. More commonly they trace a kind of enlivening conversion. A clear case in point in the nonjazz world is Jefferson Airplane's psychedelic-era hit "White Rabbit," which features a gradual crescendo over an insistent bolero groove. The ramping up of musical intensity suggests a persona who experiences a progressive heightening of sensations after ingesting hallucinogenic drugs. Or one could substitute "sexual awakening" for Jefferson Airplane's "tripping," to understand how some listeners have heard similarly *becoming* ends in Maurice Ravel's famous *Bolero*. The bottom line is that, unlike the consistent performance model that gives rise to *being* subjectivity, one could not swap later portions of "White Rabbit" or *Bolero* with earlier portions of those works without destroying the continual increase in dynamics and other musical elements necessary to create and represent a sense of heightening expectation or transformation.

BECOMING TRANE

By 1960 John Coltrane had begun to incorporate modal-based sections into his dense harmonic schemes and even to eschew functional chord relations altogether.[26] Yet despite the less-cluttered formal structures, he initially approached his newer repertoire in much the same fashion as he had his previous material. For instance, though his celebrated first recording of "My Favorite Things" runs to almost fourteen minutes, it maintains a high degree of musical interchangeability.[27] When Coltrane plays after McCoy Tyner's extended interlude (around the seven-minute mark), he simply restates the melody much as he had at the song's opening. It is almost as if Tyner's four-and-a-half-minute episode hadn't happened. It did, of course, and there is no question that the relatively inactive harmony and longer playing time generates a very different sense of temporal and physical space than on "Giant Steps" or Coltrane's other densely chordal performances. Musicologist Lawrence Kramer even describes McCoy Tyner's "My Favorite Things" solo as "virtually static . . . evoking a sense that time itself has slowed or even stopped."[28] (Another way to express the affective disparity between "Giant Steps" and "My Favorite Things" is that the former is like an obstacle course to be taken at a sprint while the latter is like an open stretch of beach on which to amble.) Even so, while the Trane persona of the original "My Favorite Things" may be less insistent than the one displayed in the more bop-oriented works, he remains firmly in the stable, *being*, mode of jazz subjectivity.

"My Favorite Things" does, however, prefigure a significant shift in how John Coltrane's groups will arrange many of their performances in subsequent years, marking the earliest recorded example I have found of McCoy Tyner soloing before Coltrane. Why note something as seemingly inconsequential as solo order? Because by choosing to play after the pianist and by utilizing certain other techniques of ensemble interaction, Coltrane and his sidemen found an effective method of fueling musical anticipation and intensity. Their approach would help to configure a new and different Trane persona, one who transforms during and via a performance.

"AFRO-BLUE"

"Afro-Blue" was recorded in 1963 and released on Coltrane's *Live at Birdland* album.[29] Like so much of the leader's post–"Giant Steps" repertoire, "Afro-Blue," composed by the Cuban percussionist Mongo Santamaria, is loosely scripted, amounting to little more than a jumping-off point in 3/4 meter. The thirty-two-bar form consists of two sixteen-bar sections in F minor, with brief (two-bar) moves to E-flat major in measures nine and thirteen of each section. Remarkably, the musicians never fully exploit the tune's openness to show off their own immense improvisational skills. Instead, each works with the other members of the group to explore longterm development at the ensemble level. The result is a gradual ratcheting up of expectation and energy rarely heard up to that time on a jazz recording, or anywhere else.

"Afro-Blue" begins in less-than-grandiose fashion. Coltrane does not even bother to count off the tune so that all of the musicians might begin together; he simply starts playing the melody. The other performers, seemingly unfazed by the impromptu opening, are on board within a few seconds. Following a statement of the song's first sixteen bars, McCoy Tyner plays a solo-cum-interlude of equal length. Coltrane, here on soprano saxophone, then plays the full thirty-two-bar theme. I have noted that John Coltrane's tendency in earlier years had been to take the initial (and sometimes only) improvised choruses. Tyner goes first on this track. He begins with the traditional single-note lines with his right hand, though the left-hand quartal voicings give his playing a more open and also more forceful feel than that of most pianists of that era. To this point drummer

Elvin Jones and bassist Jimmy Garrison maintain a strong but generally stable and understated accompaniment.

Two-and-a-half minutes into his solo (3:25 of the track), Tyner briefly forgoes the linear approach in favor of a more assertive two-handed chordal technique. Elvin Jones immediately responds with increased vigor, as if to say, "I'm ready when you are." But the pianist pulls back, returning to the previous texture (3:50), and Jones recedes in kind. At around 4:08 Tyner leaves the linear style behind for good. Indeed, it would be more accurate to say that he leaves his "soloing" behind, as the next forty seconds is a communal effort among the three rhythm section members. Tyner and Jones, especially, link up with synchronized accents of dotted quarter notes. The resulting two-against-three feel generates an ever-increasing sense that *something* is about to happen. This expectation is fulfilled with Coltrane's entrance (4:50), a high F on the last bar of the form up to a high C on the downbeat of the next chorus. He sustains that pitch for nearly eight bars. The energy trails off for a time as Coltrane explores his own eighth-note-driven lines but returns with a vengeance (6:40) as he unleashes a cascade of sound, oftentimes well outside the traditional markers of F minor. All of this activity pushes Elvin Jones to even greater levels of activity and volume. The group peaks at about the seven-minute mark. During the next three and a half minutes the musicians attenuate the energy somewhat, but such a turbulent ride ultimately requires the grand finale that "Giant Steps" didn't. The quartet embarks on an extended coda after the final statement of the melody, closing with a prodigious, crashing tumult.

COLTRANE HERO

Coltrane's playing after the "piano solo" is the key, I think, to this performance and much of his group's other music from that time. The sense of expectancy generated by the rhythm section means that a Trane persona does not merely enter again; Trane *returns*. And he returns as hero.

I am hardly the first to compare a jazz performance to heroism. Albert Murray, for one, argues that blues-and-swing-based improvisers act heroically as a matter of course in their acceptance of the task at hand, which is to create compelling music onstage in the face of possible public failure.[30] No doubt, John Coltrane embodied this sense of the hero on the 1963 Birdland date, as he did throughout his career. Whereas Murray focuses on the workaday heroism of real musicians, however, I want to point to a particular type of musical persona configured in "Afro-Blue" and similar performances. And I suggest that the quartet's arc-of-intensity approach traces a kind of musico-mythical hero's journey. Grueling, hero-making or hero-revealing travails permeate stories involving many of the world's celebrated historical or literary figures, and such tales typically involve three main parts: departure, transformation through struggle, and return.[31] "Afro-Blue" sounds just such a sequence.

The first stage of the journey requires that the hero-to-be takes leave; and so Trane does (when Tyner begins his solo). While we do not witness directly the struggle/transformation stage, we learn about it from the commentary of what I will call the Chorus (in the Greek-drama sense), configured by the combined efforts of the rhythm section. The path is a difficult one, as all real initiation rites must be, but our protagonist prevails. Completing the cycle, Trane returns from the fray stronger, wiser, and more confident than before (the saxophone entrance at the 4:50 mark), bearing an inspired message of possibility and liberation through great effort to and with the Chorus. Trane hero.

If this all seems too much to read into just one tune, consider that the Coltrane quartet repeated this performance model, even including the saxophonist's sustained high-C entrance, in its version of "Afro-Blue" recorded at the Half Note two years later. "Song of Praise" and "My Favorite Things," also from that 1965 Half Note date, follow a similar path, as do "Chim, Chim, Cheree" and "Brazilia" *(John Coltrane Quartet Plays),* "Amen" and "Sun Ship" *(Sun Ship),* and "Pursuance" *(A Love Supreme).* Given these many performances, and there must have been hundreds more like them on gigs that went unrecorded during this two-year period starting around 1963, it seems that Coltrane and his sidemen knew how they wanted to present certain tunes and that this approach felt especially "right" and effective for them. In time audiences came to recognize this as one of the quartet's musical trademarks. But the musicians did not invent this model overnight.

It is apparent that Coltrane had been experimenting with his own individual senses of intraperformance *becoming* in the years leading up to the *Live at Birdland* session. For example, on all but the first of four versions of "Spiritual" his group played at the Village Vanguard in early November 1961, Coltrane begins on tenor saxophone, gives way to solos by Eric Dolphy and McCoy Tyner, and comes back to solo on soprano saxophone.[32] The fact that Coltrane repeated this solo order and horn change on multiple performances of the same tune indicates that he did not switch to soprano because of a bad tenor reed or other technical matter. He was going for something musically. None of these Vanguard "Spirituals" fully enact that arc of intensity I described on "Afro-Blue," chiefly because the rhythm section maintains a consistent approach, but the impulse toward such an end is certainly in place. (It is clearly audible in Coltrane's soprano entrance on the November 2 version.) By the quartet's 1963 Birdland appearance, each of the band members had devised his own means to achieve that effect, individually and, most important, collectively.

Significantly, writers began to use the hero metaphor to describe Coltrane's work from around that time. Shortly after Coltrane's death, Whitney Balliett called *Crescent,* recorded in 1964, Coltrane's "best recording" and summed up the saxophonist's career as "a *heroic* and lyrical voice at the mercy of its own power."[33] Martin Williams explored the hero concept at much greater length. As with Balliett, Williams singles out *Crescent* as exemplary: "There for the moment at least, [Coltrane] seemed to have profited by the years of complex harmony and by the years of modality, to return like a hero from a perilous but necessary journey, ready to share the fruits of his experience. Harsh dangers and exotic beauties are related on the title piece, *Crescent,* and the once 'impossible' saxophone sounds seem natural and firmly established techniques. Reflections and evaluations of the journey take place on *Wise One.* And *Bessie's Blues* might be called a joyful celebration of the new insight the hero had provided."[34]

Williams's comments are worth unpacking, as they seem to point to two different sorts of hero on *Crescent.* Descriptions such as "harsh dangers and exotic beauties," "reflections and evaluations," and "a joyful celebration" can all be read as referring to a kind of heroic musical persona: Trane. But the proposal that "he seemed to have profited by the years . . . to return like a hero" and the analysis of the saxophone technique apparently refer to Coltrane himself. This is a crucial difference, for I hold that John Coltrane is understood as he is in some circles because audiences do not merely hear his music as *sounding* a metaphorical hero's journey; instead, they take the equation one step further and begin to understand the saxophonist himself as embodying such a person.

This situation brings us back to the art-equals-the-artist phenomenon I noted at the beginning of the chapter, and it echoes a similar scenario surrounding another larger-than-life musical figure. The musicologist Scott Burnham has shown how the *Eroica* Symphony and some of Beethoven's other compositions came to form a European heroic style in which the music "usually invokes the necessity of struggle and eventual triumph as an index of man's greatness, his heroic potential."[35] Though told through their own musical aesthetics and techniques, the Coltrane quartet's "Afro-Blue" and similar works share with this European romantic tradition a sense of striving and attainment. What is more, Burnham demonstrates how certain nineteenth-century writers produced narratives in which "Beethoven himself is acknowledged as the hero of the *Eroica* Symphony. This pronouncement transforms the symphony from the portrayer of heroes to an act of heroism, and Beethoven from the portrayer of heroes to hero himself."[36] In similar fashion a careful reading of Martin Williams's piece on *Crescent* demonstrates how meanings can shift from heroic Trane subjectivity "in the music" to John Coltrane himself as hero.[37]

It is no coincidence that *Crescent* and *Live at Birdland* were recorded within a year of one another. This is Coltrane's "heroic period." The struggle-and-triumph narrative that Whitney Balliett and Martin Williams heard in *Crescent* and I hear even more clearly in "Afro-Blue" must have resonated with the attitudes and aspirations of many listeners around 1963, which Monique Guillory has rightly characterized as "a watershed moment of social change in the United States."[38] Recall that in October 1962 James Meredith became the first African American student to attend the University of Mississippi. The summer of 1963 saw Martin Luther King lead the March on Washington. The following year Bob Dylan released "The Times They Are A-Changin'," and Sam Cooke recorded his civil rights anthem, "A Change Is Gonna Come." Coltrane's music would soon influence and inspire many in the so-called counterculture, all corners of which were pushing to transform the perceived social order. This set of musical and historical circumstances helps to explain why John Coltrane represented, and continues to represent, "change" for so many people. It is not simply that the saxophonist played in a variety of styles—Charles Mingus arguably covered more stylistic ground than Coltrane, though we hear Mingus's oeuvre as "breadth." No, we understand Coltrane in this way because much of his music was *about* search and transformation at a crucial moment of flux in the United States.

SID HARTHA

TRANSCENDENT

The jazz scholar John Gennari has described Coltrane's final years as guided by an "aesthetic of transcendence."[39] This designation seems so apt that I adopted it as the label for the third subjective position. The *transcendent* persona does not involve an independent self such as those heard in *being* and *becoming* subjectivities. It requires, instead, that the musical persona's "ego" gives way to a larger totality. On the level of performance, *transcendent* musical subjectivity can form when a musician blends in with fellow players such that one no longer perceives individual voices but rather a densely concentrated mass of sound. This model is common among practitioners of avant-garde jazz styles but rarely found within the postwar "mainstream," where, as I have noted, the individual soloist fronting a rhythm section remains paramount.

Beginning around 1965, John Coltrane increased the sonic density of his performances, regularly augmenting his working quartet with additional players. Despite the larger forces, Coltrane did not provide his musicians with detailed written arrangements or other means of control. Indeed, his frameworks were often very loose, suggesting that he purposely sought and facilitated a thick and unruly affect. A. B. Spellman's review of a 1965 concert at New York's Village Gate featuring Coltrane with fellow saxophonists Archie Shepp, Pharoah Sanders, and Carlos Ward, pianist McCoy Tyner, bassist Jimmy Garrison, and drummers Rashied Ali and Elvin Jones gives an idea of just how open and raucous these shows could get:

> I think I see what Coltrane wants—an ever evolving groundswell of energy that will make the musical environment so dangerous that he and the others will have to improvise new weapons constantly to beat back all the Brontosaurs. However, if [Elvin] Jones is to be one of the two drummers, then Lincoln Center at least is needed to contain and separate all that sound. One simply couldn't hear anything but drums on *Out of This World*. I had no idea what the soloists were saying, and I doubt the players could hear each other. Garrison (who played a truly virtuoso solo to open the second set) was completely swallowed up. At one point, I saw Coltrane break out a bagpipe (another demon in the forest) and blow into it, but damned if I heard a note of what he played.[40]

Like the live gigs, the texture of some recordings from this period is so multilayered that even the most highly trained musicians can find it difficult to distinguish one player from another. Such is the case with Andrew White. An accomplished saxophonist in his own right, White is widely known and highly regarded for his detailed notated transcriptions of Coltrane solos (more than seven hundred of them when I last spoke with him in 2008), covering both commercially released and bootlegged recordings.

Tellingly, White has never set out to transcribe much of Coltrane's later work. He related to me that many of these recordings resist representation on the page owing to the impenetrability of the group sound. "Besides," he added, "Coltrane's role is more collective. He doesn't display his individual expression, so those recordings don't serve my purpose [as a transcriber]."[41] Many listeners found (and find) the later music confusing, even infuriating. Arguing that Coltrane's musical sensibilities "derailed" in the mid-1960s, the critic Stanley Crouch has recounted how some audience members walked out of the saxophonist's concerts and maintains that the last period of Coltrane's career amounts to "an artistic abyss."[42] Still, many others were (and are) deeply moved by these offerings.

"ascension"

A prime example of the late style can be heard on *Ascension,* recorded in June 1965. *Ascension* features twelve musicians, the largest group Coltrane had assembled since his more-tightly orchestrated *Africa/Brass* sessions of 1961. The ensemble produced two versions of the title tune. "Edition I" (as the first take is now known) originally served as the "master" until Coltrane changed his mind about which take he preferred. Shortly thereafter, Impulse Records rereleased the album using "Edition II."[43]

On both takes of "Ascension" the musicians do observe some boundaries of formal structure, conveyed mostly through alternating sections of soloist-oriented and ensemble-oriented passages, and through quasi-modal shifts. Yet as Ekkehard Jost points out, "the macro-structures of the total sound are more important than the micro-structures of the parts."[44] In other words, the musical whole—the ensemble's combined timbre, volume, and energy—is much greater than the sum of the performers' individual contributions.[45] Crucial to the cumulative texture of the recording is the work of the augmented "rhythm section." I use scare quotes around those last two words because the drummer and bassists opt more often to create a nonmetric churning than a steady pulse.

SAINT JOHN: THE "DIVINE SOUND BAPTIST"

Like the Trane persona of "Afro-Blue," the Trane of "Ascension" announces his presence alone.[46] But instead of venturing toward initiation and struggle as the heroic persona would, the *transcendent* Trane almost immediately relinquishes his personal identity. He enters, or realizes, an infinite state (the nonmetric sonic field of the other musicians). As a kind of "selfless" persona, he is simultaneously present and absent, at once a part of everything around him and indistinguishable from it. A discernible Trane does reemerge briefly from this unboundedness to describe and celebrate it (3:15). Yet once the ego-persona has had his say, he recedes back to that greater One-ness (5:51). I would say that he stays there to the end, but there is no end. The Infinite does not go away; we just lose our ability to perceive it.

Granted, the foregoing narrative reeks of overripe analytical incense. But I have pulled out all the rhetorical stops because anything less would fall short of conveying how and why some audiences have heard and experienced this music as they have. Nat Hentoff wrote that for Coltrane "the music was a way of self-purgation so that he could learn more about himself to the end of making himself and his music part of the unity of all being."[47] Hentoff did not point specifically to *Ascension,* but his use of the terms *self-purgation* and *unity of all being* are particularly apt with regard to that recording and so many of Coltrane's other late performances. *DownBeat*'s reviewer, Bill Mathieu, called "Ascension" "possibly the most powerful human sound ever recorded."[48] Lofty praise, to be sure, but that's just the start of it. For some listeners later albums such as *Ascension* are more than just "powerful"; they are mystical texts. In an article for *African American Review* Michael Bruce McDonald notes, "Especially toward the end of his life, Coltrane came to feel increasingly responsible for creating nothing less than a music of *theophany,* not just a music capable of conveying experiences of the sacred to those able to heed its insistent call, but one that would immanently embody, that would itself be, such an experience."[49]

We need not agree with such breathless assessments, but we should take them into account if we wish to comprehend some audiences' (including some musicians') continued fervent admiration for John Coltrane. And not just his music. As with the transference some made from Trane as heroic musical persona to John Coltrane as heroic person, so, too, with many listeners who made the shift from Trane as a spiritually transcendent musical persona to John Coltrane himself as a spiritually transcendent man: a veritable saint, in fact. Archbishop Franzo King, cofounder of the Saint John Coltrane African Orthodox Church in San Francisco, experienced an epiphany in the form of what he describes as a "sound baptism" during and via a Coltrane concert in 1965.[50] This was the same year that Coltrane recorded much of his most densely textured work, including *Ascension,* so Bishop King's feeling of baptism—of being immersed in or inundated by—the musical "spirit" makes perfect sense. King and other sympathetic listeners knew John Coltrane was present—Coltrane was the designated leader of the session, after all, and his saxophone emerged from the sonic outpouring at times—yet he no longer "appeared" in his familiar manner. Recall Andrew White's line: "He doesn't display his *individual expression.*" In this sense it is appropriate that Coltrane's recording called "Selflessness" is from 1965 and not from his hard-bop days in the 1950s.[51] In many of the later performances the saxophonist was at once indiscernible and ubiquitous. For some this music must have felt (and must still feel) like the definition of the Almighty handed down from the ancient Hermetic texts: an infinite sphere, the center of which is everywhere, the circumference nowhere. Jazz writer Frank Kofsky did, in fact, equate Coltrane with a deity (if not *the* Deity), writing, "I am not a religious person, but John Coltrane was the one man whom I worshipped as a saint or even a god."[52]

"IT'S ALL IN THE MUSIC": A CAVEAT . . .

In a video documentary about the Coltrane Church (as that place of worship is sometimes called), the Reverend Mark Dukes discusses how he came to accept John Coltrane as worthy of veneration. He recalls asking Bishop King to justify the church's position. According to Dukes, King responded, "It's all in the music." Following King's counsel, Dukes listened again to Coltrane's recordings and recounts, "When I let myself go to that place that the music was getting me to go, there I found the presence of God."[53]

Michael Bruce McDonald also believes that Coltrane's music innately sounds a sacred purpose and meaning. Building on comments made by Stanley Crouch (an unlikely ally in this argument, one would think), McDonald asserts that "the theophanic function of music is immanent within music itself, not to be found in any discursive supplement offered for the sake of comprehending a musical work."[54] Similarly, in one of the more recent books on Coltrane, Ben Ratliff writes, "Insofar as Coltrane's music has some extraordinary properties—the power to make you change your consciousness a little bit—we ought to widen the focus beyond the constructs of his music, his compositions, and his intellectual conceits. . . . *Musical structure, for instance, can't contain morality. But sound, somehow, can.*"[55]

Coltrane's music can be weighty stuff, and not just for Dukes, King, McDonald, and Ratliff (who is no starry-eyed mystic and, in fact, no fan of *Ascension*) but for thousands of people around the world.[56] Yet while I am the first to argue that scholars and critics need always to take seriously the "music itself," I differ with the above-named commentators in one important aspect: I hold that sound cannot "contain" morality or any other human quality. Neither can form, nor melody, nor groove. People bestow meanings on music. In the case of John Coltrane these meanings are shaped in large measure by timbre and other formalistic details but also by an array of other aspects. In other words, it's never "all in the music," as Bishop King declared, or "immanent in the music," as Michael Bruce McDonald would have it.

If we want to understand how *Ascension* is understood as holy and John Coltrane himself is understood as a holy man, we must pay attention precisely to "the discursive supplement"—the information and meanings circulating around and about the music—that McDonald dismissed as unnecessary. We must consider *A Love Supreme,* for instance, which was released to widespread acclaim less than a year before *Ascension* and includes liner notes proclaiming in no uncertain terms Coltrane's own religious interests and aspirations. And there's *Om,* which not only carries the numinous title but also the legend that Coltrane had ingested LSD before the recording session. This widely circulated bit of information might be disregarded as unseemly trivia were it not for the fact that, more than any other class of drugs, hallucinogens such as LSD are associated with the search for, and occasional attainment of, mystical experiences.[57] Titles and stories like these serve to strengthen public perceptions of John Coltrane's late recordings as sacred and mystical music and the saxophonist himself as a sacred and mystical figure. Imagine, by contrast, if Coltrane had released the performance he called "Ascension" as, say, "Malcolm." Audiences would certainly have heard that recording differently, most likely as an impassioned response to the recent assassination of a beloved cultural leader rather than an offering of "theophanic" musical mysticism. Listeners might have also understood John Coltrane himself as more directly engaged in the civil rights struggle of the 1960s than he currently is perceived. He would still be a hero to many. A saint? Less likely.

LISTENING AND INTERPRETATION

I recognize that some people will not necessarily hear Coltrane's performances as I have described them in this chapter. Some may not even focus on the saxophonist's playing at all; certainly Elvin Jones's and McCoy

Tyner's contributions to "Afro-Blue" are well worth the price of *Live at Birdland* in themselves. But that's also part of my point here. The Trane personas I have discussed could only emerge in the context of the other musicians who participated in these sessions. Archie Shepp, Pharoah Sanders, John Tchicai, and the others on "Ascension" were as necessary in forming the transcendent Trane persona as John Coltrane was himself. The same applies to Flanagan, Chambers, and Taylor and the *being* subjectivity of "Giant Steps." Ultimately, one can (and, I suggest, should) listen to and theorize about music in multiple ways, each of which will provide a different angle on how musicians work and how their efforts get understood and treated in the world. Listening for musical subjectivities such as I have outlined simply gives us one more tool to help account for some of the varied meanings that audiences bring to and take from jazz performances, one more way to think about the shift in public understandings that would take John Coltrane from strong and steadfast leader, through indomitable hero, to selfless mystic.

TWO

Musicology beyond the Score and the Performance

Making Sense of the Creak on Miles Davis's "Old Folks"

FOR SUSAN MCCLARY

Miles Davis's 1961 album *Someday My Prince Will Come* has never attracted the attention or accolades accorded to many of the trumpeter's other records. How could it, really, considering that the two Davis releases that preceded it, *Kind of Blue* and *Sketches of Spain,* rank among the most revered recordings in all of jazz, while *E.S.P.,* the studio debut of Davis's so-called Second Great Quintet, would follow just a few years later? By contrast to those landmark discs, *Someday My Prince Will Come* isn't generally considered much more than a blowing session.[1] Still, I suggest the record merits further attention. Not only because of the wonderful (and largely underappreciated) playing throughout, or because it marks the last time Davis would work in the studio with John Coltrane, or because the album's design features Davis's wife, Frances Taylor, in one of the earliest appearances of an African American model on a record cover (see Figure 1).[2]

Someday My Prince Will Come also warrants consideration because of a very brief moment on one track. At the end of the second A-section of "Old Folks" (approximately 1:15 from the beginning) there is a quiet but clearly audible groan of wood laboring under the weight of a person in motion. I can't tell whether the sound emanates from Wynton Kelly's piano bench, Miles Davis's chair, the studio floor, or another source altogether.[3]

FIGURE 1. Cover, Miles Davis, *Someday My Prince Will Come* LP

Nor do I know why Davis and his record producer, Teo Macero, allowed that sound to remain (it's impossible that so many well-trained ears could have failed to hear it). The musicians and studio engineers certainly had the ability to "clean up" the track, either by splicing together sections of two different takes or simply rerecording it.[4] For that reason I hesitate to designate this moment as "noise," since noise, as Jacques Attali has argued so compellingly, destabilizes and threatens order.[5] Apparently, Davis, Macero, and the powers-that-be at Columbia Records, one of the industry's major labels at the time, did not believe that the sound disturbed the otherwise clean and well-executed performance enough to scrap it. Perhaps they even liked the effect. So if a squeaky piece of furniture on a studio-made recording isn't noise, what is it? For now, I'll simply refer to it as "the creak."

One might ask why anyone should care about how to designate that sound or even that it remained on the release. That is, why single out a brief, seemingly unintended moment on one selection of a not-particularly groundbreaking album? In response I suggest that "Old Folks" presents an ideal opportunity to theorize some rarely explored issues in jazz. As the musicologist Richard Leppert remarked, "People do not employ sounds arbitrarily, haphazardly, or unintentionally—though the 'intentionally' haphazard may itself constitute an important sort of sonoric discourse."[6] And so by seeking to account for this sonority that isn't "performed" in the usual sense, but (as I will show) nonetheless matters to our understandings of a performance, we can exercise Leppert's claim and, in the process, perhaps gain an otherwise overlooked perspective on how and what jazz means.

I should note that the "Old Folks" circumstance, while relatively rare, is not sui generis. Theodore Gracyk has called attention to similarly random episodes on a handful of rock recordings. "On Elvis Presley's 'Blue Moon' (1954), we can hear a soda machine in the background; on the Beach Boy's 'Wendy' (1964), someone coughs during the instrumental segment; on Bruce Springsteen's 'New York Serenade' (1974), the piano pedals squeak; on Bob Dylan's 'Wedding Song' (1974), the buttons on his coat sleeve clatter against his acoustic guitar." Gracyk adds, "It is only within the context of knowing music by way of recording that we can even point to such details as the squeak of a piano pedal or the clicking buttons and ask about their presence."[7] Yet while Gracyk's observations suggest intriguing possibilities for a hermeneutics of unintended sounds in music, he himself has broader points to make about recording, composition, and performance in rock, and he never offers detailed interpretations of any of the instances he cites. Left unanswered are questions about how specific recordings transform their quasi-extraneous sonorities into . . . what? This chapter offers some possible answers to those questions as they pertain to one such instance in jazz.

But where to begin? Asserting that the creak on "Old Folks" deserves our attention is one thing; deciding how we should deal with it is quite another. The typical "toolbox" used by today's music scholars carries an array of techniques designed to account for harmony, form, and other larger-scale aspects of a performance or composition. That same toolbox, as impressive as it is, does not appear to hold anything capable of theorizing a single, humble sonority. Musicologist Richard Taruskin has raised this problem in another context, and his thoughts on it are worth quoting at length:

> Our training as scholars gives us very precise and efficient ways of dealing with generalities. We have a vocabulary for them, and the process of framing them involves reassuringly scientific methods and criteria, many of them quantitative and exact. We have no such aids in dealing with uniqueness. . . . And nothing is less scientific than the evaluation not of quantities but of artistic qualities, the specific details, the "divine details" as Nabokov would say. These must be apprehended by imaginative response, empathic identification, artistic insight—all euphemisms, of course, for intuition, which word embarrasses and antagonizes the scholar in us. Unwilling to claim intuition as a guide . . . we often tend to flee from characterizing the uniqueness of a piece in performance, and seek refuge in our objective knowledge, which is in all cases a generalized one. Since it is never possible to talk about the unique with the same objectivity as one can about the typical, we are tempted to ignore distinguishing characteristics and instead parade our basic knowledge of style as if it were specific insight.[8]

Averse as I am to ignore this "divine detail," a "distinguishing characteristic" of Davis's track, I am going to do what any self-respecting jazz musician would do in this situation: proceed by "imaginative response." In other words, I'm going to improvise. Below I offer three ways in which we might tease out some of the meanings revealed and configured by the creak, devoting one section each to how people listen to, evaluate, and perform jazz.

LISTENING: THE RECORD EFFECT

As a point of departure I want to return to Theodore Gracyk's observation that this sort of theoretical study would not make sense—could not even take place—without the advent of recording technology. This may seem like an obvious point, but it remains an enormously significant one nevertheless. Susan McClary has shown that because recording brings to light "parameters such as timbre, timing, and inflection that had always escaped the printed text, . . . its emphasis switches from the composer of the written document to the performer, whose actual nuances we hear."[9] That is to say, we are less concerned with who wrote "Old Folks" than with who played it and how it was played.[10] Even further, the "nuances" we hear on this particular recording include a sonority the musicians did not (I assume) intend to produce. The engineers at Columbia's 30th Street Studio captured *all* of the sounds made in the room while Miles Davis and his group recorded "Old Folks," a situation that takes us one intriguing step beyond the composer-to-performer shift that McClary described.

And then we listen back. Recordings not only catch and store sounds; they also allow us to hear those sounds as many times as we wish. This repeatability cannot help but affect what listeners will perceive and consider. Even a devoted Miles Davis fan checking out Davis's group every night during an extended stint at a nightclub with an unstable piano bench (or whatever it is) in 1961 would not hear the creak as we do on *Someday My Prince Will Come.* Each time the quintet played in the club, that sound would occur during a different part of the set, and an ever-changing array of clatter—cash registers, audience chatter, doors closing, etc.—would also accompany the performance. What is more, if the creak sounded too loudly and too frequently, it might begin to annoy listeners (and also the band members!), at which point it *would* enter the realm of "noise." By contrast, hearing this one version of "Old Folks" a number of times allows the creak to become an expected, perhaps integral, part of the listening experience, even if it wasn't a part of the musicians' intentions or awareness during the recording session.

In some ways the "Old Folks" creak shares certain traits with other audio media phenomena. For example, record buyers in the LP era grew accustomed to an initial pop and crackle when the turntable needle hit the surface of the vinyl, just as they came to recognize the unique patterns of scratches and skips that eventually marked their own well-worn discs. For the few of us who admit to owning eight-track tapes in the 1970s, the abrupt *click-click* that signaled the move from one track to another, sometimes in the middle of a tune, became an accepted (or at least predictable) part of the musical encounter, almost a part of "the music itself." Similarly, Thomas Porcello has written about the "print through" audible on analog tapes where, during moments of little or no other sonic activity, one hears a faint "pre-echo" of the music to come. Porcello describes his own listening experiences: "That tiny audio shadow had the power to generate a visceral inner tension. . . . And because of the very fact of foreshadowing—the building of anticipation, tension and desire attendant to the partially-known object—the eventual impact of the events was that much more intense."[11] What distinguishes the creak on "Old Folks" from these other situations is the fact that it occurred in the studio with the musicians, indeed, as a direct result of one of the musicians, though that player almost certainly did not mean to produce it. Thus, the creak is not solely "about the technology," as LP scratches, eight-track clicks, and analog print-through are, but is also in some ways about physically playing an instrument, a fundamental distinction to which I will return.

The "Old Folks" moment may also suggest the ideals of John Cage, who so famously challenged us to hear all sounds, "whether intended or not," as music.[12] On closer examination, though, Cage's aesthetics don't fit very comfortably here, either. For the circumstances within which and through which the creak occurs (jazz musicians playing a Tin Pan Alley tune in a studio setting) and comes to our attention (a commercial recording) resist Cage's goal of a music "the continuity of which is free of . . . the literature and 'traditions' of the art."[13] It is safe to say that most listeners of the *Someday My Prince Will Come* version of "Old Folks" are aware that they are hearing a Miles Davis record, or at least a jazz record, and one safely within the traditions of the jazz art, at that. So even if the creak happened by chance, this hardly qualifies as "chance music."[14]

Again, we are left to ask: what do we do with this thing? As one example of how the sound on "Old Folks" could work—indeed, has worked—to shape meanings, I offer my own history with the track. I realize it is impossible to describe my full experience of this, or any, music. We are facing Charles Seeger's infamous "linguocentric predicament" or engaging in what Susan McClary has cleverly dubbed "effing the ineffable."[15] Still, "Old Folks" has resonated with me on a fairly definable level, one that relates directly to the topic at hand.

"Old" Music

I first heard the *Someday My Prince Will Come* LP around 1980, when I was an undergraduate jazz piano major at the University of Miami. For my friends and me at that school, Miles Davis epitomized jazz. We pored over each of his records, learned the tunes, and memorized the solos, all in an effort to incorporate into our own playing his groups' various approaches to phrasing, timbre, groove, and other elements. But among all those dozens of cuts, "Old Folks" always stood out to me, representing something more than "great jazz" to admire and emulate. In a nutshell the track sonically signified advanced age. Not that it sounded like a recording from long ago, mind you; I mean that it expressed "oldness." And I am certain that the record's creak contributed to my interpretation. Although that sound only lasts for about a second, its presence made everything about the performance seem weary and "slower," just as I imagined my own future self would eventually feel or be.

Now, I expect few people hear this recording exactly as I do. Even so, as the philosopher Mark Johnson has shown, while "there is . . . no single, god's eye way of carving up the world, . . . it does not follow . . . that we can carve it up any way we wish."[16] Johnson's research on the connections among physical activity, metaphorical language, and human cognition reveals that what people take to be their own innermost thoughts and feelings are always structured by their daily interactions with other people and things "out there" in the world. The most seemingly abstract theoretical concepts are *embodied* in many ways. Picking up on the work of Johnson and others, the music theorist Joseph N. Straus has argued that "we make sense of music, we understand it, according to patterns of bodily perceptions, activity, and feeling."[17] In such ways any number of factors could help to explain why I hear the creak on "Old Folks" as "aged," rather than, say, "agile." Perhaps the straining wood somehow connected in my mind with the sound of creaking joints, or a rocking chair, or a door slowly opening in a dilapidated house, all of which have been used in films and TV (and, in the case of the rocking chair, retirement-party gifts) to denote the elderly.

Other features contribute to the way I experience this recording. The deliberate tempo (around fifty-three beats per minute) certainly heightens the "gray" effect. The band plays so slowly that the entire five-minute, twenty-second performance consists of just two passes through the thirty-two-bar form. Here we find ourselves on somewhat more familiar musicological ground, as musicians and audiences in the West have long equated a slow tempo with old age and its inevitable aftermath (think "September Song," "Taps," Chopin's *Funeral March*). The song's title is relevant, as well. Had the creak occurred during "Teo," "Drad Dog," or any other track on the album except "Old Folks," it is entirely possible that I would hear the recording differently, perhaps as just another of the "great Miles tunes," albeit one with a weird squeak.

The mood (and so my interpretation) of "Old Folks" would also differ enormously had the performers chosen another approach to playing the tune. As on so many of his ballads, Miles Davis eschews rapid-fire lines here in favor of legato articulation, carefully modulated dynamics, and an economical use of notes, including long stretches when he plays nothing at all. In fact, had he or any of the other musicians decided to fill measures fifteen and sixteen leading up to the bridge of the first chorus, as many less "space"-conscious players would, we might not even hear the creak.

Just as crucial to the effect is Davis's trademark use of the Harmon mute. Scholars have commented on how that timbre suggests a brittleness and vulnerability diametrically opposed to the chest-pounding bravado of so many other trumpeters.[18] And it's true; a degree of frailty—another sign of old age—does characterize Davis's Harmon-muted sound. But we should not equate or confuse the "vulnerable" atmosphere with the performers who evoked that atmosphere. Davis was only thirty-five years old and well past his heroin addiction at the time of this recording. His chops are in fine form. So unlike Billie Holiday's swan song, *Lady in Satin*, Chet Baker's late work, or the final performances of Judy Garland, the allure of which for many listeners seems to be the audible deterioration of the "tragic" performer, any abject quality heard in "Old Folks" relates to the musical subjects who inhabit the world of the track, not from the age or physical shape of the actual musicians who created that world.[19] Indeed, the mood lifts briefly (reminiscences of younger days?) as the rhythm section switches to a double-time feel at the top of the second chorus during Hank Mobley's notier sixteen-bar tenor solo and Wynton Kelly's buoyant eight-bar solo. The last A-section returns us to the "elderly" ambiance, however, with Davis's muted-trumpet melody and the rhythm section's original somnolent groove closing out the track. Notice, especially, Jimmy Cobb's languid brushwork on the snare drum: a methodical *shhh . . . shhh . . . shhh,* like the shuffling of slippered feet across a floor.

So the musicians' deliberately paced performance, the choice of timbres, and the name of the song help to shape the "aged" meaning for me, yet the point remains that the brief creak on "Old Folks" also contributes to that effect.[20] It is a remarkable example of a sonority expressing in a way that the composition and the musicians' interpretation of it cannot or do not do on their own. How better to appreciate the enormity of the shift from the printed score to recording technology on our ways of experiencing and understanding music than through this sound, a part of our musical awareness that goes beyond both the printed composition and the performance?

Another angle from which to consider the creak is to ponder what its presence on *Someday My Prince Will Come* reveals about musical values and practices. Lore has it that jazz thrives on real-time performance—scholar John Gennari calls this the music's "most fundamental and enduring article of faith"—even as certain recordings have become the genre's primary historical and pedagogical texts.[21] Softening this apparent contradiction, jazz recordings tend to cloak their constructedness. Gabriel Solis put it this way: "Never mind that the process of recording inherently involves significant sound manipulation; the point is that the aesthetic of jazz is such that recordings are engineered to create a simulation of live sound, to present the impression of 'being there.'"[22]

To help bridge the gap between the world of the studio and the world of the stage, many musicians, including Miles Davis, have released "live" recordings. The applause, MC introductions, and other sounds on these discs serve a valuable function by enhancing that "being there" quality Solis noted, allowing listeners to imagine they can feel what it was like to sit among the performers and their audiences on those special nights. Some artists have even sought to reproduce the spirited atmosphere of the nightclub within the more acoustically controlled setting of the recording studio. Cannonball Adderley brought friends, food, and libations along when he made the *Inside Straight* LP at Fantasy Studios. On *Mingus Presents Mingus* Charles Mingus recreates his standard nightclub patter in the studio even though no listeners were present at the session. He verbally introduces songs, and even admonishes his (imaginary) audience members not to rattle the (imaginary) ice in their (imaginary) drinks.[23]

Miles Davis and his producers never adopted either of these "semilive" strategies. But more than once the trumpeter's recordings have included snippets of his singularly raspy speaking voice, giving us an aural glimpse "behind the scenes." On the 1956 Prestige release *Relaxin' with the Miles Davis Quintet* we hear Davis blow a brief flourish on his trumpet before chastising bassist Paul Chambers, who was warming up: "When you see the red light on, everyone's supposed to be quiet." The trumpeter then instructs pianist Red Garland to set up "You're My Everything." After a few seconds of Garland's single-note-line-with-left-hand-accompaniment intro, Davis whistles the take to a stop and directs the pianist to "play some block chords, Red." Turning his attention to the control booth, Davis says,

"Alright, Rudy [Van Gelder]," to confirm that everyone is still ready to record. Then back to Garland: "block chords, Red." The pianist obliges with a two-fisted opening, and the track progresses without further interruptions.[24] Elsewhere on that album Davis barks tersely to producer Bob Weinstock, "I'll play it and tell you what it is later," before launching into "If I Were a Bell." From the recording industry's earliest days, music executives have routinely exerted control over their artists' repertoire, sound, and style.[25] And given that the mid-1950s was a time of sanctioned racist policies in the southern United States and a de facto white-dominated racial order throughout the rest of the country, the fact that we hear Miles Davis, an African American musician, giving orders in such a brusque manner to Bob Weinstock, a white record executive, is particularly striking. In this instance, and others like it, Davis's voice serves to reinforce understandings of the trumpeter as not merely the recording session's titular leader but, more important, its artistic visionary, as well. Yet while the spoken material on *Relaxin'* documents a historically significant moment of black-male authority, no such cultural work pertains in the case of "Old Folks." We don't even know where the creak originates, and the rest of the album aspires to nothing more (or less) than a typical "quiet-on-the-set" studio session. The creak does, however, boost Miles Davis's credentials in another realm . . .

Wrong as Right

Jazz's advocates have long extolled the music's unplanned or "loose" moments. Take the pronouncements by the jazz historian Mark Gridley both that "improvisation is essential to jazz" and that "improvised parts sometimes sound more casual and less organized than the written or memorized parts."[26] Likewise, in his study of jazz, revealingly titled *The Imperfect Art,* Ted Gioia claims, "If jazz music is to be accepted and studied with any degree of sophistication, we must develop an aesthetic that can cope both with that music's flaws as well as its virtues."[27] Gioia even argues for "an aesthetics of imperfections" to counter the criticisms of those who feel that jazz somehow falls short of the standards set by European classical artists (who almost always perform wholly precomposed material and therefore do not have to decide which notes to play).[28]

Few jazz scholars or musicians would disagree with the basic tenets of these writers' positions. I certainly don't.[29] In fact, I would expand Gioia's thought by proposing that jazz people do not just excuse certain flaws but actually hail them as virtues. How else to explain the revered status of the original "Lester Leaps In?" "Lester" is an undeniably swinging cut, but no more so than any of the other collaborations between Count Basie and Lester Young. What gives this track its unique appeal (and its title) is the moment when Young continues his saxophone solo for a second chorus though Basie clearly expected to take over. Consider, too, that instant in "Giant Steps" I described in the previous chapter when John Coltrane roars back on top of Tommy Flanagan's faltering piano solo. Flanagan's tentativeness makes Coltrane's watertight performance sound all the more compelling and impressive. I will show how all this relates to "Old Folks," but first I want to reflect briefly on what may be the clearest example of the aesthetic of imperfections in action: Ella Fitzgerald's live recording of "Mack the Knife."

Originally released on the 1960 *Ella in Berlin* album, "Mack the Knife" opens with the sound of audience applause followed by Fitzgerald's presong patter.[30]

[Spoken]: Thank you. We'd like to do something for you now. We haven't heard a girl sing it. And since it's so popular, we'd like to try and do it for you. We hope we remember all the words. . . .

Fitzgerald sings the first three choruses with no audible difficulty, taking her typically joyous and spirited liberties with the phrasing. But then she gets stuck:

Oh, what's the next chorus,
To this song, now?
This is the one, now
I don't know.
But it was a swinging tune,
And it's a hit tune,
So we tried to do "Mack the Knife."

Ah, Louis Miller,
Oh, somethin' about cash
Yeah, Miller, [laughs] . . . he was spending that trash [laughs]
And Macheath dear, he spends like a sailor
Tell me, tell me, tell me:
Could that boy do something rash?

Oh, Bobby Darin and Louis Armstrong
They made a record, oh, but they did.

And now Ella, Ella, and her fellas
We're making a wreck, what a wreck,
Of "Mack the Knife."

[à la Louis Armstrong]
Oh Snookie Tawdry [scats using nonsense syllables . . .]
[scatting . . .]
Just a jackknife has Macheath, dear
[more scatting]

So, you've heard it
Yes, we've swung it
And we tried to
Yes, we sung it
You won't recognize it
It's a surprise hit
This tune called "Mack the Knife."

And so we leave you, in Berlin town
Yes, we've swung old Mack
We've swung old Mack in town
For the Darin fans,
And for the Louis Armstrong fans, too
We told you look out, look out, look out
Old Macheath's back in town![31]

There are a number of remarkable aspects to this highly extemporized performance. First, Fitzgerald's explanation that she chose to do "Mack the
Knife" because "it's so popular" and "it's a hit tune" reminds us that not
all jazz musicians have avoided "going commercial," or at least admitting
that they're doing so, even in the years since bebop. Second, Fitzgerald
reveals that a singer's sense of ownership (professional, not legal) of a song
can involve a gender component. She sings in the sixth chorus that both
Bobby Darin and Louis Armstrong had covered "Mack the Knife," but
her spoken introduction informs us that no woman had yet laid claim to
the tune, implying that if another female singer had scored a hit with this
song, Fitzgerald might not have taken a shot at it.[32] Third, and directly related to the aesthetics of imperfections issue, there's the singer's admission,
"We hope we remember the words." For a performer in most any other
genre to admit onstage that she is in less-than-full command of her material would be seen as unprofessional, at best. In this case, however, Ella's

confession helps mark her version as charmingly off-the-cuff or, in a word, "real." The track veritably screams, "Now *this* is jazz!"

It seems we like to hear our jazz artists struggle at times (which helps to explain why Art Tatum and Wynton Marsalis—virtuosos whose playing always seems so effortless—are derided on occasion for sounding cold, aloof, or soulless). And yet, unlike the bloodthirsty spectators of motorcycle-jumping events (or opera divas), we also want our performers to succeed in the end. As a result, and though jazz folks would hate to admit it, the live-and-spontaneous ideal is sometimes more lip service than reality. Above all, listeners want to hear "good music," as do the musicians themselves.[33] The mere existence of "alternate takes" from throughout jazz history attests that every generation has resisted releasing just any performance, no matter how spontaneous or impassioned the musicians may have felt at the time.[34] To achieve the desired results, jazz artists have routinely edited their work in the studio, with "fixes" ranging from punching in small fluffs to redoing entire solos. Given today's nonlinear digital recording technology, even formerly untouchable domains such as intonation and rhythmic imperfections can be altered with a few computer keystrokes from a skilled recording engineer, though, again, jazz's pure-improvisation aesthetic is so powerful that musicians will rarely boast of (or even admit to) their efforts in this regard.[35]

The aesthetic tension between "clean" and "natural" can also inform and reveal how musicians and record producers expect their finished products to sound. A short verbal exchange in the studio captured during the making of Davis's *Kind of Blue,* recorded in 1959 (though released fifty years after the original sessions), highlights these opposing ideals.

Following some clatter and a brief word with saxophonist Cannonball Adderley, Davis addresses the producer, Irving Townsend, who is in the control booth:

DAVIS: You know your floor squeaks, you know. You know what I mean? Can you hear me?
TOWNSEND (SEEMINGLY UNCONCERNED): Yeah.
DAVIS: Let's go.
JOHN COLTRANE (MATTER-OF-FACTLY): Surface noise. It's all part of the tune, man.[36]

Which brings us back to "Old Folks." Davis recorded both *Kind of Blue* and *Someday My Prince Will Come* in Columbia's 30th Street Studio.

While I hear no evidence that the "Old Folks" creak resulted from the same squeaky floor that Davis noted in the *Kind of Blue* sessions, we do get in this studio dialogue a sense that Davis expected the studio personnel to be aware of (and presumably to be concerned about and to fix) what he heard as a sonic *problem.* Granted, the analog recording technology in 1961 was not nearly as sophisticated as today's digital capabilities. Still, as I've noted, the creak could have been excised one way or another. So why would Davis and Co. leave this one in? Maybe he and the others came to agree that "it's all part of the tune," as Coltrane said about the earlier *Kind of Blue* squeak. Besides, the rest of "Old Folks" is creak-free, and the musicians play it beautifully.

Or, just perhaps, they heard the extraneous sound as working in the record's favor. Similar to the patchy moments on "Lester Leaps In," "Giant Steps," and "Mack the Knife," the apparently unrehearsed, unintended, wooden groan validates the track's authenticity. Even better, it gains this prestige without any of the musicians having to take the fall for making an error. Keeping in mind the competing jazz aesthetics of flawless execution and enthusiastic impulsiveness, we can see how this seeming imperfection on "Old Folks" grants the record a subtle aura of spur-of-the-momentness in a way that the musicians' performance does not.

PERFORMING JAZZ: THE "WORK OF ART" AND THE MUSICAL BODY IN RECORDED MUSIC

Finally, I want to reflect on what "Old Folks" tells us about the place—or absence—of performers' bodies in recorded audio media. I have noted that Miles Davis's voice sometimes remained on his albums, his spoken words serving as preludes or codas to his groups' performances. Other jazz recordings contain sections when instrumentalists sing (or grunt) along with their playing. Although some listeners disdain such moments as aural intrusions, others accept them as tolerable, even integral, aspects of the musical experience.[37] The straining creak on "Old Folks" functions somewhat like performers' vocalizations in that they both involve sounds that could be interpreted as separate from "the music." But these situations are not identical, for the creak is at once less personal than the voice—we do not know who or what made it—and yet somehow more physically present. After years of hearing entertainers, reporters, and politicians on radio or as voice-over on television and in films, audiences have come to accept disembodied speaking as a natural part of their soundscapes. By contrast, the creak on "Old Folks" conjures the less-common image of a musician shifting weight while playing. Suddenly we are aware that this track did not simply emanate from the ether, as music from radio or other sources so often seems to. Someone—literally some *body*—created this sound. In that brief moment we find an almost palpable sonic manifestation of a performer's physical presence within an audio recording and, with it, a rare, aural-only trace of the corporeal activity of jazz music making.

In his perceptive analysis of James Brown's "Super Bad" David Brackett has shown how "studio recordings typically efface the signs of production by seeking to minimize the effect of human *performance*."[38] In other words most records are so sonically pristine and our modes of listening to them so divorced from the time(s) and place(s) of their making that we can forget that the sounds we hear result from people operating instruments. Given that music helps to orient us physically in time and space, and to move us literally (through dancing, finger snapping, toe tapping, and head nodding) and figuratively (through structuring and evoking emotions), it is ironic that the ones who so often elude our musical awareness are the very ones called on to create that music.

Arguing along these lines, Suzanne Cusick has lamented that among her fellow scholars of the European classical tradition,

> music, an art which self-evidently does not exist until bodies make it and/or receive it, is thought about as if it were a *mind-mind* game. Thus when we think analytically about music, what we ordinarily do is describe practices of mind (the composer's choices) for the sake of informing the practices of other minds (who will assign meaning to the resulting sounds). . . . We end by ignoring the fact that these practices of the mind are non-practices without the bodily practices they call for—about which it has become unthinkable to think.
>
> That is, we have changed an art that exists only when, so to speak, the Word is made Flesh, into all art which is only the Word. Metaphorically, we have denied the very thing that makes music music, the thing which gives it such symbolic and sensual power.[39]

Given that European-oriented cultures have long adhered to a supposed mind-over-body hierarchy ("I think; therefore I am"), it should surprise few to learn that the situation Cusick describes persists in the Eurocentric world of classical music. The erasure of the body seems paradoxical in jazz, however, since African American–based music cultures have rarely acceded to that so-called Cartesian split. Performers of jazz—and also funk, soul, r&b, rock, gospel, disco, and hip-hop—have always prided themselves on creating sounds that inspire listeners both to cogitate and to actuate. (Aretha Franklin and her band propel us to the dance floor even as she admonishes, "You better *think* 'bout what you're trying to do to me!") Instances such as we hear on "Old Folks" can help us to wake up to that paradox and possibly recover some of the body in jazz music.[40]

It is worth pausing at this point to acknowledge just how much the way people write about, talk about, and value jazz is intertwined with physicality. Designations such as "hot," "sweet," "cool," and "hard (bop)" draw on people's experiences in the world to shape how we understand certain sounds and styles. The same goes for any number of song and album titles, including Miles Davis's own "Walkin'" and *Cookin'*. Musicians regularly use terms like *rushing, dragging, laying back,* or *pushing* to describe rhythmic momentum. Honorific titles such as *monster, giant,* and *heavyweight* reflect the imposing, even intimidating, presence of highly skilled jazz performers. (Saxophonist Johnny Griffin's nickname, "Little Giant," simultaneously describes Mr. Griffin's diminutive physical stature—he stood just five feet tall—and his immense improvisational abilities.) Using the same yardstick, less-skilled players are derided as "weak," "lame," or "lightweight."[41] When all is said and done, how we conceive of jazz is as much about the body as it is about the "soul."

As one small step toward reclaiming the centrality of the performing musician, I want also to reclaim the meaning of "the work of art." I do not mean that much-bandied phrase as it is typically understood: a noun, a thing, to be observed, contemplated, or admired. Rather, I'm using it as a verb. Here, the work of art refers to the physical (and also mental) effort necessary to create the sounds we hear as music. Of course, people must find deep satisfaction from this labor or they would not choose to spend whole lifetimes engaged in it. The musicologist and cellist Elisabeth Le Guin has even invoked the term *carnal* to convey a sense of the pleasure she derives from the intricate movements of her head, arms, legs, fingers, back, and shoulders while playing.[42] Make no mistake, though: it takes formidable corporal strength, coordination, and agility to bring any performance to life.

For an audible example of the type of bodily exertion I'm talking about, listen to Buster Bailey's clarinet solo on "St. Louis Blues" from the 1941 recording by John Kirby and His Orchestra. Bailey takes five choruses over the twelve-bar form, four of which consist of one continuous note—the G two octaves above middle C—sustained through the technique of circular breathing. No doubt, everyone associated with this session knew Bailey would utilize this "gimmick," but that detracts not one bit from the appeal and excitement of the performance. Midway through his solo, Bailey's tone waivers slightly; he's on the verge of losing control of his breathing. I'm certain that Bailey did not mean to falter there, but his brief slip draws attention to the physical demands he places on himself, even as it heightens the "can-he-do-it?" effect for the listener (there's that "aesthetic of imperfections" again).[43]

Even more remarkable in this respect is Rahsaan Roland Kirk's one-man interlude on "Pedal Up." Recorded live in 1973 and released the following year on *Bright Moments,* "Pedal Up" is a tour de force of dexterity and sheer aerobic vigor. Kirk sustains his circular breathing for more than four minutes while simultaneously playing independent lines on two woodwind instruments (as well as a rattle of some sort) and, for good measure, referencing both Strayhorn's "Satin Doll" and Beethoven's *Für Elise!*[44] It's an astonishing feat. Yet while the breathing techniques displayed by Buster Bailey and especially Roland Kirk foreground physical stamina, determined efforts permeate all worthwhile jazz, and this perhaps explains why Miles Davis not only released a record called *Relaxin'* but also one called *Workin'.* We can easily forget this "work" aspect of art when hearing recorded music, except in those rare moments, like in "St. Louis Blues," "Pedal Up," or, more subtly, "Old Folks," where the musician's body-in-action cannot be denied.[45]

⎯

I have offered three ways to interpret the creak on Miles Davis's "Old Folks." But this chapter has not come close to exhausting the potential meanings and implications of that sonority. No essay could. People continually determine, debate, reassess, and change what sounds mean (what *everything* means). Even so, perhaps this brief foray will encourage other scholars to expand that musicological toolbox a bit, to search for still more ways to account for those "divine details" and "distinguishing characteristics" that no one plays but that recordings allow us all to hear. For there are countless other intriguing moments to consider—the audience member's ebullient "yee-aaa-hh!" in the middle of Davis's "Stella by Starlight" performance at Lincoln Center, for instance, or the whispers and tinkling glasses behind Bill Evans's Village Vanguard gigs. Just a few of the sounds we hear over the music, between the music, as music: (im)perfect.

THREE

Sex Mob and the Carnivalesque
in Postwar Jazz

FOR MORE THAN A HALF CENTURY NOW a large contingent of musicians, writers, and educators has worked to reverse early perceptions of jazz as vulgar entertainment, arguing instead for its acceptance as art music, replete with the same markers of sophistication and gravity that have come to represent highbrow European forms and styles. The pianist and author Billy Taylor expressed this sentiment quite clearly when he wrote, "Though it is often fun to play, jazz is *very serious* music," this in an article titled, tellingly, "Jazz: America's Classical Music."[1] If we look and listen closely enough, however, it becomes apparent that not all jazz styles reflect the high-art principle. This chapter explores one of the music's "lower" manifestations: the *carnivalesque*.

The notion of the carnivalesque as I use it here derives in large measure from the literary theorist Mikhail Bakhtin, who argued that François Rabelais' unapologetically undignified sixteenth-century novel *Gargantua and Pantagruel* must be understood in the context of a raucous festival tradition in Europe that dates to antiquity.[2] In Bakhtin's view Rabelais created his ribald, coarse, and irreverent literary world in order to celebrate corporeal existence—this body in this lifetime—while challenging notions of "eternal truths" and seriousness so often espoused by those in or seeking power. And despite the vast historical, geographical, and cultural distances that separate us from Rabelais' literary creation, Bakhtin's conception of the carnivalesque can help us make sense of the (not-infrequent) indecorous outbursts in the supposedly staid milieu of recent jazz, while it sheds new light on other meanings and practices prevalent throughout the genre.

The roots of carnivalesque jazz run deep. Most obviously, jazz grew up alongside Mardi Gras, North America's most (in)famous carnival celebration, with its masks and revelry, its drunkenness, carnality, and flaunting of religious and societal norms. Yet while it is easy enough to hear and see a boisterous and earthy spirit in the polyphonic, poly-bodied mayhem of New Orleans street parades, that spirit is often overlooked in most current jazz contexts. Focusing on some of the sounds and images proffered by the New York–based band Sex Mob and a colorful and compelling assortment of that group's forebears and contemporaries, I show in this chapter how a carnivalesque aesthetic persists to this day as a foil to modern jazz's oftentimes severe, elitist, or solipsistic attitudes. Specifically, I suggest that in valuing revelry over veneration, and guileless laughter over glib hipness, Sex Mob and like-minded musicians reject "importance" and ironic distance, two traits often associated with postwar jazz.

CARNIVALESQUE

To begin, I want to emphasize a few general points. First, this study concerns the carnivalesque—that which echoes or borrows elements of carnival-like festivities—not carnival itself. Contemporary jazz, even the most outrageous, almost never evokes the fluid, nonhierarchical bustle of true carnival. Bakhtin notes, "Carnival does not know footlights, in the sense that it does not acknowledge any distinction between actors and spectators. Footlights would destroy a carnival, as the absence of footlights would destroy a theatrical performance."[3] By contrast, today's jazz musicians "know footlights." That is, the conventions associated with formal performances almost always apply: gigs begin and end at agreed-upon times; musicians generally appear on a stage, physically separated from their listeners; some jazz venues will not even permit audience members to converse amongst themselves (let alone talk to performers) while the music is playing; dancing to jazz is largely a thing of the past.[4] Which is simply to say that jazz is a thoroughly professionalized activity. And with the exception, again, of parade bands in New Orleans, as well as some dances during the 1930s where performers and audience members rubbed elbows, it always has been.[5] To witness this professionalization in action, one need only visit the Crescent City's annual Jazz and Heritage Festival, with its costly tickets granting patrons access to watch and listen to, but otherwise not interact with, internationally known artists who appear on meticulously scheduled, corporate-sponsored stages.

Second, the tunes, grooves, and sounds I discuss here derive mostly from African American musical traditions. Thus, "carnivalesque jazz" refers only to those elements that resemble some of the attitudes and aesthetics that Bakhtin associates with the ancient European festivals, not any specific activities, musical or otherwise, originating in Europe's past. As I show, these shared traits include laughter; an embrace of popular culture; an emphasis on the public or crowd rather than the private or individual; irreverence toward anything deemed sacred, serious, or timeless; and the larger-than-life manner of presentation that Bakhtin calls "grotesque realism."

Third, there is a difference between identifying carnivalesque elements in art or literature and finding and describing those elements in music. Bakhtin was able to cite clear examples of these features in Rabelais' writing and in paintings of the period. Although I do discuss aspects of the carnivalesque as evidenced in the daily language of jazz people and through some visual imagery, we must accept that music does not convey meaning in the same ways that words and pictures do. Consequently, I base much of my argument on *sounds*. And not just notes—timbre is a vital component of any and all musics, but it is significantly more so in a seminotated genre such as jazz and absolutely central to the carnivalesque versions of that genre. So I implore readers to listen to the recordings I describe, for only in hearing this music can one fully understand and experience the points made here. These caveats aside, we can turn to the topic at hand, beginning with the crucial notion of grotesque realism.

JAZZ DISCOURSE: OFFICIAL AND UNOFFICIAL

Bakhtin uses the terms *grotesque* and *grotesque realism* to describe a theme running through many fifteenth- and sixteenth-century European paintings and stories in which "the bodily becomes grandiose, exaggerated, immeasurable," a theme that emphasizes "fertility, growth, and a brimming-over abundance."[6] Rather than the everyday notion of the grotesque as something to be shunned or feared, it refers in this case to a hyperaccentuation of physical properties and actions usually understood as favorable or genial. The carnivalesque's grotesque elements often highlight that which Bakhtin calls the body's "lower strata," the biological parts and processes involved in sex, fecundity, and the ingestion, digestion, and elimination of food and drink. There are dozens of such passages in Rabelais. In Book III, for instance, the character Panurge sings the praises of a certain sauce that "purged the bladder, swelled the genitals, righted the foreskin, hardened the gland, rectified the penis. . . . It set the belly in apple-pie order, so a man could belch, fart, poop, piddle, shit, sneeze, sob, cough, throw up, yawn, puff, inhale, exhale, snore, sweat and wangle the ferrule to his heart's content."[7] Not simply a means of eliciting giggles from prurient readers, Rabelais' grotesque episodes unveil the absurdity of self-righteous attitudes from the prudish or powerful, while celebrating the regenerating cycles of life and death.[8]

The jazz world is replete with its own references to the grotesque and lower strata, yet these are rarely to be found in trade magazines, radio broadcasts, liner notes, history books, or video documentaries. Such media put forth jazz's "official" discourse, and the tone there remains virtually always "respectable," as does that of most jazz scholarship, my own work included. Even the U.S. government contributes to this elevated (and thus elevating) manner:

> Whereas, it is in the best interest of the national welfare and all of our citizens to preserve and celebrate this unique art form: Now therefore be it *Resolved by the House of Representatives (the Senate concurring), That* it is the sense of the Congress that jazz is hereby designated as a rare and valuable national American treasure to which we should devote our attention, support, and resources to make certain it is preserved, understood, and promulgated.[9]

Journalists, scholars, record executives, and members of Congress are not the only ones who stick to the official line. Musicians typically clean up their language onstage or during interviews, and for very good reasons. Above all, they want to enhance the general respect, and so, too, the remuneration, accorded to themselves and others in their profession. Many seek to reverse the long-standing, oftentimes racist, perceptions of jazz as the refuge for antisocial, narcotic-addicted, untrained "naturals." To counter these negative stereotypes, proponents depict the jazz musician's craft as a physically, intellectually, and even spiritually demanding one, with excellence attainable only through years of dedicated effort.[10] I do not mean to suggest that such claims are false, by the way. To play jazz at a high level *does* require thousands of hours of practicing and performing; but the same goes for any number of other skills. Hitting a baseball thrown by a professional pitcher, for instance, is an immensely difficult undertaking (just ask basketball legend—and failed baseball outfielder—Michael Jordan). Yet baseball players rarely use their excellence as a wedge to differentiate themselves from, or place themselves above, their fans. Despite the millions of dollars major leaguers earn each year, baseball people call their sport "America's pastime." Like the baseball community, performers and fans of blues, bluegrass, polka, zydeco, and country music, genres that demand their own types of knowledge and skillfulness to play convincingly, generally promote their music as a product of and for "the people," while jazz proudly sets itself apart as the exclusive province of the urbane and erudite.[11]

However, in jazz's less-monitored spaces—the rehearsal hall, backstage green room, or bar area—one can hear an unofficial language in play, and this communication draws freely on the lower strata and grotesque. Performers are exhorted to "play with some balls" or cautioned by a well-meaning mentor or colleague not to "shoot your load too soon" during a solo. While these phrases reflect jazz's male-centric and oftentimes inexcusably sexist biases, it is quite clear that they get their points across via the lower regions, as does the less gender-specific compliment, "You play your ass off."[12]

"Gutbucket," "nasty," "filthy," "funky," "raunchy," and "dirty," all of which are synonymous in everyday speech with rottenness or stench, are similarly invoked in unofficial jazz discourse to describe sounds or styles and are used regularly to express admiration or approval.[13] As the source of all that energy (and excrement) the realms of food, drink, eating, and the belly pertain here, too. Bands that sound good can be described as "cooking," "greasy," or "tasty." Musicians adroit at improvising melodic lines over harmonic progressions are sometimes said to "devour (or eat up) the changes." A number of jazz terms contain the same sort of ambivalence—involving a combination of praise and insult, or destruction and creation—that Bakhtin finds throughout Rabelais' stories. Laudatory labels such as "monster" and "giant" reflect this two-sided notion, as do lines like "that band's burning," "on fire," "killin'," or "tearing it up." Likewise, one can "play some serious shit" (a positive trait) or just sound like shit (a negative one); a musician can sound "bad" (meaning good) or bad (not good). Or consider "sick," "stupid," "crazy," and "ridiculous," all of which are widely used to denote positive qualities in a performer or performance. The same goes for "motherfucker," among the highest commendations— or lowest insults—a musician can receive.

Jazz musicians' autobiographies tend to fall somewhere between the official and unofficial discourses. Charles Mingus's *Beneath the Underdog* contains sections extolling jazz as serious art but also wildly grandiloquent passages not too different from those found in Rabelais, including an extensive list of terms for male genitalia and a depiction of sex organs taking on extraordinary physical properties.[14] The memoirs of many other jazz people also contain language drawn from the lower strata. To be clear: not all of the sex, drugs, and turmoil in these autobiographies belong to the carnivalesque or grotesque. Some of those passages are just the author's (or editor's) take on the less-domesticated, and sometimes highly romanticized, aspects of the artist's life. Yet even these accounts remind us of the close relationship of unofficial jazz discourse to the lower strata, a rare enough glimpse since that language is typically kept from the public.[15]

WHAT'S IN A NAME?

All of this brings us to Sex Mob. The trumpeter and composer Steven Bernstein (b. 1961) formed his quartet in 1995 for a series of gigs he was to host at the Knitting Factory, the primary performance venue for New York's so-called downtown scene.[16] Like Tim Berne, John Zorn, and other musicians in that time and place, Sex Mob had an eclectic repertoire and casual mode of dress and demeanor that presented a striking alternative to the more refined jazz styles favored by the neoclassicists uptown at Lincoln Center. But even more than its SoHo peers, Sex Mob embraced, and continues to embrace, an unselfconsciously joyous, raw, sometimes vulgar approach to jazz and so stands as a prime exemplar of the carnivalesque.

Quite simply, Sex Mob does not bother with the "official" front. Just the ensemble's undignified name counters the long-standing jazz tradition of donning an aristocratic, cerebral, or spiritual title (think Joe "King" Oliver, Stan Kenton's Progressive Jazz Orchestra, Steve Coleman's Mystic Rhythm Society, among others). Obviously, the "Sex" part of the band's name derives directly from the lower strata. The interconnections between the terms *sex* and *jazz* reach back a century or more; indeed, according to some accounts, these two words were virtually synonymous in the music's early days. The second half of the ensemble's name also counters official jazz rhetoric. Steven Bernstein literally relinquishes his position as leader to the mob. Given that *mob* can substitute for *group,* we might see the name "Sex Mob" as a lighthearted take on the generic term "jazz group." Understandings are rarely so simple, of course.

For decades, use of the "jazz" designation has caused consternation in certain circles. Some African American musicians and writers, in particular, have resisted the label precisely because of its connections with sex, which, they argue, denigrate performers and their work. These commentators prefer labels such as "black music," "black art music," "African American classical music," or "creative music."[17] As white musicians, the members of Sex Mob have never faced the complicated, sometimes degrading, and even physically dangerous conflation of music, blackness, and hypersexuality in the public imagination, and perhaps they have not considered the potential discomfort or animosity their group's name might arouse in some listeners, performers, or other jazz participants. As Bernstein explained it to me, that name resulted largely by accident during a brainstorming session about how to title his late-night Knitting Factory performance series. Initially he considered calling the band Slide Mob, in honor of the slide trumpet he planned to feature at the gigs. Slide Mob gradually morphed into Sex Mob, and the tag stuck. More important than the name's origins, however, are the ways people have come to use and understand it. In what has become a kind of unofficial group motto, it has been written that Sex Mob's "main commitment" is to "bring the sexy thing back into instrumental music."[18] So rather than sweeping under the rug some of jazz's supposedly ignominious origins, the group celebrates an earthy heritage of the music. Incidentally, this is a position not every black intellectual would oppose. Amiri Baraka, for one, has approvingly reinforced these libidinous connotations, writing, "Jazz is *jism,* come music, creatinging music."[19]

However one views it, the Sex Mob moniker represents, at the very least, a marked change from conventional jazz practices. And references to the lower strata only begin with the group's name. The title of its 1998 recording, *Din of Inequity,* a playful twist on "den of iniquity" conjures images of immoderation, scediness, and loud volumes. So, too, do the album titles *Dime Grind Palace* and *Sexotica.* "Kitchen" from *Dime Grind Palace* celebrates food, while songs such as "The Grind" *(Solid Sender),* "Call to the Freaks," and "Herbert's Weiner" *(Dime Grind Palace)* invoke the carnal.[20] Bernstein reaches deep into the lower regions with his six-part composition "Human Bidet" from *Solid Sender.*[21]

FIGURE 2. Front panel, Sex Mob, *Din of Inequity* CD

Sex Mob also projects a grotesque/carnivalesque aesthetic through the
visual material accompanying its recordings. The cartoon cover of *Dime
Grind Palace* shows a raucous house party of humans and anthropomor-
phized animals in full swing. Music, sex, and drinking abound. The cover
panel of *Din of Inequity* depicts a horned, devilish creature playing slide
trumpet (Figure 2), unquestionably a reference to Bernstein himself, as
he is the only prominent jazz musician ever to make that the primary
instrument of choice. The CD booklet features other similarly outlandish
drawings, including a character wearing what appears to be a condom on
his nose as a mask (while his head explodes!), and the patently grotesque
depiction of seven bemused cartoon figures standing atop the distended

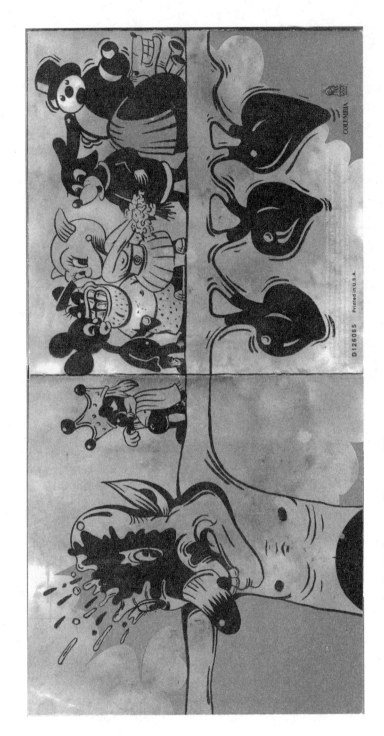

FIGURE 3. Inner panels, Sex Mob, *Din of Inequity* CD

arm of the condom-masked character, from which hang three beating hearts (Figure 3). Such images might not seem out of place on the cover of a recording by Frank Zappa or other rock provocateur, but they differ greatly from typical visual depictions of the jazz world. As such, Sex Mob's iconography reflects and helps to configure an alternative, and in this case decidedly seamier and more mischievous, understanding of jazz than that to which we have become accustomed.

SOUNDING THE LOWER STRATA

In keeping with the brazen spirit of their titles and graphics, Sex Mob's timbres turn traditional notions of musical beauty on their heads. Steven Bernstein forgoes the clear tones and precise articulations on which so many trumpeters pride themselves, but he also eschews a "sensitive" sound, such as that often associated with Miles Davis, Chet Baker, or Art Farmer. Instead, Bernstein's playing is strident, messy, and remarkably elastic. His use of the slide trumpet almost guarantees that the intonation will feel slippery and unstable. The effect can be clownish at times, but it can also have a powerful edge. Likewise, Sex Mob's saxophonist, Briggan Krauss, broaches no honeyed sonorities and only rarely favors a bebop-driven linearity; he chooses instead to deploy an arsenal of multiphonics, vocalizations, and forays into extreme registers. Perhaps the most appropriate descriptor of these horn players' sonic aesthetic is *visceral,* a word that derives from a Latin root pertaining to intestines.[22]

While Bernstein's and Krauss's sounds are readily identifiable as their own, their work does echo some early jazz stylists, especially Duke Ellington's brass growlers from the Cotton Club era, as well as free-oriented players from later generations, including Ornette Coleman, Albert Ayler, Roswell Rudd (who guests on *Dime Grind Palace*), Carla Bley (for whom Bernstein has worked), Don Cherry, and, above all, Lester Bowie. Along with Bowie's scattershot trumpet style, Bernstein picked up on the elder musician's penchant for playing seemingly lightweight pop tunes in an unselfconscious manner (Bowie's repertoire included "The Great Pretender," "Blueberry Hill," and "It's Howdy Doody Time"). This blithe embrace of popular forms and idioms is another defining trait of the carnivalesque, a point to which I will return.

Bernstein has been known to play his instrument through a "bullet" microphone and a small amplifier, a setup favored by Chicago blues harmonica stylists like Little Walter and James Cotton to simultaneously cut through and give voice to the noisy, crowded, working-class bars and dance hall parties of black urban neighborhoods after World War II. Bernstein and company may not come from or play to rough-and-tumble African American communities, but the sonic affect is much the same. For Sex Mob, too, creates "city music." The group's sound comes from and speaks to gatherings of people, jostling and partying, and is most at home in a cramped nightclub, midsummer, with its smells of stale beer, sweaty bodies, and clammy bathrooms (making it the most accurate sonic manifestation of the original Knitting Factory!).

LAUGHTER, HIPNESS, AND THE PUBLIC SPHERE

I have already shown how and why certain individuals and institutions have reshaped a genre that in the 1910s and 1920s had been vilified as crass noise and by the late 1930s was widely enjoyed as this country's most popular sound into "America's classical music." But it bears repeating that the serious-izing (if I may) of jazz was an important, perhaps even necessary, step toward establishing long-denied respect for African American people and cultures. The aspect of dignity that James Reese Europe, James P. Johnson, Duke Ellington, Teddy Wilson, Jimmie Lunceford, Mary Lou Williams, Nat Cole, and others brought to their craft played an undeniable, fundamental, and irreversible role in this process. Such decorum, both audible and visible, also laid the foundation for the formidable achievements of jazz's modernist contingents after World War II.

Still, the gains made in these efforts were not achieved without a price. One of the chief casualties of jazz's elevation in prestige has been the loss of much of its former merriment. John Lewis, Lennie Tristano, Bill Evans, and Max Roach, surely among the most highly regarded and influential jazz figures of the past sixty years, all shunned a sense of fun in favor of presenting themselves and their music as high-minded. One could even argue that the exalted reputations of these musicians could not have been possible without their stoic demeanors. This mode of presentation has become even more indelibly engrained as jazz has moved into college music programs. I pick up the topic of jazz education in a later chapter, so I will only note here in passing that, as with European classical music in conservatories, the serious-art ideology is now part of the package jazz students inevitably acquire as they absorb and develop the skills expected of the professional musician. To be sure, jazz performers can be seen smiling or joking around backstage and even sometimes onstage. But the public version of jazz humor is typically filtered through the aesthetic of hipness. I'm not referring to those valuable qualities of hipness that denote wisdom, acute awareness, or vast stores of knowledge. Rather, it's the sense of detachment or superiority that often accompanies the hipster. And in these guises, jazz doesn't laugh. It smirks.

PERFORMATIVE HUMOR VERSUS PARTICIPATORY LAUGHTER

Scholars have largely ignored the role humor has played in jazz. I hope this chapter serves as one small step toward correcting that oversight. To start, I want to differentiate between a *participatory* brand of laughter, which characterizes the carnivalesque, and the more prevalent *performative* style of jazz humor. By *performative* humor I mean a joke or a gag deliberately presented to an audience: someone says or does something intended to elicit a chuckle from someone else. In this case the person delivering the comic bit need not be seen as sharing in the audience's merriment. In fact, displaying any sense of levity may be counterproductive to the comedic effect. Think of the realm of professional comedians. From Harold Lloyd and Buster Keaton through Jack Benny and Gracie Allen, up to the almost comatose Steven Wright, many of America's most successful funny people have based their acts on appearing deadpan or oblivious to the situation, even while their audiences roared. Others, most notably, Lenny Bruce, Redd Foxx, George Carlin, Richard Pryor, and Chris Rock, have separated themselves by adopting an exasperated, satirical, or angry tone.

Jazz humor, at least since the rise of a modernist aesthetic, often works in a similar fashion, with the performer standing apart from the audience's experience of the musical joke. Thelonious Monk rarely so much as cracked a smile onstage. Listeners were expected to dig the wry wit of his compositions and playing; those who didn't get it were simply dismissed as squares.[23] Same with Sonny Rollins, Dexter Gordon, Charlie Parker, Art Tatum, Lester Young, and the other great improvisers who were savvy and skilled enough to be able to express ironical "winks" as part of their improvisational excursions. Some players did deliver their humor more obviously, but even these performers typically presented their material through the filter of hipness or satire. Check Slim Gaillard's repertoire, Dizzy Gillespie's vocal performances, or some of Charles Mingus's work. For instance, on "Original Faubus Fables" (1960) Mingus and his bandmates assume a broadly mocking tone as they lambast Arkansas' governor Orville Faubus and other political figures for their bigoted or cowardly stances during the school integration struggles of the time. The performance's acerbic drollery can be heard in the vocal mannerisms of Mingus and Dannie Richmond, as well as the quasi-Weimar-cabaret atmosphere of the opening sections, especially in the exaggerated dynamics and glissandi from the horn players Ted Curson and Eric Dolphy. Parts of "Original Faubus Fables" can evoke knowing smiles, but this is not "funny music." Instead it brings to mind what Freud described as humor's "*liberating* element," because the ego "refuses to be hurt by the arrows of reality or to be compelled to suffer," or perhaps the more matter-of-fact motto, "You gotta laugh to keep from crying."[24]

Musicians have an unquestionable right to comment on injustices when they see them. Irony and satire serve as powerful weapons in this battle.[25] Yet as vital as "Faubus" and similar performances remain, they do not involve the type of unfettered participatory laughter I am talking about. Different from performative satire, which, in the scholar Jure Gantar's words, "must arouse contempt for its target," participatory laughter acknowledges the uncertainties and foibles of the human condition, *including one's own*.[26] Herein lies a crucial distinction between carnivalesque jazz and the vast majority of other postwar jazz models, whether uptown, downtown, or anywhere else: the carnivalesque in jazz celebrates people, warts and all. Not that this attitude lacks teeth—as one scholar so evocatively put it, "Carnival laughter is the laughter of peasants with pitchforks"—but it is, principally, an act of affirmation and celebration open to everyone.[27]

"MACARENA"

An audible example of carnivalesque jazz's participatory spirit is Sex Mob's recording of "Macarena" *(Din of Inequity)*. The most well-known version of that song, by Los Del Rio and the Bayside Boys, was a global phenomenon, selling more than 110 million copies and spending fourteen weeks atop the U.S. pop singles chart in 1996. Along with the hefty sales came the almost inevitable backlash. "Macarena" was instantly derided as "a guilty pleasure," appealing only to the lowest common denominator of the listening public.[28] No doubt, the negative reactions were based in large part on the sheer number of units sold (something that appeals to so many people can't *really* be good, right?). Further damning the track is its absence of traditional markers of musical authenticity. It was created from digital samples, not from "acoustic" instruments; it sounds happy; and, worst of all, it was intended for dancing. In other words "Macarena" is a latter-day disco hit. Few, if any, genres have faced more heated opposition among music's critical establishment than disco. In reality, though, disco stands as only the most notorious of a long line of popular dance idioms that have been vilified as "bad music."[29] Even beyond the commercialism or authenticity issues, moving one's body to music has been widely viewed as either morally suspicious or incurably vapid. Given these understandings, few tunes would seem less likely for a jazz group to cover than "Macarena." And yet Steven Bernstein and his colleagues not only take it on; they embrace it.

Sex Mob's "Macarena" starts with Bernstein asking his guest guitarist, London McDaniels, "Do you wanna play that phrase you were playing?" And they're off. Such an inauspicious introduction brings to mind Bakhtin's assertion that "even in its beginning [carnival atmosphere] has no serious or pious tone. Nor is it set in motion by order; it opens simply with a signal marking the beginning of merriment and foolery."[30] McDaniels and bassist Tony Scherr bump into one another, as each tries to establish a groove in the key of F. Things are so loose here that the musicians can't even seem to agree on a tempo or definitive downbeat until almost a minute into the performance. The instability does not seem to bother Bernstein and saxophonist Briggan Krauss, however, as they trade good-natured splats and splays with one another. Eventually, drummer Kenny Wolleson and guest organist John Medeski settle into an undeniable, body-rocking pulse. The mixture ferments and escalates until we hear Bernstein's voice again, this time cueing the band to "go on" to the next section. Suddenly, what had felt wobbly to the point of near collapse, comes together. The group modulates as one up a step to G, as the horn players' unison melody statement soars joyfully. Falling back to F, we hear a brief but powerful organ solo from Medeski. Another statement of the tune in G, and a short outburst from Bernstein in F, leads back to a more confident version of the opening guitar-and-bass riff. The track closes with a quiet reiteration of the melody on electric guitar. Sex Mob's "Macarena" traces a familiar performance model—soft to loud to soft to loud to soft again. In this case that model happens to be enacted on a well-known pop song.

"IF IT'S PERFECT NOTES YOU WANT, DON'T GET THIS BAND!"

Had Sex Mob wanted to present their "Macarena" as a satirical commentary on the banality of disco-pop culture, they could have taken any number of approaches. Most obviously they could have mockingly referenced the dance groove of the original or given a derisive edge to the melody (à la Curson and Dolphy on Mingus's "Original Faubus Fables"). Yet there's no evidence of cynicism or dismissive sneers here. It's simply a group of musicians going about the jazz business of playing, and playing with, the given material, albeit in an unusually boisterous and lighthearted spirit. Moreover, if this were Sex Mob's only such performance, one might consider "Macarena" an anomaly: some jazz cats tossing off a goofy pop tune in the studio before getting down to serious business. Yet this is much the same untidy, noisy, body-activating, start-in-the-middle approach these musicians take on a large portion of their repertoire. Actually, it's the band's stock in trade. Bernstein purposely strives for a kind of carefree ungainliness, as he very rarely rehearses his ensemble. In another example of the aesthetics of mistakes I cited in the previous chapter, the performers learn the music in the studio just before they record. Bernstein adopted this practice because, as he put it, "listeners are tired of hearing the finished product all the time. There's a segment of the population who misses the mystery of discovery, and so would rather hear a performance with mistakes than a perfected performance. We don't use ProTools. If it's perfect notes you want, don't get this band."[31]

Bernstein chooses his "cover" material with two thoughts in mind. First, he needs to make sure a song is compatible with the technical idiosyncrasies of the slide trumpet (the physical configuration of that instrument makes flawless execution of intricate passages nearly impossible or, at any rate, defeats the whole purpose of using the slide).[32] Second, he looks for songs that are widely known and easily recognizable. He believes that playing familiar compositions allows the public to follow more readily the musicians' improvisational choices, making the experience more enjoyable for both player and listener. Thus, rather than ignoring, lecturing, or berating audiences as some jazz artists have been known to do, Bernstein looks for ways to connect more readily with them and, as he describes it, to "take them on a journey." Toward this end Sex Mob's repertoire includes pieces from a range of prominent sources, including James Brown ("Please, Please, Please"), the Rolling Stones ("Ruby Tuesday"), Johann Strauss ("On the Beautiful Blue Danube," tucked away in "Exit Music" from *Dime Grind Palace*), and the soundtracks to James Bond films.

Not everything Sex Mob plays sounds as fun as "Macarena" or these other tunes. The group's version of Buffalo Springfield's "For What It's Worth" *(Solid Sender)* displays the same characteristic looseness but conveys a greater sense of urgency, while "Mothra" (*Dime Grind Palace*) sounds downright dark. Still, given the raucous joy audible on so many cuts, it is clear that Sex Mob's aesthetic leans heavily toward the unregulated, laughing attitude I have described. And by performing "Macarena," as well as Abba's "Fernando," Carly Simon's "Nobody Does It Better," and other unabashedly pop-py songs alongside compositions by jazz royalty like Duke Ellington and Count Basie, Sex Mob also forswears the notion that popular songs are "guilty pleasures," a loaded term that the musicologist Robert Walser has described as "music that one can enjoy only as long as one can feel superior to those who produce and support it."[33] To understand how Sex Mob's playfulness upends the hierarchy that would place jazz (and by extension the people who produce and support it) above other genres (and by extension the people who produce and support those genres), it is worth exploring the concept of "timelessness" as disseminated throughout jazz discourse.

THE CARNIVALESQUE VS. "TIMELESSNESS" IN THE OFFICIAL JAZZ REALM

For jazz to achieve and maintain its position as a classical music, it must be understood as not only serious but also transhistorical. Words like *eternal* and *timeless* serve to form just such understandings. Instances of these terms in the jazz media are too numerous even to begin cataloging. No doubt, such designations help to provide long-overdue recognition for the musical achievements of a number of skilled composers and performers from past eras. But to describe Dexter Gordon, Billy Strayhorn, or others as intelligent, creative, or sophisticated is one thing; to label them and their music as "timeless" is quite another, for it removes these artists from the very historical and cultural circumstances that made their music possible.

More troubling, when someone like Wynton Marsalis, the proponent par excellence of jazz "timelessness," adopts the looks and sounds of his long-dead heroes, he and his colleagues extol a narrow and self-defined vision of jazz's past as a way of legitimizing and marketing their own activities today. In this way Marsalis's stance exemplifies Bakhtin's assessments of state- and church-sponsored celebrations: "The official feast looked back at the past and used the past to consecrate the present. . . . The official feast asserted all that was stable, unchanging, perennial: the existing hierarchy, the existing religious, political, and moral values, norms, and prohibitions. It was the triumph of a truth already established, the predominant truth that was put forward as eternal and indisputable. This is why the tone of the official feast was monolithically serious and why the element of laughter was alien to it."[34]

It is no coincidence that Marsalis gets the most "face time" in Ken Burns's documentary *Jazz*. Marsalis was the main musical consultant for that series. Nor did it happen by chance that the final selection on the documentary's five-CD companion is the Lincoln Center Jazz Orchestra's 1998 version of "Take the A Train," a "faithful" recreation of Strayhorn's original from the 1940s (which also appears in that set). Marsalis is the founder and artistic director of Jazz at Lincoln Center and the leader of its orchestra. To be sure, a neotraditionalist performance deserves inclusion in any documentary or audio compilation as an apt symbol of jazz in the 1990s. But I am hardly the first to notice that when Burns and Marsalis chose to fill the final disc of their CD set with Lincoln Center's "A Train," as well as a cut from Marsalis's own quartet, a track from bop saxophonist Dexter Gordon's 1970s "homecoming" period, and two selections from Ellington's last decade, they necessarily squeezed out any number of other justifiable representatives of the music's last forty years. It does not really matter whether Ken Burns, a self-avowed neophyte of jazz history, was aware of the narrowness of the narrative that bears his name. The point is that his documentary and its many multimedia spin-offs still stand as the most visible, most elaborate, and most powerful purveyors of an official discourse of jazz timelessness.[35]

Clearly, Sex Mob represents a very different take on "the jazz tradition" from that espoused by Marsalis and Burns. But it does not do so by ignoring the music's past (after all, the group has recorded such Ellingtonia as "Come Sunday," "Black and Tan Fantasy," and "The Mooche," as well as Basie's "Blue and Sentimental" and a tribute to Artie Shaw); it just refuses to view the work of earlier generations as relics to be worshipped obsequiously. Instead of an eternal longing for what Ralph Ellison once suspiciously described as jazz's "Golden Age, Time Past," the openness that marks carnivalesque jazz celebrates this life, this day, this moment.[36] Gary Giddins has noted that in Sex Mob, Steven Bernstein "presides over a band that interprets ancient jazz as an old-time religion, only without the solemnity—more like old-time paganism really."[37] As with all pagan rites, carnivalesque music foregrounds the body, in all its sexy, smelly, temporary glory, a body that, not coincidentally, has been largely contained since jazz became an "intellectual," or at least a "listening," music. Bernstein grew up in Berkeley, California, and that town's zen-in-tie-dye ethos rubbed off on him. In a 1999 interview he remarked, "I'm part of the psychedelic generation. I see a lot of colors, and I want my music to be colorful, to exemplify a psychedelic form. . . . But then again combining that psychedelic concept of structure with the fire of, say, Roy Eldridge and [Louis] Armstrong—guys who play instruments like you thought they were going to bust it—gets the audience dancing in a very physical way."[38]

Which brings us back once again to the uncomfortable relationship postwar jazz has had with popular culture. Enhancing the music's prestige has meant not only pulling it "up" so that skeptics would have to recognize the tremendous skill, creativity, and energy of its performers. It has also meant pulling jazz *away* from its roots in and as popular music. Of course, jazz performers and composers—including the "serious" ones—have always drawn on commercial songs and styles. Tin Pan Alley, the center of America's popular music industry throughout the first half of the twentieth century, provided the raw material for a large percentage of jazz performances. But commentators have often downplayed this connection, either by ignoring outright the publishing-industry origins of the compositions or by telling us how this or that player "transcends" the supposed banality of what the bebop record producer Ross Russell once dismissed as "the horrible products of the tunesmiths."[39] In the post–Tin Pan Alley era jazz's many intersections with rock, funk, r & b, soul, rap, and country have likewise met with resistance. Musicians who openly incorporate and celebrate pop music or other aspects of popular culture in their jazz run the risk of turning off their more art-minded peers (and journalists and academics), even while—or perhaps because—they sometimes draw large and appreciative audiences. Not that Sex Mob will ever top the charts; there's probably too much messiness and clatter for them to hit it really big. Still, this is far from an underground phenomenon. The group's *Sexotica* earned a Grammy nomination in 2007 for Best Contemporary Jazz Album, and the mere fact that its recordings were distributed for a time through Sony/Columbia—alongside and at the same time as Wynton Marsalis—suggests that someone high up in the music industry thought they could move a fair number of "units."

John Janowiack's review of *Din of Inequity* for *DownBeat* reveals how these issues of seriousness and credibility can play out in the jazz media:

> Bernstein's slide trumpet (slumpet?) sounds like Roswell Rudd on a
> good day after a strong whiff of helium or, to put it another way, like

a mischievous schoolboy making funny noises with a balloon. That's intended as a compliment, oddly enough, since his musical musings are infused with wit. . . . [Bernstein is] like a circus geek who gets off on shocking us with his audacity. I can just picture him as the kind of kid who would bring weird treasures to school to get the attention of classmates. ("Hey guys, check this out. It's a slumpet!") Far too subversive for show-and-tell, he could only show it off during recess to a few cool kids, the kind who grow up to be . . . well, they never grow up, they just hang out at the Knitting Factory a lot. Sex Mob is a novelty act, to be sure, and we can only take it as seriously as they let us. And that seems to be the whole point. Despite a decidedly unserious vibe, this album is performed by some seriously clever musicians who deal in outlandish surprises.[40]

Janowiack seems perplexed. He likes the album, but he also has difficulty accepting the musicians' playfulness as anything other than a "novelty act" or even thinking of these accomplished professionals as adults. *Din of Inequity* suggests too much fun and too little decorum, so Sex Mob must go the way of jazz's other loud aunts and uncles who embarrass the respectable side of the family: it must be ignored or, at best, referred to with a condescending rolling of the eyes.

Given writers' unease with or reluctance in dealing with this sort of jazz, it becomes easy to overlook just how many well-known musicians have invoked the carnivalesque aesthetic as a significant part of their presentations. I've already mentioned Carla Bley, Lester Bowie, and Roswell Rudd. Others, including Joey Baron, Han Bennink, Willem Breuker, Don Byron, Olu Dara, the Dirty Dozen Brass Band, Bill Frisell, Charlie Hunter, Roland Kirk, Henry Threadgill, Matt Wilson, the World Saxophone Quartet, and lesser-known artists like the Extra Action Marching Band, Gerry Gibbs, March Fourth Marching Band, and the Microscopic Septet, have also conjured a wildly festive mood. Taken together, this is an impressive group of creative people, and should give us pause to consider why notions of the prosaic and profane, of laughter and effusive playfulness, don't figure more prominently in narratives like Ken Burns's *Jazz* (but, of course, we do know why).

LAUGHTER AND FERTILITY: SOME CLOSING THOUGHTS ON CARNIVALESQUE JAZZ

Roswell Rudd once proclaimed, "all jazz is fun music."[41] Yet while Rudd's good-natured take on his craft is refreshing, it is, as we know, far from accurate. Not all jazz is fun, nor should it be. The irrefutable intensity and single-mindedness evident in the music of Max Roach, John Lewis, and other brooding or refined musicians have given audiences new ways of seeing, hearing, thinking about, and acting in the world. Dignified, rigorous, or seething presentations will continue to play a significant role in the future development of the genre. But when jazz becomes all-consuming in its gravitas, it loses some of the humanity that it so often proclaims as its province. Worse, too often the music wears the facade of seriousness without delivering the revelatory goods, leading only to preciousness (and usually tedium, to boot).

The art historians Timothy Hyman and Roger Malbert have suggested that "carnivalesque art is fuelled by an absence and a need; and it may be precisely where laughter is most forbidden that the carnivalesque becomes most meaningful."[42] Laughter may not (yet) be forbidden in jazz, but it is undoubtedly in short supply, which is why the carnivalesque matters to jazz. The carnivalesque welcomes laughter. It *breeds* laughter, and in doing so it rejects and liberates from the mannered and the intimidating. It nurtures an acceptance of one's all-too-human quirks and failures (and so those of others, as well).

The current tendency among so many scholars, journalists, teachers, musicians, and fans to equate jazz authenticity and quality solely with musical weightiness patently misrepresents the true breadth of jazz styles, attitudes, and identities prevalent over the past half century. But that is the least of the problems with this sort of narrative. Noting a similar tendency in the world of literature, Milan Kundera has forebodingly predicted of Rabelais' future readers: "with a heavy heart, I imagine the day when Panurge no longer makes people laugh."[43] Likewise, I fear that the motivation to elevate jazz on the ladder of cultural hierarchy is so strong that some day jazz people will no longer laugh with and through their music. Woe to us if that day ever comes. As Bakhtin chided in one of his later essays, "Only dogmatic and authoritarian cultures are one-sidedly serious. . . . Everything that is truly great must include an element of laughter."[44] If jazz ever cleans up its act entirely, if it loses the open, honest laughter of the gloriously sloppy, puerile, carnivalesque (which is to say, if it becomes respectable and "classical" through and through), we will have lost with it a powerful weapon against despair, arrogance, and cynicism. Lost, too, will be an invaluable source of the music's continued vitality and relevance. For although the carnivalesque may be "dirty," this dirt provides the soil in which jazz can still grow.

PART TWO

Place and Time

FOUR

Race, Place, and Nostalgia after the Counterculture

Keith Jarrett and Pat Metheny on ECM

JAZZ HAS LONG BEEN IDENTIFIED as an urban genre. Certainly the standard historical narratives trace a metropolitan lineage: New Orleans to Chicago to Kansas City to New York, with other cities inside and outside the United States also playing prominent roles. Dozens of song and album titles helped to establish and reinforce these interpretations, celebrating a favorite municipality, neighborhood, thoroughfare, or landmark. One commentator even described jazz as the "expression of the dynamic of the modern city and modern life through its complex dissonant sounds and dynamic energy," implying that jazz is not only made in cities but is itself a sonic representation of urban living.[1] Using these city-centric understandings as a backdrop, this chapter addresses a decidedly different geocultural milieu for jazz, one that, while oftentimes located in urban areas, evokes various idealized visions of an America far removed from the bustle and hum of the metropolis.

Of course, practitioners of folk, country, and other American styles have long extolled the virtues of rural or untamed spaces. Composers of European classical music, too, have a well-established tradition of valorizing nature, which, as the musicologist Richard Leppert has shown, was often "placed in binary opposition to culture."[2] Yet while an idyllic theme in some music genres may be fairly commonplace, jazz has been so closely linked to the city for so long that a style suggesting anything other than a cosmopolitan sophistication seems contrary to expectations. As I will detail, nonurban approaches to jazz differentiate themselves from their urban cousins through evocative album cover images and programmatic titles, as well as a gamut of melodic shapes, timbres, chord progressions, and rhythms that, perhaps inevitably, borrow from the other genres I have mentioned. But the implications of this music go beyond sounds, pictures, and song titles. Taken as a whole, the recordings described here represent a moment in postwar jazz notable for being rooted in or gesturing toward the musical styles of white rural and middle America. This phenomenon plays a prominent role in helping us to discern both where a handful of influential jazz musicians have come from, literally and figuratively, over the past few decades, and in explaining some significant aesthetic and cultural shifts in jazz since the 1960s.

AN UNLIKELY "FUSION"

From 2002 to 2004 Norah Jones's CD *Come Away with Me,* released by jazz stalwart Blue Note Records, provided a seemingly ubiquitous sonic background for patrons at upscale emporiums around the United States. The disc's lead single, "Don't Know Why," and its title track garnered extensive airplay, helping to catapult it to the top of both *Billboard*'s Contemporary Jazz chart and its Top 200 album chart. Not that commercial success for breathy, young, and attractive female singers of jazz-inflected material was particularly new; Cassandra Wilson, Diana Krall, and Jane Monheit trod similar paths in the years immediately preceding Jones's triumph. What set *Come Away with Me* apart was the inclusion of so many characteristics typically associated with country music, most obvious in her rendition of Hank Williams's "Cold, Cold Heart" but also throughout the rest of the disc via the acoustic guitar work and Floyd Kramer–like piano fills.[3]

Now, prior to *Come Away with Me,* and aside from the efforts of a small coterie of other artists, the words *country* and *jazz* had rarely been uttered in the same breath, least of all by members of the mainstream jazz contingent. For decades jazz people had derided country-related styles as an artistic wasteland. To these advocates such sounds hardly qualified as music at all. This was pabulum, by and for white hicks, the antithesis of jazz's presumed worldliness.[4] Buddy Rich's acerbic declaration that he was "allergic to nothing but country music" typifies the dismissive attitude.[5] The degree to which the practices and understandings of these two genres

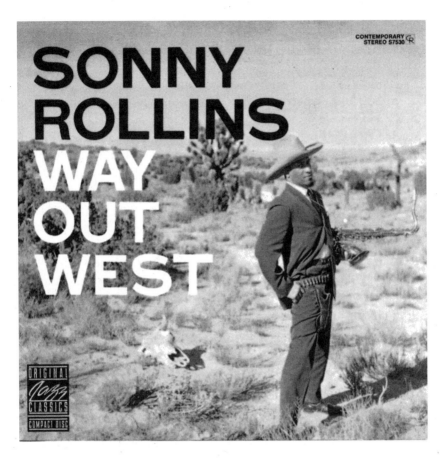

FIGURE 4. Cover panel, Sonny Rollins, *Way Out West* CD

have traditionally diverged can also be seen in Sonny Rollins's 1957 release *Way Out West* (Figure 4). The cover of that album famously shows the saxophonist standing in a desert attired in chaps and a ten-gallon hat. A holster by his side, Rollins carries no six-shooter; his saxophone serves as his "weapon." Although the record's cactus-and-sagebrush setting would seem perfectly natural for a release by, say, Gene Autry (a.k.a. "The Singing Cowboy"), it is clearly meant in this case as a play on ethnic and musical stereotypes. Beyond the tongue-in-cheek, pseudo horse-hoof drum figures in "I'm an Old Cowhand" and "Wagon Wheels," *Way Out West* makes very few musical allusions to actual rural-American styles. In other words there's no "country" here, and the only real "western" connections are to Los Angeles, home of the recording studio, record company, and the session's drummer, Shelly Manne.[6]

Norah Jones's *Come Away with Me,* by contrast, forgoes jazz's characteristic disdain for or condescension toward country music (and most other popular genres). It brings these worlds together in a straight-faced and engaging way and in the process has drawn a large and diverse listening audience. As it turns out, Jones's project was only the most popular instance of such blending in the new millennium. In his 2003 article for the "roots music" magazine *No Depression,* Geoffrey Himes pointed to Seattle as the hub for other musicians who combine country, folk, and jazz.[7] Himes provides interviews with and commentary on the scene's principal performers—keyboardist Wayne Horvitz, pianist and singer Robin Holcomb, and guitarist Bill Frisell (who guests on Norah Jones's disc)—and offers discerning insights on the music these artists create and the circumstances that enabled the sounds. He suggests, for instance, that since neither Seattle's jazz scene nor its country music scene had ever attracted much attention beyond the regional level, the musicians there have not felt tied down to set notions of purity or tradition in either genre and are thus freer to experiment. Himes devotes extensive space to Frisell, focusing particular attention on the guitarist's 1997 release, *Nashville.*

By the late 1990s Bill Frisell (b. 1951) had already established a reputation as a compelling performer, composer, and bandleader on a number of genre-blurring projects. Yet *Nashville* seemed different, even for someone who appeared to revel in musical diversity. Most noticeably, Frisell recorded the project in Tennessee, not New York or San Francisco, where he had made almost all of his previous discs, and he featured a number of local players. So unlike his *Have a Little Faith* from 1993, which presented works from a broad range of North American composers (Aaron Copland, Madonna, Bob Dylan, Stephen Foster, Muddy Waters, Sonny Rollins, and Charles Ives, among others) but delivered in a postmodern style typical of New York's downtown scene, *Nashville* highlighted bluegrass- and country-oriented musicians at home, geographically and stylistically, and so seemed to uphold a quirky sort of country authenticity even while it won the *DownBeat* Critics' Poll as Jazz Album of the Year.[8]

Frisell hails originally from Denver and, recalling the *Nashville* sessions, told Himes,

When I grew up in Colorado, country was around the periphery all the time . . . but I tried to ignore it and even actively resisted it. When I was a teenager, the rock 'n' roll that I liked—stuff by Dylan and the Byrds—had a lot of country in it, but as soon as I discovered jazz, I became a total jazz snob and shut the door on everything else.

But when I did this Nashville project, I realized I had heard a lot of country music over the years, and I realized I really liked it. And when I let myself like it, I became fascinated with trying to find what it had in common with jazz. I started listening to a lot of older music from the early part of the century, the Harry Smith *Anthology [of American Folk Music]*, the Library of Congress recordings, and the old blues guys.[9]

Frisell's comments are instructive, both in the way they highlight the hierarchy upheld by some that would place jazz above country and other styles ("I became a total jazz snob"; "when I let myself like it") and in the specific idioms that he wanted to explore (for example, early field recordings revered as the authentic lineage of the genre, *not* the "urban cowboy" sound of many current Music City stylists). Himes applauds Frisell and the other members of the Seattle scene for the quality of their work but stops short of crediting them with instigating this sort of nonurban jazz. For that he cites Munich-based ECM Records.

In a 2001 article published in the *Chicago Tribune* (and covering much of the same ground as the 2003 *No Depression* essay) Himes wrote, "It was ECM that first inspired the notion of 'pastoral jazz.' Just because jazz had always been an urban music—reflecting the jittery rhythms, metallic horns and surging energy of American cities—didn't mean that it always had to be. In ECM's signature sound—the patiently unfolding arrangements, the softly glowing tones and the slurred legato phrasing—perceptive observers spied the possibility of a rural jazz, a shared improvisation reflecting farms and forests rather than streets and skyscrapers."[10]

True, some of the musicians who recorded for ECM, including Bill Frisell, had evoked open spaces, American and otherwise, long before *Come Away with Me* and *Nashville*. But Himes's observation raises some far-reaching questions: How and (more important) why did these jazz artists evoke musical "farms and forests" in the first place? Above all, what does this pastoral aesthetic suggest about jazz's shifting identities and meanings? To begin to address these issues, it will help to retrace the founding of ECM Records amid the broader cultural scenes of the 1960s and 1970s and to focus on the key roles played by two ECM artists—Keith Jarrett and Pat Metheny—in fashioning an idyllic vision of both jazz and North America.

ECM, "THE LAND," AND THE DUAL LEGACY OF THE 1960S

Those who labor in the earth are the chosen people of God, if ever he had a chosen people, whose breast he has made his peculiar deposit for substantial and genuine virtue.

THOMAS JEFFERSON
"Notes on Virginia," Query XIX (1785)

As Jefferson's words reveal, the roots of an idealized ruralism run to the very founding of the United States. A similar sentiment persisted in the nineteenth century as reflected in the Transcendentalist writings of Thoreau and Emerson, as well as the paintings of Thomas Cole and other members of the Hudson River School. The turn of the twentieth century saw Theodore Roosevelt establish the national park system and John Muir publish his successful series of wildlife essays. Three decades later, visual artists Thomas Hart Benton, Grant Wood, Andrew Wyeth, and Walker Evans were depicting a spacious nation stocked with hearty, if stoic, inhabitants; Roy Harris, Ferde Grofé, and Aaron Copland were composing the art-music equivalent of the bold North American landscape painting; and Woody Guthrie was fashioning songs describing "the dystopian landscapes of the all-enveloping, all powerful dust storms; the testing mountain and desert landscapes of the road; and the utopian landscapes of the West."[11]

The Americanized pastoral jazz that ECM fostered in the 1970s and beyond echoes these and other early expressions of an open and free rusticity. That music can be heard, too, as an extension of—and, somewhat paradoxically, a reaction against—the collectivist principles of the 1960s counterculture.[12] In a move that is now almost as mythologized as (and was unquestionably influenced by) Thoreau's escape to Walden Pond a century earlier, a highly visible, mostly white and middle-class, contingent of young people embraced the virtues of communal agrarian living.[13] Correspondingly, a number of well-known rock musicians who had previously churned out revved-up blues-based material began producing tunes that incorporated bluegrass- and country-related instrumental textures, their album covers featuring folksy images.[14]

Yet while such bucolic sounds and scenes attracted scores of rock-oriented performers and their listeners during the mid-to-late 1960s, they had little hold on most swing, bop, and avant-garde musicians of the time. Jazz proponents reveled in their urbanity and generally ignored rural musical styles and gestures.[15] Especially suspect were country and bluegrass, genres typically associated with white communities in the South. Musicologist Olivia Mather shows in her study of country rock how media coverage of the battles between civil rights advocates and segregationists "tainted country music's reputation for many years to come, specifically through the connection of several country artists to George Wallace's campaigns, but also through a kind of guilt by association, where the music of white, working class Southerners was equated with racist and reactionary politics."[16]

Even so, a few young jazz musicians did express a kinship with the ideals of the emerging country/folk/rock–based youth movement. Among this cadre was Keith Jarrett (b. 1945), a white pianist and composer, who, after spending a brief time with Art Blakey's Jazz Messengers, began making a name for himself in a group led by the African American saxophonist Charles Lloyd. Lloyd's quartet enjoyed a strong following among the burgeoning "flower-power" communities on the West Coast. While few could have predicted the ensemble's remarkable success with these audiences, in hindsight we can see that this affinity was not completely peculiar. As Ian Carr points out, two of Lloyd's sidemen, Jarrett and the drummer Jack DeJohnette, "had grown up with ears attuned to the Beatles and rock music, and so were solidly of the sixties generation."[17] Jarrett himself confirmed this empathy in a 1987 interview, recalling, "I shared a lot of the questions that people [who] came to the Fillmore had. Outside of music, I mean, just the questions, the life-size, universe-size questions."[18] Jarrett began recording as a leader in the late 1960s. Many of his self-penned compositions from the time betrayed strong influences from Ornette Coleman and other free-jazz musicians, but his version of Bob Dylan's "My Back Pages" (*Somewhere Before*, 1968) and brief venture as a folk guitarist and singer (*Restoration Ruin*, 1968) reflect his sympathetic stance toward the more idyllic visions of the counterculture. These predilections would return, though in somewhat less idealistic guise, in a number of his ECM recordings just a few years later.

END OF AN ERA

Having suffered repeated tragedies and defeats—the back-to-back assassinations of Martin Luther King Jr. and Robert Kennedy, the inability to end the conflict in Vietnam, the Manson Family murders, the violence at the Rolling Stones' concert at Altamont—many young Americans began distancing themselves from their former wide-eyed optimism. And while Tom Wolfe's famous designation of the 1970s as "The Me Decade" oversimplified the realities of the time, there's no question that the post-Woodstock period witnessed a hunkering down of sorts.[19] The drastic degree to which attitudes in popular music drifted away from the "Aquarian" spirit can be witnessed in Nick Lowe and Elvis Costello's 1974 plea to their now-cynical contemporaries, "(What's so Funny 'bout) Peace, Love, and Understanding," as well as the rise of smaller, more closely knit regional sounds. The 1970s marked the rise of punk, disco, and rap, three signature styles representing different urban communities on the East Coast. More apropos to this discussion, listeners at that time heard heated anti-Dixie denunciations from California-based singer-songwriter Neil Young ("Southern Man" and "Alabama") just as the United States witnessed the brief-but-bright ascendency of Southern rock, with its proud anthems "Sweet Home Alabama" (Lynyrd Skynyrd) and "The South's Gonna Do It Again" (Charlie Daniels Band). In the Midwest the band Kansas combined progressive rock with American-folk elements. In California Gram Parsons, the Eagles, Linda Ronstadt, and others fashioned what became known as country rock.[20]

This is not to say that Keith Jarrett or similarly guided jazz performers and composers were taking their cues directly from any of the above-named musicians. Rather, artists from a number of regions, disciplines, and genres participated in, drew on, and helped to configure a broadly reemergent reverence for "the soil." For example, 1970 saw both the first Earth Day celebration and the unveiling of Robert Smithson's *Spiral Jetty*, the best-known representative of Land Art. The ecopolitical organization Greenpeace was founded one year later. The environmentalists' bible, the *Whole Earth* catalog, first published in late 1968 by Stewart Brand, "reached its zenith of cultural influence in 1972 after Brand won the National Book Award and *The Last Whole Earth* reached the best-seller lists."[21]

Concomitant with this ruralist turn in the arts, politics, and society the erstwhile bassist Manfred Eicher formed ECM Records.[22] From its very first release in 1969, ECM established a reputation as home to a serious and introspective brand of jazz, and the company quickly garnered worldwide acclaim for its minimalistic album cover designs and audiophile sonic qualities. Canada's *Coda* magazine soon hailed ECM for producing "the most beautiful sound next to silence," a line the label adopted as its motto.

Eicher proved remarkably adept at finding creative musicians from Scandinavia, Brazil, and other largely overlooked regions. Many of these artists explored styles reminiscent of or rooted in the folk music of their own native lands, the "open-spaces" quality of their compositions and performances feeling even more capacious thanks to Eicher's predilection for a reverb-drenched sound. This combined sonic and visual aesthetic worked. By the end of the decade, ECM had become one of the most commercially viable and instantly recognizable jazz labels on the planet, with Keith Jarrett and Pat Metheny two of its best-selling artists.

ROMANTICISM AND THE AMERICAN "FOLK"

As of this writing Keith Jarrett has released more than sixty recordings through ECM, covering an array of genres and instrumental combinations. While Jarrett's first efforts for the label (*Ruta and Daitya* and *Facing You*, from 1971) received strong support from both critics and fans, he did not achieve his current jazz-megastar status until 1975 with *The Köln Concert*. This recording has sold more than three million copies to date, a staggering sum for any jazz recording and completely unprecedented for a solo-piano release.[23] Such an achievement appears even more astonishing given that the record does not feature any songs, per se, just four episodes labeled "Part I," Part IIa," "Part IIb," and "Part IIc." The pianist explores a wide spectrum of moods and styles in this concert, including extended modal vamps and rhapsodic passages resembling mid-nineteenth-century European romanticism (which fostered its own pastoral tradition, of course). But he also devotes significant portions to evoking a specifically Americanized rural sound. Listen to the country-gospel feel beginning around 21:15 of Part I, or throughout virtually all of Part IIa.

Many of Jarrett's other solo recordings draw from and reach for a similar sense of place. He designated one section of his 1981 concert in Bregenz, Austria, as "Heartland" (note the change from *Köln,* where he'd labeled each section numerically). Here he blends plagal cadences and other harmonic devices seemingly pulled from the Anglo American hymnal with his 1960s folk-revivalist inflections. Even more telling, a 1987 Tokyo concert, released as *Dark Intervals,* features a segment called "Americana," on which Jarrett suggests the "noble" film-score rhetoric of the Hollywood western, a hint of country rock, and, again, ample plagal cadences. While distinctions mark each performance, both of them stand in apparent homage to Middle America as the embodiment of humble, quiet dignity.

Beyond these programmatically titled nods to an idyllic United States, the absence of song forms throughout Jarrett's solo concerts evoke metaphorical "wide open spaces"—rhythmically, formally, harmonically, even acoustically (through that aforementioned reverb)—more readily than typical bebop-informed jazz performances do.[24] Although jazz critics and analysts have sometimes appropriated the "organic" analogy from classical music when describing bop-based approaches, such improvisations rarely "grow" as Jarrett's solo work so often does.[25] As I noted in chapter 1, musicians who favor bop aesthetics usually generate interest by creative manipulation of small-scale elements over a repeating song form and a steady pulse. And though recent scholars disagree on the extent to which bebop musicians from the middle of the last century viewed their own music as an overtly political statement, Afrocentric or otherwise, it is hard to argue with L. D. Reddick's assessment from 1949: "Bop is essentially modern and urban."[26] In contrast to bebop's crowded cityscape, the sections of Jarrett's concerts I described (and there are many more throughout his solo recordings) convey expansiveness.

"COUNTRY" MUSIC

The American pastoral ideal is equally audible on Jarrett's ensemble albums for ECM, most notably the highly acclaimed *Belonging* (1974) and *My Song* (1977).[27] *Belonging* features the loping figures of "Long as You Know You're Living Yours," as well as "The Windup," which, according to Ian Carr, "is inspired by the kind of boisterous 'hoedown' found in some American square dancing."[28] Merely the title of Jarrett's "Country" *(My Song)* suggests a rural setting; and the tune's compositional makeup leaves no doubt that we're dealing with a distinctly North American location.

"Country" comprises four sixteen-bar sections, arranged AABB, in the key of E-flat. The harmonic scheme never strays far from basic I, IV, V, and vi chords, moving briefly only to the key of A-flat in the B sections before quickly working back to the tonic. The melody is equally straightforward, every note staying within the E-flat-major scale. Jarrett's piano work relies mostly on triadic and add-2 harmonies, his chord voicings largely devoid of flatted fifths, raised ninths, or other tension-heightening "alterations" that typify bop-based playing. His group adheres to a relaxed straight-eighth-note rhythmic feel, with bassist Palle Danielsson and drummer Jon Christensen providing a steady, unadorned foundation. After a sixteen-bar solo-piano introduction, saxophonist Jan Garbarek enters with the song's theme. Aside from the intro, the track's only solos are a subdued thirty-two-bar foray by Danielsson, followed by a slightly more assertive sixteen bars from Jarrett. The absence of extended solo passages enhances the tune's aura of simplicity and is a striking departure from the many jazz recordings since the 1960s that feature long and elaborate improvised excursions.

The fact that "Country" is an undeniably pretty tune explains some of its appeal (it helped *My Song* crack the *Billboard* pop charts in 1978).[29] But there is more to the cut's allure than a nice, well-played melody. The Arcadian title, transparent structure, and unhurried performance express a kind of vigilant tranquility that must have resonated with the environmentalist attitudes of its time, sounding a post–Earth Day, photos-from-space, awakening to the fragility of the planet. For Jarrett's musical portrait here is not of vigorous masses conquering the land, or of awe-inspiring vistas, but rather of a quietly Edenic—and perhaps now lost—domesticity. It is indicative of the overall mood that *My Song* not only features a tune called "Country" but also one called "The Journey Home." Not to be overlooked here is Jarrett's vehement, almost zealous, insistence on playing only "acoustic" instruments. Never mind that the grand piano remains one of the greatest achievements in musical technology of the past two centuries; in the wake of the widespread use of electric instruments by rock and, increasingly, jazz musicians in the 1960s and 1970s, Jarrett's piano-only stance came across as more "natural," and so a significant component of his pastoral aesthetic.

Curiously, Keith Jarrett is the only participant in this all-American brand of jazz to have been born, or even reside, in the United States. *Belonging* and *My Song* were recorded in Norway by (along with the pianist) two Norwegians (Garbarek and Christensen), a Swede (Danielsson), and two Germans (sound engineer Jan-Erik Kongshaug and producer Manfred Eicher). Jarrett has stated that he composes with his fellow musicians in mind, and of these particular recordings he noted, "I basically wrote for Jan [Garbarek]—for his sound—and for me. And I knew that Palle [Danielsson] and Jon [Christensen] would feel perfectly fine."[30] Clearly, then, one does not have to come from a certain place or time for one's music to sound like or evoke that place or time. This situation echoes that of another American musician famous for evoking untamed lands, Aaron Copland. Copland, who played the most prominent role in shaping how the art music world (and also Hollywood composers) would represent the American wilderness, grew up in Brooklyn. Despite composing such seemingly site-specific fare as *Billy the Kid* and *Appalachian Spring,* he had little or no contact with the American West or the mountain regions of the Southeast. And like Copland's imaginative sonic renderings, Jarrett's ECM recordings seem to draw their pastoral imagery almost exclusively from Euro-American notions of "the great outdoors."[31] Also similar to Copland (but not Bill Frisell's *Nashville*, Norah Jones's *Come Away with Me*, or, as we will see, some of Pat Metheny's work), Jarrett's compositions and performances often suggest folklike melodies to convey their rural or rustic qualities, but they never fully embrace the less-refined aspects of actual folk musics.

The remarkable success of Jarrett's pastoral compositions and performances proved that one could create (and sell) something called jazz in the 1970s without having to be or sound like a New York–based hard-bop or free-jazz stylist. And by emboldening musicians everywhere to explore their own local forms and melodies, Jarrett's work helped to accelerate and legitimate the development of what has been called variously European jazz, Euro jazz, World jazz, even glocalized jazz, a point I take up in my final chapter.[32] For our current purposes it is important to note that Jarrett's Anglicized ruralist aesthetic attracted a large following and influenced a generation of jazz musicians in the United States. Included among this throng is Pat Metheny, one of the best-known jazz artists of the past thirty years. And while Jarrett's influence on Metheny is clear, the guitarist did find his own path. Or perhaps I should say "paths." For Metheny's American-pastoral bent manifests itself in a number of ways, shaped in large measure by the performance setting in which he puts himself. As I will show, these variations do not merely reflect different orchestrational approaches to the same sense of place but reveal contrasting notions of the United States—and jazz—beyond city limits.

GUITAR HERO

It is no coincidence that Pat Metheny (b. 1954) and Bill Frisell, two of the more prominent figures in pastoral jazz in the United States, play guitar. The guitar is the only instrument that regularly serves a front-line role in folk, blues, country, rock, and jazz, so guitarists are often able to move among and incorporate elements of each of these genres. Three years younger than Frisell, Metheny nevertheless received the earliest widespread attention of the two, and he has sustained an impressive level of commercial and critical success since his 1974 debut on ECM as a sideman for the vibraphonist Gary Burton.[33] Burton himself had explored rural American idioms in the 1960s and early 1970s, most notably on his albums *Tennessee Firebird* (1966) (which featured both Chet Atkins and Roy Haynes!) and *Country Roads* (1969). Metheny's invitation to join Burton's group must have been based in part on these musicians' shared fondness for and ability to play a wide array of American styles.

Metheny was raised in the Kansas City suburb of Lee's Summit, Missouri. A devoted Beatles fan from a very early age, he experienced a jazz epiphany at twelve years old after hearing his older brother's copy of Miles Davis's *Four and More*. From that point he jumped headlong into his adopted genre, listening, practicing, and gigging extensively. After high school Metheny attended the University of Miami for one semester before being asked to teach there. From Miami he moved to Boston, becoming the youngest instructor ever at the Berklee College of Music and, shortly thereafter, joining Burton's group. An avid listener, he readily absorbed the sounds of his new East Coast surroundings. Even so, as one *DownBeat* critic noted in 1979, "Metheny's music springs directly from the American heartland in which he grew up," an interpretation aided, no doubt, by the imagery and discourse with which the guitarist surrounded himself.[34] Given just some of Metheny's song titles from around this time— "Missouri Uncompromised," "Midwestern Night's Dream," "(Cross the) Heartland," "Country Poem," "Ozark," "The Fields, the Sky," "Farmer's Trust"—it would be nearly impossible for jazz journalists and others *not* to notice and emphasize these roots.

DAYBREAK

In 1979 ECM released *New Chautauqua,* a one-man album featuring Metheny on a variety of guitars. The record's title references the Chautauqua Movement, which, from the 1870s to the 1920s, provided Americans in the hinterlands with religious, artistic, intellectual, scientific, and political food for thought.[35] In keeping with the rustic setting of that original institution, the cover photo of *New Chautauqua* depicts an empty stretch of highway flanked on one side by a grove of trees, on the other by a swath of green field. Superimposed above the scene in a somewhat indistinct photographic negative is a small shot of Metheny holding a guitar in what appears to be a performance venue or recording studio.

The portrait on the album's back cover offers a much clearer, and even more evocative, image (Figure 5). Here we see the guitarist posed on a

Within the image:

ECM-1-1131

NEW CHAUTAUQUA

PAT METHENY

ELECTRIC 6 AND
12 STRING GUITARS
ACOUSTIC GUITAR
15 STRING HARP GUITAR
ELECTRIC BASS

SIDE I

NEW CHAUTAUQUA 5:17

COUNTRY POEM 2:31

LONG-AGO CHILD /
FALLEN STAR 10:17

SIDE II

HERMITAGE 5:37

SUEÑO CON MEXICO 5:36

DAYBREAK 8:40

ALL COMPOSITIONS
BY PAT METHENY

RECORDED AUGUST 1978
AT TALENT STUDIO, OSLO
ENGINEER:
JAN ERIK KONGSHAUG
COVER PHOTO + DESIGN:
DIETER REHM
PHOTO:
JOJI SAWA
PRODUCED BY
MANFRED EICHER

AN ECM PRODUCTION

©℗ 1979 ECM RECORDS GMBH

MANUFACTURED AND DISTRIBUTED BY
WARNER BROS. RECORDS INC.
A WARNER COMMUNICATIONS COMPANY ⊙.
3300 WARNER BLVD., BURBANK, CALIF. 91510
3 EAST 54TH STREET, NEW YORK, N.Y. 10022

ALL RIGHTS RESERVED. UNAUTHORIZED
DUPLICATION IS A VIOLATION OF ALL
APPLICABLE LAWS.

PRINTED IN U.S.A.

FIGURE 5. Back cover, Pat Metheny, *New Chautauqua* LP

wooden stool. Bathed in sunlight streaming through a window, Metheny's famously tousled mane of hair haloes his smiling face. He's barefooted, wearing a cotton T-shirt and faded denims (Levis or Wranglers, certainly not Sergio Valente or any of the other "designer jeans" favored by disco fans in the 1970s). Metheny cradles a steel-stringed acoustic guitar, long the preferred instrument for performers of country and folk music but virtually unused in jazz settings. The overall impression here is casual, youthful, genial, and unmistakably white, a striking contrast to the images of serious African American men that the jazz world had witnessed on record covers and fan magazines since the 1930s (or would see again with the neoclassicists beginning in the 1980s). The guitarist's laid-back look also differs from the tie-dye shirts, sub-Saharan dashikis, or Arabic galabayas that some players, including Keith Jarrett, adopted in the late 1960s and early 1970s as a sign of solidarity with the civil rights movement and "anti-Establishment" values.[36]

New Chautauqua's photographic images find their aural equivalent in the record's compositions and performances. The title cut commences with alternating triads of B and A over an E pedal point vigorously strummed with a flat pick on the acoustic guitar. Metheny's choice of E as the tonic key maximizes his use of open strings and, combined with the strumming technique, helps to forge the connections to country and folk styles. The song retains this flavor even after Metheny enters with the theme, which he has overdubbed using an electric hollow-body guitar, modified by subtle electronic effects. This added timbre would not be out of place in a jazz-rock fusion setting of the time (in fact, it was Metheny's preferred sound with his Group), yet the acoustic-guitar underpinnings, strumming, and triadic harmony guarantee that we will hear this as rural-flavored music.

That feeling pervades the entire disc to the point that the jangling, finger-picked "Country Poem" would have sounded more at home as sonic backdrop to Ken Burns's *The Civil War* documentary than to that filmmaker's *Jazz* series. In this regard it is worth considering just how *New Chautauqua* came to be defined as jazz at all. Perhaps, as young as he was, Metheny had already established his name in that genre. Or maybe it is because ECM was known as a "jazz label," so anything distributed under that brand would be placed automatically in the jazz bins of record stores.[37] Whatever the cause or causes, Pat Metheny presented a strikingly different look and sound for jazz and, even more than Keith Jarrett's work, signaled a profound shift in how the music could be practiced and understood from that point forward. Suddenly, the small-town, Anglo-America associations of T-shirts, blue jeans, bare feet, and strummed steel-string acoustic guitars were no longer antithetical to jazz. Quite the contrary: for many, Pat Metheny embodied the genre. Even at the time of the album's release, the jazz critic Larry Birnbaum recognized (and also seemed uncomfortable with) *New Chautauqua*'s cultural underpinnings: "with its churchy bluegrass and neo-Romantic sensibilities, Metheny has fashioned a cleanly orchestrated rhapsody in white, bearing none but the most tangential relationship to Afro-American traditions."[38]

While *New Chautauqua* stands as an unambiguous example of a bucolic strain in American jazz during the 1970s, in one way it remains an anomaly in Pat Metheny's oeuvre. For unlike Keith Jarrett, who has devoted much of his career to solo performances, Metheny has spent most of his time working alongside other musicians. Of these, it is worth discussing two individuals in particular—Lyle Mays and Charlie Haden—each of whom played key roles in helping the guitarist configure differing variations on the pastoral jazz theme.[39]

Charlie Haden, born in Shenandoah, Iowa, in 1937, spent the majority of his formative years in Springfield, Missouri. As a child he soaked up the sounds of hillbilly and white gospel music while singing and playing ukulele as Cowboy Charlie on the Haden Family Singers radio show. He recounted those early years in a 1984 interview with Rafi Zabor: "I saw a special view of country America that you don't get in the city. I used to go to houses in rural Missouri and people would be on their porches singing and playing fiddles and blowing into moonshine jugs, playing washboards and spoons. My grandpa used to play the fiddle under his chest instead of his chin and he used to tell me stories about Frank and Jesse James, the Younger Brothers and the Daltons. My grandma told me about Wild Bill Hickok in Springfield, Missouri."[40]

Like Metheny, Haden became aware of jazz as a teen through an older brother. After taking up bass, he moved to Los Angeles in 1956 and soon thereafter began working with Ornette Coleman. Many musicians, critics, and listeners at that time viewed Coleman as an iconoclast whose presentations were either deliberately intended to shock or were a disturbing product of an anxious cold war era.[41] Haden heard the saxophonist differently. In Coleman, Haden found a kindred spirit, a performer who, like himself, possessed both a thorough understanding of bebop's modernist principles and an abiding love for rural American music traditions. The clearest illustration of this empathy can be heard on "Ramblin'," from Coleman's *Change of the Century,* recorded in 1959, where Haden's bass solo consists almost entirely of the traditional song "Old Joe Clark."

Haden reexamined that same melody two decades later as the second half of a quasi medley called "Two Folk Songs," the opening cut of Pat Metheny's *80/81* album. Notably, the first of the "folk" tunes on that pairing was not a long-established staple of musical Americana, à la "Joe Clark," but rather an original composition by the guitarist himself. That is, similar to Bob Dylan's (and also Keith Jarrett's) folk-revivalist work from the 1960s, Metheny composed his own take on American "roots" music. And like many other such tunes, "Folk Song #1" (as it appears in published form) paints an idealized vision of rural life as unadorned and unpretentious.[42] The composition is built of hummable, three- and four-note melodic motives over a harmonic progression of D, C, G, and A triads. The structure follows an unusual variation of the AABA form: the eight-bar bridge section is framed by eleven-bar A sections, each of which features one bar in 5/4 meter, with the others in the typical 4/4. Presumably, Metheny chose these irregularities to approximate the looseness of Depression Era southern vernacular styles. Of course, "Folk Song #1" differs markedly from the unpolished offerings of, say, Jimmie Rodgers's blue yodels or Robert Johnson's Delta blues in that Metheny composed the uneven phrase length and maintains it in every A section, whereas Rodgers, Johnson, and similar musicians tailored their phrasing to the circumstances of each performance.

As published in the *Metheny Songbook,* the resulting composition looks like a clever, if unremarkable, musical representation of homespun America. Like all orally/aurally-based genres, however, that which appears rather dull on the printed page can come to life when played, and at nearly twenty-one minutes long "Two Folk Songs" stands as one of the more fascinating recordings of the early 1980s. Alongside Metheny and Haden on this track are saxophonist Michael Brecker and drummer Jack DeJohnette. The musicians play the complete form of the composition only twice, before and after Brecker's tenor solo. Rather than blowing over the tune's uneven phrase lengths, the form for the sax solo consists merely of a repeated two-bar cycle (D triad for one bar, C triad for two beats, and G/B and G/A for one beat each), all in 4/4 time. Metheny's decision to pare down this section clearly freed the players to stretch out. At the time of this recording Brecker's reputation rested mainly on his position as co-leader of the Brecker Brothers, a popular funk and fusion group, as well as his work as a top-tier session player. In those situations he demonstrated dazzling virtuosity and harmonic sophistication, while proving himself a dependable font of concise, clean, and "soulful" passages. He could have turned to such techniques on "Two Folk Songs." But he takes a different tack, delivering vocal-like gestures reminiscent of "New Thing" artists of the 1960s.

Mention must be made, too, of the close interaction among the rhythm section players. As on "New Chautauqua," Metheny begins "Two Folk Songs" with strummed steel-stringed acoustic guitar. Again, prior to Metheny's emergence, this technique had gone unused in jazz contexts.

Yet given the barebones harmonic progression and Haden's character-istically spare bass lines, the timbre sounds appropriate here. In a 1982 interview Metheny revealed that he "was thinking . . . in terms of c & w [country and western]" on that tune, and he noted that it "came from an idea I had to get that real energetic strumming thing happening as a rhyth-mic element for Jack [DeJohnette] and Charlie [Haden] to play against."[43] It worked. The groove energizes DeJohnette, in particular, whose kinetic drumming almost overwhelms the rest of the band at times, while some-how remaining supportive. His drum solo (beginning around the 10:20 mark) serves as a transition to "Old Joe Clark" (13:18). Haden's statement of that song's melody carries the group toward a majestic marchlike sec-tion for Metheny's acoustic guitar solo and a long diminuendo as Haden returns with the closing theme.

In other hands "Two Folk Songs" could have come off as a trite nod to an imagined rural utopian past. These players chose instead to bridge the two typically opposed worlds of modernist jazz and rural Americana. The Ornette Coleman Quartet may have suggested such a connection in the late 1950s, but Metheny and his sidemen explored the idea to its fullest. Indeed, this track helps shed new light on "Ramblin'," showing us how Coleman's group was not just playing at the cutting edge of the avant-garde, as jazz lore so often has it, but was also simultaneously working through and giving voice to the varied and deeply interwoven strands of North American music.

Of *80/81*'s seven other selections, only "The Bat," "Every Day (I Thank You)," and "Goin' Ahead" draw directly on pastoral jazz timbres and har-monies, with the gently finger-picked, solo acoustic-guitar performance of the latter song revisiting the terrain of *New Chautauqua*. Yet these cuts, when placed alongside "Turnaround" (an Ornette Coleman–composed blues head), "Open," and "Pretty Scattered," further contextualize and re-inforce the country and avant-garde associations promised by "Two Folk Songs." Moreover, these last two selections feature the saxophonist Dewey Redman, who, like Charlie Haden, had recorded with both Ornette Cole-man and Keith Jarrett.[44] Given the strong country-folk flavor of the re-cord, the mere presence of two African American musicians—Redman and DeJohnette—destabilizes prevalent understandings of ethnic, geo-graphical, and musical identity. I do not want to overstate the case, but it is safe to say that by the time of this album's release, popular conceptions of the geocultural domains of the United States had all but ossified into a rural = white, black = city polarity. (Think, on the one hand, of the television shows *Green Acres, The Beverly Hillbillies, The Real McCoys, The Andy Griffith Show,* and *Petticoat Junction,* on the other of *The Jeffersons, Sanford and Son,* and *Good Times.*)[45] The inspired performances from this ensemble disrupt such a binary, recalling in many ways the close interaction of black and white vernacular musicians before the Great Migration—what Greil Marcus has called the "old, weird America"—when country, blues, folk, Tin Pan Alley, and jazz overlapped to a great degree.[46] In this way, *80/81* encourages us to question stereotypes of the rural United States as eternal and immutable, to see it as a more multifaceted, unpredictable, and tempestuous region.

"GARAGE" BAND

Lyle Mays, another midwesterner (born in 1952 in Wausau, Wisconsin) has served as keyboardist and co-composer for the Pat Metheny Group since that ensemble's inception. Early on, Mays evinced an atypical jazz keyboard style. Unlike the soloist-synthesizer virtuosity displayed by Jan Hammer, Chick Corea, and other fusion proponents that preceded him, Mays tends toward warm, sustained "pads." Likewise, in his piano playing Mays eschews a bebop-type linear conception (here he differs from Metheny, who can run changes with the best of them). His playing reveals, instead, the unmistakable influence of Keith Jarrett's American-pastoral work, particularly in his propensity for triadic and "add-2" voicings.[47] In addition to the synthesizers and piano, Lyle Mays may be the only jazz musician to have made the autoharp a permanent part of his performance arsenal. Although used sparingly, that instrument's shimmering resonance blends well with Metheny's guitar timbres and helped establish the group's distinctively idyllic sound.

The Pat Metheny Group released five albums for ECM between 1978 and 1985, with their eponymous first record from 1978, sometimes known as "The White Album," probably best known today. Describing his motivations around the time of that release, Metheny noted, "I feel myself leaning all the time toward rock—not rock, exactly—but a more American influence, all the time."[48] While the first record features notable pastoral jazz elements (especially in "Phase Dance," "Aprilwind" and "April Joys"), those traits are even more pronounced on the group's highly successful follow-up, *American Garage* (1980). Mays and Metheny collaborated as co-composers for four of the five tracks on this record, and their work here offers a markedly different take on the pastoral theme from that heard on the discs previously discussed. For while *American Garage* steers clear of the crowded downtowns of the United States, it also avoids both the gentle acoustic confines of *New Chautauqua* and the fierce folk/blues/free-jazz crossroads of *80/81.*

The cover of *American Garage* features a photo of a grassy lot filled with camper trailers, the vehicles' aluminum bodies glittering in the sun. Overhead, a gentle bank of puffy white clouds dots an otherwise clear blue sky (Figure 6). Given understandings in the United States of campers as the preferred mode of travel for weekend vacationers, one might wonder why Metheny and the ECM brain trust would choose to use this image on a jazz record. Are we supposed to understand it as a sardonic critique of a tired and timid nation? If so, the message is lost, as the photo suggests nothing less than a sincere tip of the cap to a quiet American pastime. The back of the record sleeve features a staged portrait of the musicians "rehearsing" next to an old station wagon in the garage of the album's title (Figure 7). Note Lyle Mays's placement in the shot. In lieu of the usual array of instruments Mays used in the group's live shows, we see only one electronic piano, an amp serving as a stand. Atop the keyboard sits a well-worn baseball glove, with a ball visible inside.

Of course, the point of this photograph is not for us to think of Lyle Mays as a dedicated baseball player. Instead, the presence of the mitt encourages us to see the keyboardist and these three other somewhat shaggy young men as the newest incarnation of that all-American laboratory of postwar dreams: the garage band, albeit with a jazz twist.

The visual garage-band motif finds its sonic counterpart in the introduction of the album's title song. Drummer Danny Gottlieb slashes out four measures of quarter notes on the half-open high-hat cymbals. One of the band members counts off in typically exuberant rock 'n' roll fashion: "One. Two. One, Two, Three, Four!" It is an intriguing gesture for a jazz record, offering possibilities for a new kind of fusion, perhaps a "punk jazz."[49] Yet after an energetic opening section, the tune falls into a restrained quasi-funk groove in G major. The momentum does pick up again during Metheny's guitar solo (which features a brief nod to the Beatles' "Get Back") but the preceding sections had permanently tamed the performance. Any connections from the song's name and opening count-off to garage-band rock aesthetics—which value transgressive "energy" and abandon above all—is attenuated by the quartet's tidy rendition.

PAT METHENY GROUP

AMERICAN GARAGE

ECM

FIGURE 6. Front panel, Pat Metheny Group, *American Garage* CD

The title track is not the only innocuous cut here. From the Copland-esque introduction of "(Cross the) Heartland" and multisectional "grandeur" of "The Epic," to "Airstream," a paean to the brand of trailer pictured on the album cover, *American Garage* sounds a safe and hospitable jazz environment, as far removed from a hardened dustbowl terrain as it is from a smoky urban nightclub.

To jazz listeners today, the album's blithe earnestness may feel forced, much like the highly orchestrated festivities that surrounded the commemoration of the nation's bicentennial a few years before the record's release. Still, *American Garage* connected with many at that time, topping *Billboard's* jazz charts in 1980, and we should not underestimate its

ECM 1155
422 827 134-2

FIGURE 7. Back panel, Pat Metheny Group, *American Garage* CD

significance, then and since.[50] For here we see evidence of another consequential shift in jazz's place in the United States. I mentioned earlier that
the conventional narrative has jazz traveling from city to city, and I have
noted a few important examples of a rural strain that emerged at various
points in the music's history. But in *American Garage,* and the many efforts
it inspired, we find jazz musicians establishing a third path. This one runs
alongside the music's traditional urban centers yet remains safely removed
from them, tracing a metaphorical migration for at least one segment of
jazz and its audiences: the exodus to suburbia. And like the actual movement of large portions of American society after World War II, this is a
decidedly white flight from the city.

AMERICAN NOSTALGIA

I must say to you that the state of the Union is not good: Millions of Americans are out of work. Recession and inflation are eroding the money of millions more. Prices are too high, and sales are too slow.

GERALD R. FORD

Address before a Joint Session of the Congress Reporting on the State of the Union (January 15, 1975)

To this point I have not mentioned the one word hanging over so much of this music: nostalgia. The scholar Svetlana Boym notes, "Nostalgia (from *nostos*—return home, and *algia*—longing) is a longing for a home that no longer exists or has never existed. Nostalgia is a sentiment of loss and displacement, but it is also a romance with one's own fantasy."[51] I would add that nostalgia suggests a kind of "timelessness," as well, as if the imagined home were both safe and *eternal*, though, of course, such imaginings are always very much of their time. The pastoral jazz aesthetic emerged in full force during a particularly troubled period for urban centers in the United States. The 1970s saw the infamous *New York Daily News* headline, "Ford to City: Drop Dead," images of Los Angeles engulfed by smog, and cynical jokes about Cleveland's Cuyahoga River catching fire.[52] It is understandable, then, that Americans would place their hopes and dreams somewhere outside the nation's metropolises. New York's jazz professionals were not immune to this mood, and a number of prominent musicians actually changed their living situations, relocating to smaller communities upstate, or to Pennsylvania, Connecticut, or New Jersey.[53] Those who stuck it out in the boroughs faced an increasingly difficult situation as clubs closed or presented different forms of music. Others, like the saxophonist Sam Rivers, dug in their heels, producing their own shows in former warehouse spaces. The "loft scene" that resulted gave voice to the region's anxieties, featuring an edgy sound with a decidedly Afrocentric orientation.

In contrast to these hardened realities pastoral jazz offered a vision of a clean and secure America. Teens and young adults from the suburbs heeded the call, buying records and filling seats in concert halls. This was no mean feat for a jazz group at the time (or since). Yet, like the Charles Lloyd Quartet's following in the 1960s, it was also not entirely surprising. For in Pat Metheny and his colleagues, white, post-Watergate-era youth had found a jazz role model in their own image: raised on rock music but now slightly "above" it; long-haired but not chronically alienated; and almost certainly college bound. To these audiences Metheny offered some of the hipster cachet associated with jazz but without the dangers, real or imagined, of the city. Given the guitarist's phenomenal commercial success, it was inevitable that scores of other musicians and record companies would follow his lead. These efforts would help to shape the subgenres eventually known as New Age and smooth jazz. More consequentially, though, I suggest that pastoral styles also helped fuel the exponential growth of college-level jazz programs in the United States.

I take up the subject of jazz education in the next chapter, but it is relevant to point out here that by the 1970s America's suburban youth were expected to attend college even without any clear goals of what they would study. And though the first major jazz programs in this country's colleges date to the middle 1950s, supported by campus visits from Stan Kenton, Woody Herman, and Dave Brubeck, the growth rate of such programs picked up meaningful momentum only during the 1970s and 1980s—just as Keith Jarrett and Pat Metheny were producing their most pastorally inflected work. From 1972 to 1981 the number of schools offering jazz studies degrees grew from fifteen to seventy-two, an increase of nearly 500 percent. By 2002 the number of programs would nearly double again, to more than 120.[54] To be sure, some musicians associated with free jazz and other approaches in the 1960s and 1970s did help to increase the presence of jazz-oriented courses and workshops in American higher education.[55] Still, the gains made by those individuals—many of whom held positions in newly created departments such as African American Studies or Ethnic Studies—cannot fully account for the skyrocketing increase of and enrollment in jazz programs nationwide, not least because these programs were (and mostly remain) populated predominantly by white teachers and students.

As we have seen, the racialist aspects of Pat Metheny's look and sound were not lost on the jazz press of the time. Commenting in 1979 on the Metheny Group's successes, *DownBeat* contributor Neil Tesser opined, "It is a matter, I think, *not* of white musicians asserting their paleness or some such nonsense, rather it is a matter of no longer apologizing for this background, as white musicians have felt more free about incorporating their separate roots into improvisational music."[56] Tesser foresaw Metheny becoming "the Brubeck of the 80s." "Like Brubeck," he explained, "Metheny offers a driving, valid, and determinedly white music; like Brubeck, he has counted on college audiences as a major constituency in the early part of his journey, and has already begun to exert considerable influence on developing guitarists and composers."[57] As a result of this deurbanization, even suburbanization, of jazz, Middle America "discovered" a newly acceptable musical genre for formal study. Jazz had long been virtuosic, complex, and serious enough to warrant attention from journalists. Now it was close enough to home—stylistically, geographically, and ethnically—for white, rock-nurtured students and their tuition-paying parents to feel comfortable.

NEW AND OLD DREAMS: SOME CLOSING THOUGHTS

As in all music genres, stylistic shifts in jazz portend more than just new possible combinations of notes, chords, timbres, or grooves to play. They also suggest broader transformations in participation and meaning. Pastoral jazz openly reflected the hopes and fears of this country's young, white, middle class in the 1970s and 1980s. Undoubtedly, the success of this aesthetic prompted much of the backlash by jazz's neoclassicists throughout the 1990s (both Jarrett and Metheny are conspicuously absent from Ken Burns's *Jazz* documentary). Yet while we can applaud the efforts of Wynton Marsalis, Stanley Crouch, and others toward reminding the nation of jazz's distinguished black American urban legacy, we should also recognize that the neoclassicists' other agenda—to elevate jazz's place on the cultural ladder to a level of equality with that of European classical music—could not have succeeded as well as it has without first establishing a foothold in America's Heartland. In the end, the emergence of an idyllic jazz in the 1970s can be understood alternately as a reawakening of a long ruralist tradition, a newly found respect for an imperiled planet, a return for some to musical and cultural "roots," or a nostalgic fear and rejection of degraded urban centers. Whatever the case, the affects of this trend are still being heard and seen in jazz today.

FIVE

Rethinking Jazz Education

IN A SCENE FROM THE 2004 Hollywood thriller *Collateral,* Vincent, a self-assured professional assassin (played by Tom Cruise), enters a Los Angeles jazz club with Max, a smart but timorous cab driver (Jamie Foxx), whom Vincent has forcibly enlisted to shuttle him from one hit job to another. The two men sit down at a table, ostensibly to listen to the band, which is led by a trumpeter named Daniel (Barry Shakaba Henley). It turns out that Vincent is not only a murderer but also a jazz aficionado. He lectures Max—no fan of the music—on the finer points of improvisation and, once the band finishes for the night, invites Daniel to their table. Daniel and Vincent commiserate on the current state of live jazz. Recalling a better era, Daniel described one life-changing evening—July 22, 1964—when his hero, Miles Davis, sat in with him at that very club. Only after Daniel finishes his reminiscence, and the wait staff, customers, and other musicians have left, does Vincent reveal to the two men that he has been hired to kill Daniel, who has run afoul of an international drug cartel. Daniel pleads with Vincent to let him go (as does Max). Apparently softened by Daniel's skillful musicianship, Vincent offers the trumpeter a way out. He just needs to provide the correct answer to one question:

VINCENT: Where did Miles learn music?
DANIEL (DEFIANTLY): I know everything there is to know about Miles.

MAX (TRYING TO HELP): Music school! He got it in music school, right?

DANIEL: His father was a dentist. East Saint Louis. Invested in agriculture. Made plenty of money. Sent Miles to Juilliard School of Music. New York City. 1945.

MAX (RELIEVED AND IMPRESSED BY DANIEL'S KNOWLEDGE): *Damn!*

Vincent swiftly pulls out his handgun and fires three bullets between Daniel's eyes. Revealing a degree of sorrowfulness, Vincent swoops in before Daniel's head crashes down and gently rests the dead trumpeter on the table. Meanwhile, the action has visibly traumatized Max. Hadn't Daniel replied correctly to Vincent's question? Miles Davis *did* attend Juilliard, right? Yes, but Vincent had another answer in mind.

VINCENT (SOTTO VOCE): He dropped out of Juilliard after less than a year. Tracked down Charlie Parker on 52nd Street who mentored him for the next three years.

Vincent has taught Max an important lesson: real music—like real life— occurs on the streets, not in a school.

A pair of my earlier publications explored the ways in which the educational backgrounds of college-based jazz instructors influence what and how these instructors teach and, thus, what their students will hear as "good jazz."[1] Although there is a great deal more scholarship to be done on the aesthetics and pedagogical techniques emphasized within institutionalized jazz programs, this chapter looks at a different side of music education. Namely, it explores how conservatory-style training for jazz musicians is generally understood by and represented in the broader jazz world, especially among the music's historians and journalists.

Why return to the topic of jazz education when most of the individuals involved in that field remain little known beyond their immediate regions? I do so because, by nearly any measure, college-based programs have not only replaced the proverbial street as the primary training grounds for young jazz musicians, but they've also replaced urban nightclubs as the primary professional homes for hundreds of jazz performers and composers. As I will show, however, this far-reaching and seemingly inexorable move from clubs to schools remains ignored, marginalized, or denigrated throughout a wide range of jazz discourse. And by examining some deeply held conceptions of both jazz history and music education, I hope to encourage jazz people to reconsider the roles schools now play in the development and dissemination of their favorite music.

DISCOURSE AND ANTIDISCOURSE

In January 2007 the *New York Times* featured an article on the front page of its Sunday Arts and Leisure section titled "Jazz Is Alive and Well, in the Classroom, Anyway." Timed to correspond with the thirty-fourth annual conference of the International Association of Jazz Education (IAJE), scheduled to meet in New York the following week, the piece tells of a jazz boom within America's high school and college music programs.[2] The article's author, Nate Chinen, relates some remarkable statistics: the 2007 conference was expected to draw more than eight thousand attendees from forty-five countries, and IAJE membership had quadrupled over the last two decades.[3] While Chinen closes his piece on an optimistic note, suggesting that the rise of college programs may help to sustain local jazz scenes throughout the United States, he also evinces wariness about the merits of this trend. He writes that the profusion of information available to jazz students today "might be a mixed blessing," and he cites the Berklee College of Music faculty member Bill Pierce's concern that "you can learn every Coltrane solo there is without ever listening to a record. I'm not saying that's a good thing. But it's there."[4]

Pierce's comment alludes to the increase of commercially published notated transcriptions of solos by John Coltrane and other canonical jazz figures. No doubt, Pierce worries that young musicians who base their learning on written representations of improvisations miss out on an important musical experience. In this case they couldn't hear the beauty of John Coltrane's recorded saxophone timbre or how Coltrane played within the context of the other performers in his band. Pierce is correct, of course, but he does not appear to recognize how his attitudes and values have been shaped by his own historical situation. That is, Bill Pierce was nineteen years old when John Coltrane died, and he never attended a Coltrane performance himself.[5] Someone who *had* seen Coltrane play in person might argue that recordings offer just a limited glimpse into the power of Coltrane's music. Charles Mingus once commented along these lines when he said, "It's a funny society that's raised mainly on hearing records, they very seldom get the chance to know what the difference is, hearing live music."[6] Pierce's valorization of recordings over published transcriptions reveals how easily we can forget that one's historical, cultural, and geographical location influences how we study, hear, teach, and create music (and everything else).

My point is not that transcriptions make better learning tools than records, rather that each generation of musicians uses the information available to it in the way it sees fit, and apprehensions over a specific pedagogical method should be understood in that light.[7] More important, I use this example to show that even parties who would seem to be sympathetic to jazz education—Pierce earns much of his livelihood from teaching at Berklee—tend to downplay its materials, techniques, and effectiveness. As I have suggested, a great number of other musicians, critics, and scholars also seem suspicious of college-based jazz education, favoring instead those customs, modes of learning, and venues prevalent during earlier eras or in other places. Christopher Small's position on this couldn't have been clearer: "formal courses of training for jazz musicians may signal the end of jazz as a living force; an art that is truly living resists the codification, the establishment of canons of taste and of practice, that schools by nature impose."[8] The outstanding pianist (and longtime freelance educator) Hal Galper has voiced a similar lament: "Used to be, back when there was less music theory available, the players developed more individual playing styles because of the lack of information, through the painful process of trial and error. I'm not promoting musical ignorance as a viable process for developing individuality but the delicate balance of how much to and not to teach a student should be a constant challenge for a teacher. An effective teacher should know how to get out of the way of a student's development. This is impossible in a classroom."[9]

Others are more circumspect in revealing their positions. In *Jazz Styles: History and Analysis* Mark Gridley points to the roles America's colleges and universities play in teaching and supporting jazz at a time when much of the country appears ambivalent about the music. His comments are worth quoting at length, as they both summarize widely held perceptions of the recent state of jazz in the United States and reveal a characteristic reluctance among writers to delve further into the music's changing practices and locations. Gridley writes:

> With the exception of a few standouts, jazz had less exposure and fewer performance outlets during the 1990s and the beginning of the twenty-first century than at any other time in its history. The number of

nightclubs featuring jazz on a regular basis was smaller than ever before, and the fees paid to the musicians in them were lower. . . . A number of eminent jazz musicians acquired full-time positions as college instructors and would not have been able to remain in the field of music without such jobs. Hundreds of excellent jazz players, including more than a handful of world-class musicians, served as adjunct instructors in colleges and universities. *In fact, most of the jazz improvising going on in America during this period occurred in high school and college bands. . . . And the level of musicianship among many young players was so high that a number of high school and college bands were better than some professional bands.*[10]

Few would argue with Gridley's assessments. It is worth asking, though, why he would wait until literally the very last sentences of his 349-page textbook to point all this out to us. If colleges (and even high schools) have served as the most vibrant centers of jazz over the past generation or longer, why not note this trend earlier in his book, and why devote only one paragraph to this situation while spending seven pages on a section called "Strategies for Album Buying"?[11] Certainly, a shift of this magnitude would seem to bear more extensive comment in a history text.

Other examples reveal similar attitudes. In *Jazz: The First 100 Years* Henry Martin and Keith Waters note, "The growth of jazz pedagogy . . . over the past three decades has been astonishing." Even so, these authors give roughly the same attention to this "astonishing" development as they give to discussing the styles of Big Bad Voodoo Daddy and the Brian Setzer Orchestra.[12] Ted Gioia's *The History of Jazz* makes virtually no mention of music schools, nor does Ken Burns's ten-part PBS documentary. Gary Giddins's 2004 collection *Weather Bird* consists of 146 short essays covering a wide range of topics, including the programming policies at the annual JVC Jazz Festivals and the fluctuating reception of jazz within the hermetic world of the Pulitzer Prize's selection committees. Yet in a tome that runs to 632 pages and bears the subtitle *Jazz at the Dawn of its Second Century,* Giddins never broaches the topic of jazz education.[13] Lest one imagine that conservatory-style jazz programs emerged too recently for historians to concern themselves with the matter, we should bear in mind that the Berklee School (now College) of Music opened its doors in 1946—roughly the same moment when Charlie Parker, Dizzy Gillespie, and others were introducing bebop to the world—and that the National Association of Jazz Educators (precursor to the IAJE) was established in 1968, more than forty years ago, or half of the entire history of recorded jazz.

Not all writers have avoided or mistrusted jazz education. Charles Beale's essay for the *Oxford Companion to Jazz* provides an evenhanded take on the history of and issues surrounding jazz pedagogy.[14] And one group of scholars has even commented, "One of the wondrous oddities of our current moment is that the best advice to a serious jazz player in training is not to drop out and study in New York's nightclubs but to attend one of the several conservatories where excellent jazz instruction, by accomplished jazz artists, is richly available."[15] Yet most authors who have addressed this topic at any length seem skeptical, at best, of the relevance of America's college-level programs. In his 2005 book, *Is Jazz Dead?* Stuart Nicholson opens the chapter called "Teachers Teaching Teachers: Jazz Education" by observing, "The institutionalization of jazz education in the final decades of the twentieth century has meant it is now playing an increasingly important role in shaping jazz in a way it did not in the past." He cites the saxophonist and educator Bill Kirchner's remarks that "jazz education—with all its imperfections and limitations—is the best way we now have of sustaining the mentoring process and enabling students to interact with their peers."[16] After this seemingly dispassionate introduction, however, Nicholson abruptly trashes the whole of jazz pedagogy in the United States for what he sees as a fatal overemphasis on bebop- and modal-based forms and styles: "By copying the work of past masters, many students can acquire a superficial understanding of the art of improvisation, but they lack the deeper understanding of the processes involved that ultimately leads to originality of concept and execution."[17] To counteract these supposed faults, the London-based Nicholson proposes that American jazz education be reoriented to function more like the jazz programs in Europe. In particular, he asserts that America's jazz students should incorporate a greater study of European classical styles. To support his position, he points out that Charlie Parker enjoyed listening to classical music and had expressed an interest in studying composition with Nadia Boulanger and Edgard Varése.[18]

To be sure, Parker, and also Fats Waller, Billy Strayhorn, Charles Mingus, and many other important jazz musicians from previous generations, studied and drew inspiration from European art music, just as scores of jazz performers and composers continue to do today. And it is true that, as Nicholson notes, "classical music provides a huge reservoir of musical knowledge to build upon."[19] But it is equally true that jazz artists have learned and borrowed from the music cultures of South America, the Caribbean, Japan, India, and Africa, as well as other sounds from across the United States, including rock, gospel, blues, and country music, a broad palate of potential influences that Nicholson chooses not to document. Nicholson's Europhilia, evident not just in his chapter on jazz education but throughout his book and beyond, suggests that he is less interested in encouraging young American musicians to develop their own jazz styles than in simply having them replace a bopcentric approach with a Eurocentric one.[20] (Moreover, we might consider why Nicholson thinks that it is a bad idea for jazz musicians to emulate "past masters" of jazz but a good idea for them to emulate "past masters" of classical music.)

Gary Kennedy's "Jazz Education" entry in the second edition of *The New Grove Dictionary of Jazz,* published in 2002, takes an equally dim view of America's current college programs. Unlike Stuart Nicholson's preference for European-based models, though, Kennedy favors the practices of African American teachers and institutions of the late nineteenth and early twentieth centuries. His essay begins with an admiring historical overview of instruction and skill acquisition among important black musicians from the 1890s through the 1960s, followed by a section on the growth of jazz summer camps and the earliest college programs in the 1940s, 1950s, and 1960s. When his chronological account of the subject approaches the present day, Kennedy's tone turns decidedly less sanguine: "Even fifty years after the movement began, 'jazz education' has yet to reach any of the serious artistic goals that the term would imply. Much of the reason for this *failure,* at least in the USA, is that most undergraduate-level jazz programs are concerned more with creating generic professional musicians and educators than jazz musicians."[21]

Kennedy is right to credit the largely overlooked teachers who nurtured the first generations of jazz performers and composers.[22] Still, his entry warrants comment for the assumptions buried just beneath the rhetoric. Most obviously, his position presumes that there exists, or existed in the past, a "real jazz" separate from the evidently pseudo version taught and performed in schools today, though he never specifies the qualities that differentiate authentic from inauthentic styles. Nor does he describe the performance practices, sounds, tunes, or venues that supposedly separate "generic professional musicians" from "jazz musicians." Kennedy's disparagements seem particularly puzzling when one considers that they appear in the three-volume *New Grove Dictionary of Jazz.* I have compiled a sample of American musicians, born since 1950, who studied jazz for at least some time at one of this country's colleges or universities (see Appendix I).[23] The information comes directly from *Grove* itself, so that dictionary's editorial staff, of which Kennedy was a member, evidently considered these individuals sufficiently authentic and accomplished to merit inclusion in the compendium. This list plainly illustrates the impact of school-trained performers and composers on all aspects of jazz over the past four decades or more and makes it difficult to justify Kennedy's description of jazz education in the United States as a "failure." We should be clear, too, that there are a great many other very fine musicians whose names do not appear in *Grove* but who studied jazz in school and who set up shop in towns large and small throughout this country and abroad. While many of these individuals may not have earned worldwide acclaim (though some have) or may not make a full-time living in music (though some do), they continue to play, write, teach, learn, listen to, and in all manner of ways, participate in jazz.[24] Granted, standard pedagogical methods are far from perfect; I have expressed my own reservations about some of these. But evading, deriding, or ignoring jazz programs tout court hardly constitutes healthy dialogue or an honest assessment of the music's current places and practices. And if we are to effect meaningful improvements in *how* jazz is taught, we must first accept this fundamental shift in *where* it is taught (and played, and heard).

JAZZ MYTHOLOGIES

Having established a general reluctance among historians and others to credit America's music programs with playing a more positive role in recent jazz, I want to explore some of the reasons behind this reticence. Toward that end I identify four predominant myths guiding negative perceptions of jazz education. I am not using the word *myth* here in the sense of an outright misconception or falsehood. Instead, it should be understood as the stories that people tell themselves about themselves. Most important, people *believe* these stories; indeed, they live them, though usually without being aware they are doing so. As one writer described it, "Within myth, I do not see the myth itself, just as I do not see the lenses in my glasses; on the contrary, I see through the invisible or transparent myth in apprehending the world as—from my perspective—it simply is."[25] And if myths cause us to focus on things or activities from one perspective, they necessarily cause us to repudiate, ignore, or overlook other perspectives.

Myth 1: City Living

To start, there is the long-standing myth of jazz as a strictly urban genre. I have already discussed this perception at length in chapter 4 and could refer to countless other examples of a city-centric jazz narrative, so I will simply add here that as recently as 2002 *The New Grove Dictionary of Jazz* stated categorically, "The history of jazz in terms of the venues that have fostered it is the history of nightlife in different cities."[26] Periodicals such as *DownBeat* and *JazzTimes* still dedicate the overwhelming majority of their print space to the activities of a relatively small circle of urban musicians, especially those who live and work in and around Manhattan. This New York–nightclub mythology remains so deeply entrenched that the Jazz Studies program at New York University (NYU) uses it as a marketing tool. The program's Web page boasts that it is "Located in the heart of Greenwich Village, the world's Mecca for jazz music. . . . Students perform weekly at landmark venues including the Blue Note Jazz Club, the Village Vanguard, Birdland, the Jazz Standard and the Knitting Factory."[27]

Without question, the clubs of New York, as well as New Orleans, Chicago, Kansas City, Detroit, Philadelphia, Los Angeles, Paris, Copenhagen, Tokyo, and other large cities, have served as important centers for jazz from the music's inception. Those settings have not only provided a place for performers to play in front of audiences but are also crucial locations in which musicians can establish and build professional connections. Yet while jazz performers and their fans still convene in nightclubs and concert halls throughout the world, the diminishing number of such settings has forced jazz people to find other ways and places to interact. Even NYU recognizes this trend. In the same paragraph as the one cited above, the school's promo reads, "With guidance from an up-to-date and nurturing faculty, NYU Jazz students learn to develop in new venues, realize new concepts for distributing their music and create alternatives for successful careers in the modern jazz industry."[28] America's nonurban colleges and universities have long provided such "alternatives." Names like Denton, Texas; Valencia, California; Bloomington, Indiana; Oberlin, Ohio; DeKalb, Illinois; and Greeley, Colorado, may not stir the jazz imagination in the way that New York City and other major metropolitan areas do, but campuses in these and other small towns now support and utilize jazz in ways that many larger cities don't.

In some regions on-campus concerts by visiting artists, student ensembles, and faculty groups represent some of the only live music available and so provide a service to the community while strengthening relations between "town and gown." Reaching these constituencies goes beyond simple goodwill for many schools. In an era of declining financial support from state coffers, it is no secret that colleges and universities must now raise a significant percentage of their budgets from private sources. Local audiences are increasingly seen as potential sources of that funding. And when institutions on campuses like those I have listed (and there are many others) actively integrate their jazz education programs into their efforts to cultivate donor relationships, jazz's commentators should take note. Such situations illustrate as clearly as any Lincoln Center event ever could just how deeply the music has rooted itself at the nexus of high-end politics, education, and business in the United States.[29]

Myth 2: What Is Hip (and Unhip and Nonhip)?

A second myth affecting perceptions of jazz education involves the aesthetic of hipness. The editorial preferences of the major jazz textbooks and fan publications serve more than simply to focus readers' attentions on jazz life in particular geographical areas. They also reinforce and shape understandings of how jazz is supposed to look and who is supposed to play it. Which is to say that these publications promote an *image* of jazz as much as they report on the genre's sounds. And they have tended to portray jazz musicians as not just city-based but also self-possessed, sophisticated, and utterly disdainful of the commonplace. In a word, hip.

The hip-jazz image is usually exemplified in one of two ways. First, there is the "venerable" icon from the 1950s or 1960s. In 2006 *DownBeat* ran a cover story on the seventy-one-year-old Ramsey Lewis and another on Sun Ra, who died in 1993. Not to be outdone, *JazzTimes'* cover stories that same year featured Sonny Rollins, then seventy-six years old, and Ornette Coleman, also seventy-six, while another pictured Miles Davis, who passed away in 1991. Second, there's the "hot new thing," epitomized by the June 2007 cover story in *DownBeat* with the breathless title, "Who's Got Next? Jeremy Pelt Leads a Pack of Young Trumpeters Who Demand Attention. We've Got 25 You Need to Hear." Note that these constituencies do not include figures from the 1930s or early 1940s, when jazz reigned as the favorite genre in America, nor from practitioners of the immensely popular smooth-jazz subgenre of recent decades. Hip can be young or old (or even dead), but it must always distance itself from appearing too eager to please its audiences. That most readers who purchase these magazines will never possess the hip attributes of their jazz heroes does not detract from the allure of the published image, just as it does not hurt sales of *Vogue* or *Cosmopolitan* that very few readers of those magazines will ever look like cover models.

Yet while many musicians, journalists, scholars, and fans favor this urban-hip identity, it is not the only embodiment of jazz today. An ideal way to observe a clash of disparate jazz cultures is to attend one of America's many competitive jazz festivals. These events often force a panel of judges, typically consisting of representatives from both urban jazz centers and jazz education programs, and as many as twenty different bands to face one another for eight hours a day, two or three days in a row. To sit among the adjudicators (and to watch the hip faction squirm, sneer, or wince) provides an eye-opening lesson in the breadth of practices and identities understood as jazz and reveals some of the activities and aesthetics that induce writers to disavow school programs. At least two of these traits have come to be stereotypically equated with America's college-level jazz education in general.

On one extreme of perceived unhipness lies the ensemble conductor who appears to wield a high degree of control over students (a.k.a. the infamous "band dictator"). It should come as no surprise that jazz's modernist and postmodernist contingents would look unfavorably on musical disciplinarians. As early as the 1950s, tales of Lester Young, the prototypical hip musician, enduring a disastrous stint in the U.S. Army circulated among jazz communities and engendered mistrust of authoritarians. Around that same time, Howard Becker reported on an attitude among white, bop-oriented performers that resisted any authority figure, musical or otherwise.[30] Even well-known bandleaders are not immune to jazz's contempt for hardliners: Benny Goodman, Sun Ra, and Buddy Rich have all been mocked or disparaged for their severe policies or dispositions.

On the other side of that same coin are those instructors who choose to present jazz as "fun." These teacher-directors select an upbeat repertoire while projecting an amiable stage presence. Again, it makes sense that an affable deportment and genial sound would draw the ire of hip-jazz devotees. Ever since the rise of bebop in the 1940s, a cadre of musicians, aficionados, and critics has worked to paint jazz as a serious art form. As I have noted throughout this book, such efforts have been guided in large measure by the desire to counteract racist notions that reduced creative African American musicians to charismatic but unthinking entertainers in the service of a predominantly white clientele. The "happy" band director undermines this serious-jazz stance.

It is worth noting that while the stereotypes of college jazz band directors as either militaristic autocrats or incurably cheerful naifs represent diametrically opposed models of stage demeanor, they do share at least one flaw from the hipster point of view. Both typically favor big bands, while today's hip-jazz aesthetics prefer small ensembles, with their tendency toward looser, less-scripted, moments.[31] Another related factor here involves sartorial display. Today's urban-jazz proponents tend to perform in either well-tailored suits (see the much-photographed look sported by the neo-classicists) or in the decidedly casual, even sloppy, wardrobe favored by postmodernist groups like Medeski, Martin, and Wood. By comparison, many school jazz ensembles appear in matching uniforms, much like those worn during the institution's orchestra or wind ensemble performances. If the directors of these groups do make a concession to a "jazzy" style, it is often by substituting a red or green wrap-around bowtie for the traditional black one, or going with an open-collared shirt, though some band members also complement the style by donning berets and dark sunglasses. This uniform is especially common among vocal jazz ensembles, which, as the musicologist Jessica Bissett has shown, are widely dismissed—even within college jazz programs—as the "cheesiest" of all groups.[32]

There is no question that race plays a fundamental role in all of these presentations and perceptions. Ingrid Monson has written on how the hip aesthetic draws on, amplifies, reimagines, or otherwise involves notions of a streetwise black America.[33] Yet the vast majority of teachers and students in college-level jazz education programs are not African Americans. Thus, even while a handful of self-consciously nerdy white postmodern musicians may participate in, if only by subverting, the same hip aesthetic as the sharp-dressed "cats" (the Bad Plus and Bill Frisell come to mind), many other nonblack participants do not adopt the postmodern stance and so do not accrue the honors associated with hipness. In other words, it can be hip to be square—but not to be cheesy. Simply being associated with schooling can mark students and teachers as eggheads, sheltered from the supposedly real life of the jazz streets. Beyond just *being* white (or Asian or Latino), many jazz-program participants are dismissed as *sounding* white, perhaps the most cutting insult of all among proponents of a hip-jazz aesthetic. In this regard Monson's essay is helpful in pointing to the lamentable legacy of attitudes that would equate hipness solely with notions of black "badness." She exhorts us to realize that "discipline, dignity, and social consciousness are as important to defining hipness as transgression or social marginality."[34] This caveat serves as an important reminder to guard against simplistic generalizations linking jazz, or hipness, or (more consequentially) African American authenticity with willful ignorance.

Consider, too, the gender aspect of the hipness myth. Ann Douglas has chronicled how "over the course of the nineteenth century, women gradually came to constitute the overwhelming majority of grade-school teachers in America's public and private schools, a feat accomplished in no other country, and one which was to cause immense uneasiness in the men involved in American education by the turn of the twentieth century."[35] Teaching remains "women's work" even to this day. Men make up less than a quarter of this country's three million instructors at the kindergarten-through-twelfth-grade levels; the number shrinks to a mere 9 percent when considering only K–8.[36] And while the university professor has traditionally been understood as a somewhat more "manly" occupation than the grade school teacher, the college instructor hardly conjures images of an unambiguously hearty male heterosexuality in the manner of, say, construction worker, NASCAR driver, or Wall Street trader. Add all of this to the fact that male musicians (and not just jazz musicians) have long struggled against perceptions of their profession as a feminized activity, and it may be that for those invested in a hypermasculine image of jazz, combining a teacher with a musician is simply too much. In that case, one might argue, the phrase "jazz education" doomed attitudes toward college programs from the start.[37]

We can see, then, why educators and education are largely left out of the jazz press. A magazine editor's primary responsibility is to raise the value of a publication. In order for the major jazz periodicals to draw the highest numbers of readers and advertisers, editors present what they deem to be the most attractive image of the genre. The stereotypical jazz educator just does not fit this vision.[38] But even allowing for the hip-jazz bias, jazz people may need to reassess their perceptions of college instructors. Given the ever-increasing professionalization and specialization in jazz education over the past decade, more and more programs are being led by instructors who uphold the hip aesthetic, making it difficult to argue, as even I have in the past, that those nonhip stereotypes and practices remain the rule.[39] Besides, if we may forgive magazine editors for ignoring some of the jazz identities displayed in institutional education (their professional situations are affected by such things, after all), musicologists do not have such an excuse. The scholar's job is to note significant developments in musical practices and meanings and to situate those developments within broader musical, social, cultural, and historical contexts.[40]

Myth 3: "You Either Got It, or You Don't"

A third myth of jazz education states that school training stifles innovation (Gary Kennedy, Stuart Nicholson, Christopher Small, and Hal Galper all allude to this in their criticisms). With "the new" still valued within many, if not all, jazz circles, this criticism warrants consideration.[41] It is true that college programs have yet to show an ability to turn every promising talent into an influential artist. Yet just because jazz programs cannot systematically produce musical geniuses, it does not follow that students in those programs fail to learn, improve, or otherwise benefit from their studies. In jazz, as in every other discipline offered in higher education, good teachers provide students with a foundation in what has come before, offer suggestions to shore up perceived weaknesses, and foster a challenging, creative, and supportive environment in which they can focus on their work. Values and practices differ from school to school, but in general the progress young performers make over the course of a few years, in terms of both technical facility on an instrument and ability to "say something" with that instrument, is substantial and undeniable (recall that list of school-trained players). Some students become excellent, even important, musicians; some don't climb that high . . . just like those performers trained in the informal "schools" of New Orleans, Kansas City, or Harlem in the last century. The resistance by jazz education's critics to acknowledge these improvements may have to do with their desire to mystify improvisational skill. For if anyone and everyone can learn to create music on the fly, perhaps jazz's "magic" is somehow diminished. Certainly, the romantic conception of the Great Artist receiving inspiration directly from the musical gods accounts for much of the mystical aura hovering over a number of improvisers, most famously Keith Jarrett.

What is more, teaching private lessons, improvisation classes, ensembles, history, and the like represents only some aspects of what jazz educators do. Faculty members also mentor young players on the ways and means of the music profession, and many performers land their first significant gigs as a direct result of their teachers' intercessions. During the 1970s and 1980s, the bands of Woody Herman, Maynard Ferguson, Buddy Rich, and Stan Kenton were regularly stocked with alumni of North Texas State University (now the University of North Texas) who were recommended for those jobs by their teachers. The vibraphonist and longtime Berklee

College of Music faculty member Gary Burton showed a knack for recognizing and developing future standouts; his sidemen have included former Berklee students Mick Goodrick, John Scofield, Abe Laboriel, and Makoto Ozone. Saxophonist Steve Coleman met his frequent collaborators Ralph Alessi and Andy Milne when the latter two were studying under Coleman at the Banff International Workshop in Jazz and Creative Music in the 1980s. These same relationships can develop even during brief visiting artist workshops, such as when guitarist Ben Monder "discovered" drummer Ted Poor, now a highly sought-after performer himself, while Monder was giving a master class at the Eastman School of Music, where Poor was studying. One could find dozens, perhaps hundreds, of similar occurrences.

The benefits of these interactions run in many directions. Younger players gain experience, exposure, and financial rewards by playing alongside seasoned pros, while veterans may find that the fresh energy and ideas that youthful singers and instrumentalists bring to the stage can respark their own enthusiasm. The host institutions of these musicians can also profit, as the successes of teachers and their protégés in the professional field enhance their programs' reputations and so, too, their abilities to recruit still more talented students. In turn, schools contribute by providing a physical space in which musicians can congregate and play, as well as the equipment—pianos, drum sets, amplifiers, rehearsal rooms, recording studios—that facilitates the forging of social and professional connections. In short, while colleges may never unlock the alchemical secrets of creating musical masterminds, they do offer all of the benefits of the early twentieth-century nightclub-based mentoring system that Gary Kennedy extolled in his *Grove Jazz* essay, albeit in an admittedly less colorful (but also less toxic) environment than the popular after-hours-session-in-a-smoky-gin-joint image.

Myth 4: Jazz and the "Free Market"

A fourth myth driving negative perceptions of jazz education involves market forces, specifically, that any style of jazz receiving support from an academic (or government) institution is inherently less authentic or artistically viable than that which seems to survive solely within the domain of commerce. Faculty positions have long been mocked as the refuge of individuals unfit for the so-called real world ("Those who can't do, teach"). In jazz the thinking goes that college instructors may possess theoretical knowledge *about* the music but that their playing lacks either the requisite degree of technical skill or, worse, the elusive quality known as soul. This attitude is revealed even in a well-meaning *DownBeat* reviewer's praise: "There are academians and there are academians. The Brooklyn Conservatory Faculty Jazz Ensemble are academians in name only. . . . The B. C. F. J. E. confirm that, in jazz, technique and theory don't mean a thing without the aesthetic of swing."[42] The writer's point here is that this faculty group merits acclaim precisely because its members do not "sound like teachers."

At the same time, proponents of earlier ways and places of learning do want their favorite performers to be understood as smart, skilled, and serious. One way to encourage those perceptions is to designate the street as another—parallel, hipper—version of "higher education." Hence the many references to "the Art Blakey School of Hard Bop" (or "the University of Miles Davis," or "the Jazz College of Hard Knocks," etc.).[43] In this respect critics of college programs want to have it both ways. On one hand, they would have us believe that jazz is like European classical music in that it merits study in conservatories. On the other hand, they also insist that "real jazz" survives and develops solely on the efforts of its musicians, nightclubs, and record companies, independent of any assistance from those same conservatories or what one jazz writer described in another context as "the crutch of subsidy."[44] Of course, this free-market stance flies directly in the face of the deeply entrenched, anticommercial modernist position held by many of these same pundits, resulting in a situation where musicians are expected to make a living exclusively through gigs and recordings, while not seeming to be playing for money.[45]

Tied to such attitudes is the perception that jazz education is little more than a racket organized to sustain nothing but itself. This view underlies Stuart Nicholson's aforementioned "Teachers Teaching Teachers" chapter title and has even worked its way into jazz-education circles. In a letter to the editor responding to Nate Chinen's *New York Times* piece on the IAJE conference, an instructor wrote, "One of the positive consequences of—and perhaps a contributing factor toward—the significant expansion of the jazz education industry in the past 20 years is that it has allowed musicians to maintain a career in jazz. . . . As a 50-year-old jazz musician and educator, I have benefited from this expansion, but I do wonder if at some point the jazz education industry will exist more to perpetuate the industry than the music."[46] As well intentioned as this soul-searching musician-educator seems to be, he need not wring his hands over the matter, for he is missing a fundamental point: the line that scholars, journalists, and musicians maintain to separate "jazz" from "jazz education" is blurry, even illusory. Yes, students go to class, study, practice, and rehearse in classrooms, but they also play gigs, sometimes with faculty members, sometimes with other students, sometimes with performers unaffiliated with a formal music program.[47] When students (and teachers) are not in school, they can often be found listening to recordings and attending gigs by other musicians. In other words, those studying jazz at Berklee or the University of Kentucky or the University of Oregon, or any of the dozens of other degree-granting programs in the United States, are not just waiting until they graduate to become part of a jazz scene. They *are* the jazz scene, or a large portion of it, at any rate.[48]

A case in point is the quintet KneeBody. Four of the group's members—trumpeter Shane Endsley, bassist Kaveh Rastegar, keyboardist Adam Benjamin, and saxophonist Ben Wendel—graduated from the Eastman School of Music. Drummer Nate Wood earned his degree from the California Institute of the Arts (Cal Arts). Adam Benjamin returned to school in 2005, receiving an MFA from Cal Arts in spring 2007. When the group performed at the University of Nevada, Reno (UNR) in 2006—that is, while Benjamin was still in grad school—it wasn't billed as "four professionals and a student" but simply as KneeBody. Those of us who attended their performance and clinic were astonished by the musicians' virtuosity, creativity, and, above all, the intricate musical cueing system they had devised.[49] KneeBody also profited from this visit: UNR paid the group handsomely, and a number of students bought CDs after the show.

Now, KneeBody probably would not have even been aware to contact UNR about playing there were it not for the connections made and developed over the last two decades via the jazz programs at Eastman, New York's School for Improvisational Music, and especially Cal Arts, where not only Adam Benjamin and Nate Wood but also Peter Epstein (who directs UNR's Program in Jazz and Improvisational Music) and I went to school. The lines of connection are too many and too interwoven to untangle here. Suffice it to say that the roles of teacher, student, professional performer, booking agent, colleague, festival adjudicator, friend, concert promoter, and audience member shift constantly. All this adds up to a much more complex interrelationship of music, schooling, aesthetics, and economics than the critics of the so-called jazz-education industry have recognized. And the University of Nevada is only one of many institutions that KneeBody has visited. The group's schedule for 2007 included appearances at Camden County College, the University of Sioux Falls, the University of Colorado, and the Stanford Jazz Workshops, as well as Iridium in New York and Munich's Pinakothek der Moderne. Likewise, KneeBody is just one of the more than two-dozen ensembles and individuals to have presented jazz concerts, workshops, and master classes at UNR over the past few years.[50]

CONCLUSIONS: PAST VS. PRESENT, IMAGE VS. REALITY

The image of the great jazz improviser mentored by streetwise hipsters is a powerful one; it is what drives the scene from *Collateral* that I described at the outset of this chapter. But it is time we reassess this image in the face of twenty-first-century realities. If "the most important task of the contemporary historian is to write the history of the present," as Richard Taruskin has argued, then those writing on jazz must honestly begin to address the ascent, even the centrality, of today's college-level jazz programs.[51]

I am not suggesting that cities are finished as incubators of jazz talent; musicians and audiences continue to gather in New York and elsewhere and surely will for some time to come. Nor do I mean to say that school programs are flawless incubators of jazz creativity. Indiscriminately praising institutionalized jazz education would be just as misplaced as our current tendency to ridicule or overlook it. Students, teachers, administrators, and accreditation bodies must scrutinize and assess pedagogical practices, as well as such thorny issues as the disproportionately high number of white males enrolled (and also teaching) in these programs or the astronomical tuition costs charged by some of these schools.[52] But the music's historians and other chroniclers must also take a more active and informed role in this conversation. This is crucial not just because music schools will produce the next generation of jazz stars—though that is almost certain to happen, too—but, more important, this is where jazz musicians, good and not-so-good, now gather to learn from and play with one another; where audiences listen; where individual and communal identities are formed, tested, challenged, and reformed. Which is to say, this is one of the places where jazz matters most today, at least in this country. We need not fear that formal education somehow undermines or embarrasses "real jazz" or, as Christopher Small suggested, marks the end of jazz as a "living force." The saxophonist and longtime educator David Liebman and his fellow board members of the recently founded International Association of Jazz

Schools (IAJS) are right on the money with their motto: "The future of jazz is connected with the future of jazz education."[53] Ultimately, the fact that so many institutions now provide a home for widely differing understandings of and approaches to teaching, playing, and learning this music is a cause for celebration, not despair.

SIX

Negotiating National Identity among American Jazz Musicians in Paris

Jazz is a marvel of paradox: too fundamentally human, at least as
modern humanity goes, to be typically racial, too international to
be characteristically national, too much abroad in the world to have
a special home. And yet jazz in spite of it all is one part American and
three parts American Negro, and was originally the nobody's child
of the levee and the city slum.

J. A. ROGERS

"Jazz at Home"(1925)

THIS FINAL CHAPTER BROACHES a subject that has surfaced in various
guises for decades but asserts itself now perhaps more forcefully than ever:
the increasingly complex and fluid associations of jazz's national, specifically "American," identity.[1] Without question jazz initially emerged as a
distinct genre in the United States, and the vast majority of its most highly
regarded figures were born here. Yet as J.A. Rogers suggests, the music
spread quickly, establishing a foothold in parts of Europe, Asia, Australia,
Africa, and South America by the early decades of the twentieth century.
The musician and scholar Bruce Johnson has even suggested of this diaspora, "Jazz was not 'invented' and then exported. It was invented in the
process of being disseminated."[2] The music has continued to circulate,
so much so that while the International Association for Jazz Education
(IAJE) made its home in Manhattan, Kansas, its membership extended to
thirty-five countries, including Colombia, Kazakhstan, Turkey, and other
nations far removed from the music's typical geographical representations.
These purportedly remote regions have produced some serious players.
Tigran Hamasyan, for example, winner of the 2006 Thelonious Monk
International Piano Competition, hails from Armenia.[3]

Despite this global presence, many writers and commentators tout jazz as "America's Classical Music," "America's Theme Song," or simply "America's Music."[4] Narratives linking jazz exclusively with the United States have taken hold even beyond U.S. borders. E. Taylor Atkins's excellent study on jazz in Japan shows how such understandings have led some of that country's jazz participants to experience an "authenticity complex," in Atkins's words, an anxious insecurity regarding their own place in the music.[5]

Given the intricate web of jazz practices, locations, and meanings, it is worth exploring just how various articulations of and relations to American nationality operate among America's own performers and composers. To that end I investigate some of the ways in which jazz musicians at the beginning of the twenty-first century display, discard, or otherwise represent "Americanness" in terms of musical style, subjective identity, and professional strategy. Because nationality becomes meaningful only in relation to other nationalities, Americanness in jazz remains largely invisible to us when dealing with American musicians within their own country of origin (as Stuart Hall put it, "Only when there is an Other can you know who you are").[6] So in order to bring these understandings more clearly into the open, I have focused on a group of Americans currently living outside the United States, specifically, those now based in and around Paris.

Of course, dozens of authors have chronicled the decades-long migration of American jazz performers to the City of Lights.[7] All of these accounts have provided valuable insights into the circumstances leading up to select individuals' decisions to relocate overseas, as well as the professional and personal ups and downs that accompanied such moves. Helpful as these studies remain, however, they largely overlook the questions of identity outlined above and, in any case, generally focus on earlier generations of musicians. As I show, twenty-first century performers in France encounter different circumstances and expectations from those of their twentieth-century forebears. I hope that this chapter will serve to shore up research in just these areas, deepening our understandings of American jazz musicians abroad and the notions of nationality, authenticity, and cultural hybridity that surround their presence there today.

This chapter grew out of interviews I conducted in Paris during the summer of 2002 with sixteen American musicians.[8] Subsequent discussions, interviews, and correspondences with a broad range of individuals—musicians and nonmusicians, Americans and French—augmented insights drawn from that initial interview process, as did attending numerous jazz performances in Paris. It is also worth noting that I lived and worked as a jazz musician in Munich, (then West) Germany, between 1983 and 1985 and returned to that city a number of times in the subsequent couple of years. Many of the ideas and attitudes relating to the current group of Americans in Paris resonate with my situation in Munich at that time.

In approaching this topic, I considered four basic questions:

What factors would lead an American musician to move to or remain in Paris today?

How do American musicians in that city understand and publicly represent themselves with regard to nationality?

In what ways, if any, do these representations play out in terms of musical performance and composition?

How, where, and when might musicians use nationality as a strategy to improve their chances for professional success? (I define *success* as the degree to which an individual controls repertoire and stylistic details of the music, as well as when, where, with whom, and for how much money he or she creates that music.)

In time I came to identify two groups within the overall assemblage of American jazz musicians in Paris, embodying two very different attitudes toward and understandings of national identity in jazz. This situation reflects in many ways the flexible, even apparently contradictory, narratives that both celebrate jazz as a worldwide phenomenon and hold it to specific notions of national ownership and authority. The first group, which I call the *Americanists,* comprises those players who emphasize their connections to the United States. These musicians uphold the position that because jazz originated in the U.S., those born in this country enjoy certain cultural, historical, perhaps even biological claims to jazz legitimacy. Americanists live and work within France and the broader European scene, but they maintain a professional and subjective identity separate from the country and cultures in which they have placed themselves. Occasionally, I also refer to an *African Americanist* subgroup. As the label suggests, some critics, listeners, and musicians (from a broad range of ethnicities) who hold to an Americanist understanding of jazz take the thought one step further. This faction contends that while Americans make the best jazz musicians, black Americans play more authentically than nonblack Americans. Incidentally, such perceptions took root in France almost immediately upon the music's arrival. The historian Jeffrey H. Jackson has described a 1924 lawsuit in which the director of a Paris nightclub sued for breech of contract when a jazz group showed up to play with four black performers and one white performer instead of the contracted all-black band. That the club owner won the lawsuit speaks volumes about these understandings linking jazz excellence to black-American ethnicity.[9] The second group, which I designate here as the *assimilationists,* includes those American performers who downplay or ignore their nationality, integrating as completely as possible into their adopted country. Assimilationist musicians make no special claims of authority or competence due to their circumstances of nationality or ethnicity, avowing that anyone, regardless of place of origin, can attain excellence in the jazz field.

I should note that the terms *assimilationist, Americanist,* and *African Americanist* are not in general use among those I interviewed. Moreover, musicians do not always fall neatly into one category or another, as the subjective and professional lives of the people I discuss here are often more multidimensional than simple designations can convey. For instance, as I have shown throughout this book, the category of race is rarely far from the surface in any aspect of jazz life. For black musicians, especially, this can complicate issues of nationality. Many African American performers settled in France expressly to flee the smothering pressures of a racist United States. At the same time, some also found (and find) that despite their own ambivalence, even hostility, toward the country of their birth, they cannot shake the fact that others see them as American, nor can they escape their own feeling of Americanness when surrounded by non-Americans. Members of the Art Ensemble of Chicago, for example, chose to return to the United States after living in Paris in the late 1960s and early 1970s. The group's trumpeter, Lester Bowie, remarked of the decision, "We wanted to go back to the States because we wanted to go home. . . . To me it ain't no gas to be French. I like being an American Negro."[10] And, as the scholar Eric Porter has shown, musicians may proclaim certain affiliations in one context and take an entirely different position in another context. Porter notes, "Some [African American] musicians have celebrated jazz as a racially or culturally defined black music, but many of these same figures have for various philosophical or strategic reasons also seen it as an articulation of a broader human community and consciousness."[11] With these variable notions of identity, belonging, and presentation in mind, perhaps it would be most accurate to consider the designations I outline here as poles of a continuum on which one may understand musicians according to their own relative (and changeable) positions vis-à-vis the United States. Before exploring how these notions actually play out among current Americans in France, it will help to trace briefly jazz's long tradition of roving expatriates and exiles.[12]

U.S.-born musicians were playing jazz (or, at any rate, "jazzy") music in Paris as early as the end of World War I. Among those leading bands in that city were James Reese Europe, Louis Mitchell, and Will Marion Cook, whose Southern Syncopated Orchestra featured Sidney Bechet and inspired the famous rave from Swiss conductor Ernest Ansermet in 1919.[13] These bandleaders and many of the musicians who would follow them were African American, and they quickly learned that, despite the tired primitivist stereotypes that seemed to prevail whenever they played for white audiences, Europeans largely treated them with a degree of respect rarely shown back home. Indeed, as we have seen, black jazz musicians were often viewed as more authentic than their white counterparts and could earn substantially more money. Parisians, in particular, seemed to view these performers in the same way that they viewed participants from other disciplines, that is, as "artists."

Word spread quickly in the United States that Europe provided a hospitable place not only for African American musicians to work but also to live. Dozens more jazz singers, instrumentalists, and dancers would arrive there in the following decade, establishing a set of small yet vital creative communities not unlike the Harlem Renaissance, then flourishing on the other side of the Atlantic. To be sure, the situation was far from perfect. Quality players were not as plentiful as in the States, and the dreams and rumors of a truly racist-free society never fully materialized. Yet in contrast to the shabby treatment they had often received in their homeland, many black musicians of this era found themselves celebrated as honored guests on a Continent anxious to shake off the anxieties and sorrows that the war had initiated.[14] This warm reception was nurtured by a group of enthusiastically supportive Francophone writers, including Hughes Panassié, Charles Delaunay, and Robert Goffin, who contributed some of the earliest serious jazz criticism in any language.

While the good times rolled for Americans in Paris into the 1930s, the influx slowed and the American presence faded substantially as Europe headed toward World War II. The few musicians who remained during this period faced tough times. Most hunkered down to wait out the difficult years, but at least one expatriate took a more active role. Josephine Baker joined the French Resistance, eventually earning the *Croix de Guerre* and *Légion d'Honneur* for her efforts.[15] With the Allied victory American performers were on the move once again. During the late 1940s and into the 1950s a steady stream of accomplished jazz professionals traveled from the United States to various locations throughout Western Europe. As with the first wave of Americans to land overseas, dozens of players, including prominent black figures Kenny Clarke, Dexter Gordon, and Johnny Griffin, found that Europe, and especially France, once again offered musicians plentiful opportunities for employment and inexpensive housing.[16]

Eddie Allen, an African American drummer based in Paris since 1989, has given a great deal of thought to the mutual attractions between American musicians and the French public after the Second World War. In Allen's estimation black performers felt bolstered by a French social environment that respected creative individuals and did not necessarily fear ethnic difference, while jazz music provided the French people a voice through which to celebrate their deliverance from Nazi occupation. In Allen's words, "Black people came over here to be liberated, and to *offer* liberation." Increasingly, white jazz musicians, faced with diminishing prospects in the United States, also chose to relocate. Although some of these performers, regardless of ethnicity, missed the musical vibrancy, professional camaraderie, and family members they had left behind, many experienced a gratifying life overseas. White saxophonist Brew Moore moved to Europe in 1961, living there off and on until his death in 1973. In an early-1960s interview with the critic Leonard Feather, Moore enthused, "I don't know how I lived under that tension [in the United States] so long. . . . I've never been happier or more relaxed than since I started playing here in Copenhagen."[17]

At first glance this postwar migration would seem to represent only a simple resumption of movement from the States to Europe. But in contrast to the ragtime-, New Orleans–, or swing-based styles of Paris's earliest jazz immigrants, musicians from the later contingent had honed their skills during the bebop era and thus tended to favor faster tempos and a more angular melodic shape. And because the Europeans had not yet heard the new "modern jazz" from New York, France's growing cohort of homegrown players mostly paled in comparison to the Americans. Even guitar virtuoso Django Reinhardt felt overwhelmed by the new approach. On hearing a recording of Dizzy Gillespie's 1945 bop anthem "Salt Peanuts," the Paris-based Reinhardt reportedly "shook his head with disbelief and said: 'They play so fast. I don't know if I can keep up with them.'"[18] This qualitative gap, combined with a lingering Afrophilia that stretched back to the first decades of the century and beyond, virtually ensured that French musicians and critics would stand in awe of the newest arrivals from across the pond.[19] The French filmmaker Bertrand Tavernier drew on just these understandings in his 1950s period piece *Round Midnight* (1986), a sympathetic depiction of the relationship between Dale, a black American jazz star (a composite of real-life models Lester Young and Bud Powell) played by Dexter Gordon, and his adoring fan, Francis (based on Powell's friend and supporter, Francis Paudras), played by François Cluzet.

THE FREEDOM PRINCIPLE

While bop-oriented Americans ruled the European scene during the 1950s and into the 1960s, a new generation of musicians followed in their footsteps, bringing with them the attitudes and practices of the emerging avant-garde. Don Cherry, Archie Shepp, Albert Ayler, and Eric Dolphy all spent significant time on the Continent, as did many of their protégés, including, as we have seen, the Art Ensemble and other prominent members of the Chicago-based Association for the Advancement of Creative Musicians (AACM). These performers and composers, too, found receptive audiences and increased financial opportunities through appearances at clubs, concerts, and recording dates in France. As the music scholar and AACM member George Lewis put it, Paris in the 1960s "already enjoyed a long-standing reputation for welcoming black American culture, and was now perhaps the most accommodating of any city in the world to the newest American experimental music." Lewis recounts how the Art Ensemble's first concerts in Paris "became an immediate sensation" and "proved revelatory to European audiences."[20] Writing of the buzz generated by these and other "New Thing" artists in France, Eric Drott noted, "During the peak years of public interest in free jazz, from about 1968–1972, articles on the movement could be found in a bewildering variety of [French-language] publications, ranging from underground newspapers to glossy, high-end magazines, from communist-sponsored periodicals to bulletins underwritten by the U.S. State Department."[21] In such ways avant-garde American musicians came to dominate a substantial portion of the European jazz scene well into the 1970s.

Unbeknownst to them, however, these later performers might also have brought the seeds of destruction for their own relatively privileged times overseas. For the very parameters of music that this highly creative and compelling contingent had "liberated"—above all, a consistent swing rhythmic feel and a standard set of chord changes—were also those areas where U.S.-raised musicians had excelled over their European counterparts. In a sense America's traveling free-jazz practitioners had shown Europe how to take a perceived weakness and turn it into a strength: play fewer tunes based on Tin Pan Alley song forms and use a straight-eighth-note groove, or forgo a rhythmic pulse altogether. Not surprisingly, an increasing number of European players began to use more of the classical techniques and aesthetics that had always surrounded them (and that many of the American free players themselves had also studied), while also incorporating some of the forms and melodies of local folk musics.

Record labels sprang up across the Continent during the early 1970s. And while recording continued to provide steady income for bop-oriented American players, companies such as FMP, Enja, ICP, Black Saint, Hat Hut, and ECM also began releasing material from the decidedly unswinging likes of Europeans such as Peter Brötzmann, Terje Rydal, and Evan Parker. Some of this new music suggested American-style free jazz, but increasingly it revealed other priorities, leading eventually to what George Lewis described as a veritable "declaration of independence from [American jazz] hegemony."[22] To the surprise (and, for some, horror) of many musicians, critics, and industry executives, these sounds—particularly those from Munich-based ECM—sold remarkably well. And not just in Europe. As I detailed in chapter 4, ECM's best-known artists of the 1970s were the Americans Pat Metheny and Keith Jarrett, both of whom recorded with European sidemen for a time: Metheny with the German bassist Eberhard Weber; Jarrett with the Scandinavians Jon Christensen, Palle Danielsson, and Jan Garbarek. And both Weber and Garbarek also released successful recordings together and under their own names. So while Europe-based jazz musicians, local and imported, continued to perform American styles, the growing acclaim accorded to European jazz artists encouraged others to develop their own local sounds. The musician and scholar Mike Heffley characterizes the new attitude: "Over time, [European jazz] has taken on a strength and confidence—even a certain amount of crowing—that is sounding off beyond its local scenes and language barriers, commanding attention in the global arena. European improvised music now carries musical and cultural information and implications as potentially vital, edifying, and new to American music and culture as jazz was to Europe in the twentieth century, or as Western classical (especially German) music was to America in the nineteenth."[23] By the middle 1980s, musicians, critics, and festival producers could point to a movement or subgenre dubbed variously as "European jazz," "European new jazz," "Euro jazz," or "world jazz."[24] As Heffley's observations suggest, this trend turns the familiar contrast between New World and Old World on its head. For in some jazz circles North America has come to represent the antiquated, while Continental musicians are seen as fresh and creative. The blossoming of home-grown European jazz talent brings us to the present day.

THE PARIS SCENE IN THE NEW MILLENNIUM

Once a significant percentage of Europe's jazz participants began viewing bop-based jazz styles as "a quaint anachronism," Americans abroad did not seem quite as special to many local players.[25] Hence, while the dozens of U.S.-born musicians who now make Paris their home represent the latest in an extensive jazz lineage, fewer receive the honored-guest treatment enjoyed by earlier generations. The Paris-based pianist and composer Chris Culpo recognizes this self-determination among today's European players. Culpo told me that French musicians, in particular, are "starting to go where they want to go without looking over their shoulder at us [Americans]." As Culpo concedes, the increasing competence, confidence, and commercial viability of European practitioners has drastically affected the career opportunities of those American musicians now living and working overseas. Even so, the "American" label continues to bear symbolic capital among a portion of Europe's jazz fans, musicians, concert promoters, and club owners, and some U.S.-born performers use this to their advantage when looking for and presenting their work.

WHY PARIS?

Given that European-born musicians no longer necessarily hold their American counterparts in the highest regard, I wondered what sustained the continued migration of performers from the United States. For some, the impulse to relocate was quite straightforward: Paris's architectural beauty and the charm of its café culture was simply too attractive to resist. Others noted that while the French no longer hand over their gigs automatically to Americans, Paris still remains less competitive, at least in its remaining bop-based settings, than many U.S. cities (capable drummers are in especially short supply). Fewer outstanding players on the scene means increased opportunities for skilled musicians, regardless of their national origin.

Another commonly expressed motivation behind moving to France was that country's respectful attitude toward those involved in literature and the arts. In fact, virtually all the musicians I spoke with described this as a fundamental difference between the United States and Europe. The pianist Tom McClung observed, "No one laughs at you here if you tell them you're a musician. Musician is a respectable occupation." According to Eddie Allen, "In capitalist America, 'musician' equals 'you don't have any money, so you don't have any value.' In France, 'musician' equals 'artist.'" And as drummer Steve McCraven put it, "Here they take care of their musicians; they take care of all their artists. [If] you have an instrument here, you're somebody. Elsewhere musicians struggle; here there's a place for you."

France's social welfare system supports these attitudes. Guitarist Michael Felberbaum noted, "To be a jazz musician in the States is such a marginal thing. Here it's a different story, socially and legally. You actually have a [legal] status here."[26] The trumpeter and singer Larry Browne concurred: "Art is taken for granted in France—in the positive sense. Here you get paid vacations. The government supports music and other cultural forms because these are seen as indispensable to a good life." Felberbaum's and Browne's comments refer to the state program whereby French nationals and qualified immigrants can apply for official designation as a performing artist in order to receive subsidies. While the paperwork surrounding this system can be tedious, the returns—vacation time, medical coverage, and retirement benefits—are usually enough to free a player from having to accept the "day job" so dreaded among musicians in the States.[27]

The other most commonly expressed motivation behind moving to Paris was its geographical location. Players commented that they are able to arrange tours between the Continent's towns and cities much easier than they could in the more sprawling U.S. For the drummer John Betsch, "Paris is practical. It's centrally located as far as Europe goes." Taking this thought even beyond the immediate area, Betsch adds, "From here I can get to Africa as easily as I can get to New York." Saxophonist David Murray also cited the proximity to the African continent, noting that France's geopolitical history enables a rich cross-cultural exchange. Murray explained, "Paris is great because it's so closely tied to Africa. Geographically it's closer to Africa than is the U.S., but also the French colonial exploits in Senegal and other countries have created a constant influx of African peoples and cultures." African immigrants dominate Murray's Paris neighborhood of Menilmontant, and he has made this connection a significant part of his professional life in France, producing concerts and recordings featuring African artists. Similarly, the drummer Steve McCraven employed musicians from Senegal, Madagascar, and Algeria, as well as France, the United States, and England, during a series of recording sessions in 2002.[28]

Yet if some musicians celebrate their relocation to Paris as a gesture toward Africa and its people, cultures, and sounds, a few others I spoke with took a very different view. For these individuals Paris represents a move *away from* Afrocentric influences. One white musician even described his stay in France as an "escape" from those understandings that equate jazz authenticity solely with an African American heritage. These musicians find inspiration in European-based musical aesthetics, and they share with some of their French counterparts a desire to, as they see it, "release" jazz from the too-narrow constraints of the blues, swing, and bop-based aesthetics widely propounded in the U.S. In an interview about his brief move to Paris around 2001, the white American saxophonist Scott Rosenberg told Peter Margasak, "I ran into this attitude over and over again in Europe of people trying consciously to eradicate what they identified as jazz or the influence of jazz from their playing and approach, as though it were something cancerous to be cut out. Before I went to Europe I think I even occasionally had similar aspirations. It started to seem driven by a misguided sense of purity, a kind of negative absolutism, and ultimately an intentionally created separation whose only goal was to serve some kind of strange nationalism or continentalism, and in its worst manifestation, racism."[29]

Now, I want to be very clear that I never once heard or witnessed anything resembling a racist attitude from anyone I interviewed in Paris. Quite the contrary, even the assimilationist musicians with whom I spoke freely acknowledged the enormous contributions to jazz by African American performers and composers, past and present. They simply have other aesthetic goals in mind and believed that Paris offered them a better opportunity to pursue those goals. Still, Rosenberg's account of his own experience is illuminating, and it points to those notions of identity I mentioned at the outset of this chapter. For the different geocultural orientations of these Paris-based Americans reveals the messiness of the apparently simple designation "jazz," a tag representing not only a broad array of sounds but also a wide range of cultural values. All this diversity stems from and results in a mix of peoples, of course. And although these interactions are often amicable and mutually beneficial they can also be volatile and acrimonious.

There is no absolute, one-to-one correlation between musical style and subjective or cultural identity; musicians have always adopted and adapted sounds from all the genres available to them. But the various musical affinities and approaches musicians in Paris employ do highlight the differences separating the Americanists from the assimilationists. For instance, assimilationist musicians tend to incorporate a relatively greater range of stylistic sources. They draw particular inspiration from European classical material. The pianist Chris Culpo, who had played mainstream jazz gigs in Boston and New York, came to France on a Fulbright scholarship while completing his graduate work in composition at Juilliard. At the time of our interview Culpo had just finished giving a lesson to one of his jazz piano students, and I had seen him play with the French saxophonist Jean-Charles Richard at a club called Les Sept Lezards the previous night. But immediately after our talk, Culpo went back to writing a chamber piece commissioned by Radio France. Culpo claims his professional goal is to follow "the parallel streams that influence each other: jazz and classical music. What interests me is the fusion of these two."

European influences are clearly discernible in the harmonic and timbral aesthetics assimilationists emphasize. Their original compositions typically avoid ii–V–I progressions and other markers of functional jazz harmony. Depending on the instrumentation at hand—and instrumentation tends to vary much more widely among assimilationists than among the Americanists—these performers also often engage in extended polyphonic interplay. They tend to utilize relatively smoother timbres, though sometimes incorporate rock-based sounds or some of the more abrasive sonic aesthetics and techniques of the European classical avant-garde. By and large assimilationists also prefer straight-eighth-note feels or nonmetric passages. Taken together, their timbres, harmonies, and rhythms tend to bestow on the music a somewhat brooding character.

By comparison, Americanist-oriented players uphold the concept that effective jazz requires a strong dose of bop- or postbop-based linearity, and they employ more blues inflections than the assimilationists. Americanists may cover material from other composers, or they may write their own pieces, but either way these players rely more often on standard twelve- or thirty-two-bar song forms, though they sometimes incorporate open-ended modal passages, particularly when gesturing toward one of the music's icons, John Coltrane. These performers are also more likely to uphold the traditional jazz instrumentation of trumpet and/or saxophone supported by a rhythm section of piano, bass, and drums, and prefer a swing feel more frequently than their assimilationist counterparts. The combined effect of these preferences tends to engage the body more directly, seemingly aiming the music "outward," rather than modeling a sense of interiority, as the assimilationist approach often does.

PARLEZ-VOUS?

Musical style is only one way Americanist-oriented musicians distinguish themselves from the local cultures around them. Language choice is another important aspect of this position. One performer was quite emphatic when he told me that he consciously employs language as a tool. He deliberately addresses his concert audiences only in English in order to be seen as an "outsider," this despite the fact that he is married to a French national. Similarly, the saxophonist Steve Lacy learned more than a passable version of French during his three-decade stay in Paris. Yet in an engagement I attended in June 2002, Lacy spoke only English onstage. He even introduced his longtime bassist, Jean-Jacques Avenal, as "John Jack." Lacy was certainly aware that locals made up almost all of his listeners that evening, and he knew enough French to get by in his announcements. So why choose English? When I brought this question to one of Lacy's associates, I was told that the saxophonist always found it professionally expedient to be heard as "special" and "different," and the American accent and English-language usage helped sustain those understandings.

Some musicians speak French in their daily lives but switch to English when it comes to jazz because, as they see it, that's the "natural language" of the music. The pianist Katy Roberts, who uses French in everyday situations with no accent to my ears, purposely teaches her piano students "jazz English," as she called it, asking rhetorically, "How do you translate [a term] like 'Rhythm changes'?"[30] Note that Roberts's pedagogical choices, while undoubtedly intended to provide practical assistance to her students, also subtly reinforce notions linking jazz authenticity to the United States. They seem to suggest that if one wants to understand "real" jazz, one must learn certain musical forms, and under the terms that Americans learn them.

The African American drummer Steve McCraven, a Paris resident off and on since the late 1970s, utilizes both English and French. Revealing the opportunities and complexities of a postcolonial European environment, McCraven says, "Speaking [French] has opened doors for me. It's allowed me to speak with my African brothers, to touch their culture, their music." Moreover, although cosmopolitan Parisians pride themselves on embracing ethnic difference, France's colonial history in Africa has undeniably engendered a hierarchy. As a result, "blackness" generally functions more multidimensionally in Paris than in the United States, with African American immigrants in that city typically ranking "higher" than those from sub-Saharan regions. Aware of this pecking order, black musicians from the United States repeatedly told me of instances when they purposely spoke English in order to mark themselves as American and defuse potentially dangerous situations involving anti-African police or locals.

By contrast to the practices of the Americanist musicians, assimilationists, by definition, seek to blend in with the Franco-European culture that surrounds them, so it comes as no surprise that these individuals prefer to speak French almost exclusively in both personal and professional contexts. Chris Culpo exclaimed, "We're in France! I've made an effort to learn the language. It's a matter of respect, and it's become second nature now." Culpo noticed a subtle upswing in pro-American sentiment among the French immediately following the events of September 11, 2001, but told me, "I don't carry around a big [American] flag. I'm only second generation, anyway. I feel at home whenever, wherever the music is good."[31] Glenn Ferris remarked, "You isolate yourself without the [French] language. It serves no positive purpose not to learn [it]." When I asked him about others who see English usage as a professional strategy, he replied, "Rubbish. In fact, it's the opposite: [the French people] appreciate the effort." Ferris continued, "Now that jazz belongs to the world, there are great musicians everywhere who play this music. And one of the things I appreciated here [is that] I didn't have to belong to any tribe. I could be myself. I'm circulating in an independent way through it all."

Culpo and Ferris see no need to emphasize their American roots in their professional lives. Ferris's statement that "jazz belongs to the world" explicitly undermines notions of the music as an exclusively American cultural property and carves a space for a broader sense of belonging. I should make clear that these and the other assimilationist-oriented artists I spoke with are white Americans. Given the relative distribution of the various racial groups in France, these performers are more readily able to blend in, literally, with the dominant white French population than are Paris's African American musicians, all of whom I met lean more toward Americanist identities.

Ingrid Monson has explored similar circumstances in jazz, and her work shows how seemingly inclusive stances, such as the assimilationists adopt, can at times involve a subtly racialist component. In certain cases, Monson argues, nonblack musicians may take up what she calls a "universalist" position as a way to counter a strongly African Americanist posture:

> Since whiteness tends to be a sign of inauthenticity within the world of jazz, the appeals of white musicians to universalistic rhetoric can be perceived as power plays rather than genuine expressions of universal brotherhood. If jazz is one of the few cultural activities in which being African American is evaluated as "better" or more "authentic" than being non–African American, a white musician's appeal to a colorblind rhetoric might cloak a move to minimize the black cultural advantage by "lowering" an assertive African American musician from his or her pedestal to a more "equal" playing field. It is this use of colorblind rhetoric that often provokes African Americans to take more extreme positions on ethnic particularity.[32]

Monson's observations remind us that the evidently open and ideal notion of jazz as a universal music may not always spring from a wholly virtuous position, especially where non–African American musicians are concerned. At the same time, though, we should recognize that Culpo, Ferris, and other white performers abroad who maintain a strongly assimilationist identity and position, have also walked away from the opportunity to "raise" themselves in those settings where their American roots may still be an advantage, so their beliefs and actions should not be seen as crafty or nefarious.

COMMUNITIES

Whereas assimilationists play many, even most, of their gigs alongside non-Americans, the Americanists tend to stick closer to one another and play in each other's bands. Significantly, both black and white musicians populate the Americanist side of the continuum. This represents a marked difference from much of the United States, where ethnicity often defines the boundaries separating the various jazz communities. Indeed, in the larger

U.S. cities distinct "black," "white," "Latin," and "Asian" jazz scenes can function relatively autonomously. In Paris, where there are fewer American jazz performers to go around, racial identification sometimes takes a backseat to national identification, on and off the bandstand, with working relationships serving to strengthen social relationships and vice versa. To be sure, the increased racial interaction among Americans in Paris can function beyond altruistic community building. Some white performers, in particular, may emphasize the Americanist side of the continuum because they see it as a professional advantage to do so. As one musician described the situation, "Being [known as] a 'white musician' in New York doesn't do me as much good as being [known as] an 'American musician' in Paris. [A certain prominent African American performer] probably wouldn't even talk to me in New York; here we're colleagues." In other words, musicians do not always take gigs solely to express themselves or to form interracial kinships; they also take them in order to survive professionally, and each must build networks and orient performances and behavior in a manner designed to improve his or her level of success.

Some Americanist musicians steadfastly maintain their position even while admitting that many European musicians now dismiss the bop- and postbop-based styles they favor as old-fashioned. David Murray remarked:

> Europe has never really wanted to accept the recertification of bebop in terms of what was coming out of Lincoln Center. Many European musicians are trying to include more of their own founding concepts from European cultures and interject that into jazz. . . . And when I say that they didn't follow the Lincoln Center movement, the Europeans made a wise decision, that was it, because they made themselves and their music visible. They stood up in the jazz community and we now have European jazz. I mean, I'm not carrying the flag for European jazz but I do recognize it. But every now and then, they have to hire me and people like me, just to know what the real thing is.[33]

On one hand, Murray sees it as an astute decision for European musicians to forgo the mainstream jazz model (which he equates with Jazz at Lincoln Center) in favor of their local styles. On the other hand, Murray's allusion to himself as "the real thing" reasserts his own Americanist position of authority and authenticity. In addition, his comment that Europeans continue to "hire me and people like me" points to a continuing Americanist (and/or African Americanist) bent among some French club and concert promoters. For example, in July 2009 the Paris nightclub Sunside celebrated the eighteenth anniversary of its monthlong, "American Jazz Festival," while the club New Morning, one of Europe's top performance spaces, presented its annual "Festival All Stars" series, which featured a host of American groups. (And note the English-language names of both of these venues). Americanist-oriented musicians play into these attitudes whenever possible. One performer remarked, "I'm an American, so I do try to be somewhat different from the Parisian guys." In fact, the more successful of the Americanists often choose not to play on the local Paris scene as often as they could in order that they don't diminish their "American" mystique.

Glenn Ferris approaches his situation quite differently. Ferris moved to France in 1980 and immediately set about developing contacts with players from all parts of the globe, finding the stylistic variety of the European scene more conducive to maintaining steady and creative work. While some of his projects do lean toward swing- and bop-based models, contrasting aesthetics are rarely far away. Ferris told me that he could never have imagined even forming his trio—consisting of trombone, cello, and bass—had he not immersed himself in European music styles. He concedes that a portion of France's listening public remains infatuated with the jazz-as-American notion, but he sees no advantage to distancing himself from the local French players: "Musicians in Paris don't care if you're American. If anything, they would resent musicians coming over to take their gigs." Ferris decided early on to legalize his presence in France. "I'm about as French as you can get without being a citizen," he says, adding, "There's no benefit to being outside the system; that only creates the stress of not knowing [your future]." Ferris's choices have paid off for him. He maintains a busy schedule of performing and recording with a wide range of ensembles and teaches at the government-sponsored Paris Conservatory.

WORKING THE MIDDLE

The American musicians I met in Paris consider themselves "artists." They take their jazz seriously and expect their listeners to do the same. As I have noted, this outlook is in line with the stance of the French government and other areas of French society. Yet despite these ideals, the reality remains that not all gigs allow for complete musical autonomy. Many newly arrived or less-successful performers find it necessary to accept whatever work comes their way and are at the mercy of bandleaders' and patrons' preferences when it comes to choosing style or repertoire. So while the lines separating the assimilationists and (African) Americanists may seem clearly drawn for Paris's top American players, other performers live and work between the two extremes. These musicians sometimes try to benefit from any remaining gleam of American jazz supremacy in Europe but also try to develop working relationships with French bandleaders. They want to be American but not *too* American, leading to a situation in which players may emphasize their nationality in some settings and downplay it in others.

The trombonist Jerry Edwards, a relative newcomer to the Paris scene when I spoke with him in 2002, recognizes the delicate balance he walks and concedes that playing alongside French musicians as frequently as he does diminishes any prestige still attached to his nationality. Still, Edwards chooses to take local gigs and to speak French whenever possible. He says, "The [ideal] really is to be a traveling American. But me, I want to assimilate. I love this city, and besides you have to have the French [language] thing together for business." Echoing Edwards's assessment, saxophonist Warren Walker related to me some of the advice he received from a perceptive and well-meaning French musician shortly after arriving in Paris in 2004: "Don't tell anyone you live here. Just tell them you're visiting and available for gigs." Here we see once again how a "local musician" tag in Paris tarnishes some of the luster associated with being the American outsider.[34]

The realities faced by Edwards, Walker, and all of the other individuals I have discussed here underscore just how much the musical and professional choices performers make can depend on seemingly "nonmusical" factors. They also help to explain my use of the word *negotiating* in this chapter's title. Musicians negotiate at every turn and on every level: from the working out of verbal and written contracts to the constant musical adjustments necessary to interact effectively with fellow performers. And musicians, like everyone else, negotiate social and cultural allegiances in light of new circumstances, as they explore potential identities and senses of belonging.

PERSPECTIVES

Shortly after moving to France in 1989, Eddie Allen began to feel an unexpected kinship with the country he had left behind. "I had to come to

France to find out I'm an American," he said. "I miss America; it's my country. I appreciate my culture much more now that I'm here. Now I'm an American outside of America; it gives me a different perspective." I propose that U.S.-based jazz scholars, too, can gain a different perspective by looking and listening abroad. Beyond getting a better idea of the enormous breadth of sounds now played as jazz in the world, a wider vantage point allows us to see more clearly the degree to which national identity can influence meanings and practices. Some American performers see their nationality as a marker of jazz authenticity and a professional advantage; others view their country of origin as irrelevant, a situation that should give historians and others pause before waving the "America's music" banner yet again. We see, too, that while jazz may be a global musical phenomenon, in many ways it still operates locally—U.S.-born jazz musicians in Paris face a somewhat different set of circumstances than U.S.-born musicians in Los Angeles, just as Japanese-born jazz musicians in Boston face a different set of circumstances than they do in Tokyo—and that unfamiliar surroundings and conditions compel musicians to enter and form new communities, as well as to develop new professional tactics.

More broadly, exploring this issue as it plays out among these performers serves to show how all matters of identity and meaning remain contingent and intertwined. And while this exploration of nationality points to only one angle on the realities of jazz life for one group of musicians in one time and place, I trust that the ideas offered in this chapter—and every chapter in this study—have provided, at the very least, a different perspective on jazz locations, sounds, and meanings. This may not be the most dramatic way to conclude a book, but I believe it is an honest and appropriate one. Jazz isn't done yet. Far from it. And as long as people continue to create and listen to this music—that is, as long as jazz matters—scholars such as myself, along with musicians, journalists, fans, industry types, teachers, and others will continue to narrate and debate it. So I conclude with no neatly tied bows, just an appreciative acknowledgment for the incredible range of jazzes made to date and an affirmation that the music remains alive and well.

ACKNOWLEDGMENTS

Thank you for reading my book. I'd like you to know that invaluable information and suggestions were supplied by Ralph Alessi, E. Taylor Atkins, Andrew Berish, David Borgo, Michael Branch, Stacy Burton, Hillary Case, Ravi Coltrane, Dennis Dworkin, Larry Engstrom, Peter Epstein, Phil Ford, Mary Francis, Charles Hiroshi Garrett, Daniel Goldmark, Hans Halt, John Howland, Ray Knapp, Julianne Lindberg, Louis Niebur, Lewis Porter, Kenneth Prouty, Paul Roth, Gabriel Solis, Alex Stewart, Sherrie Tucker, Warren Walker, Robert Walser, Ben Wendell, Justin Willsey, Nadya Zimmerman, and the anonymous readers at the University of California Press, *Jazz Perspectives,* and *The Journal of Musicological Research.* I also owe a huge dept of gratitude to the many good folks at the University of California Press, including Joe Abbott, Emily Park, Eric Schmidt, Heather Vaughan, and, especially, the very wise and patient Mary Francis, for all their editorial input and assistance over the years.

I presented portions of chapter 4 as part of the Thinking about Music Series at the University of Cincinnati/College Conservatory of Music. Research related to chapter 5 was read initially at the Distinguished Lecture Series for UCLA's Department of Musicology and subsequently for the Music and Culture lecture series at Case Western Reserve University. Many thanks to the faculty and students of those schools, particularly Jessica Bissett and Julianne Lindberg (UCLA), Daniel Goldmark (Case), and Jeongwon Joe (Cincinnati), for inviting me to speak and for the many ideas that emerged from the discussions. Chapters 3 and 6 began as articles I wrote for *Jazz Perspectives* and the *Journal of Musicological Research,* respectively. Thanks to the editors of those publications for allowing me to revise and reprint my essays. Work related to chapter 6 was supported in part by a grant from the University of Nevada (UNR) Junior Research Grant Fund. (This support does not necessarily imply endorsement by the University of the research conclusions.) The project also benefited from a generous International Activities Grant sponsored by UNR's University Foundation and Office of Academic Affairs.

I am deeply grateful for the support my family and I have received over the years from the UNR community, above all from Deans Eric Herzik and Heather Hardy, Provosts John Frederick and Marc Johnson, Vice Provost Jannet Vreeland, and Director of the School of the Arts, Larry Engstrom. My associates in the Department of Music and Dance are an immensely creative and productive lot. Special thanks to Andrea Lenz, Louis Niebur, Julia Bledsoe, Cynthia Prescott, and fellow members of the Collective: Larry Engstrom, Peter Epstein, Hans Halt, and Andrew Heglund. My students have been a constant source of inspiration and insight. Deserving special recognition are Jessica Bissett, Brian Landrus, Julianne Lindberg, Matt Mayhall, Sam Minaie, Paul Roth, Gavin Templeton, Zach Teran, and Aaron Wolf. Thanks, too, to Clay Alder, Craig Bellis, Julia Bledsoe, Claudia and Roberto Castañeda, Tony Czarnik, Lance Dresser, Dennis Dworkin, Erika Frick, CeCe Gable, Chuck Garrett, Ray Knapp, Dent Hand, Susan McClary, Danna O'Connor, Bob Oesterreich, Rob Walser, CJ Walters, Steve Zideck, and my other wonderful friends, neighbors, and guardians in and beyond the Reno/Tahoe area. To the many musicians I interviewed, those with whom I played, those to whom I listened (in person or via recordings): It's understating the case to say that without your work, my work would not have been possible.

Above all, thank goodness for Ralph Alessi, James Carney, Scott Colley, Ravi Coltrane, Larry Engstrom, Peter Epstein, and Daniel Goldmark, who've been there for and with me through thick and thin. Ditto for Clint, Marie, and Annette Case; James and Diane Saul and their kids (and now grandkids); Ted and Valorie Ake and their kids; and Stuart Ake and Shelley Okimoto. Finally, I want to thank my parents, Theodore and Beatrice Ake, who nurtured my love of music from early on, paid for the lessons, drove me to rehearsals (or let my rock 'n' roll bands rehearse in their living room), and even helped carry my old Hammond M3 to gigs.

—

I wrote this book during an extremely tumultuous time in my life. David Abraham Case Ake was born to my wife, Hillary Louise Case, and me on September 2, 2005. Hillary was diagnosed with cancer five months later and died in our home on December 11, 2006. Through all of this—the joys, wonders, and inevitable anxieties surrounding the birth of our son, and the despair, fear, and hope-against-hopelessness of Hillary's illness and death—there were two constants. The first is the incredible love and assistance from the friends, family, and colleagues mentioned above. The second is the strength and renewal I have found in listening to, playing, teaching, composing, and writing about music, mostly (but not exclusively) jazz. Music is too often characterized as a pleasant accessory to "real life." If you're reading this book you probably don't need me to tell you this, but just to be sure: music plays an absolutely central role in maintaining one's sense of balance, purpose, and promise. There is nothing more fundamentally real than that.

Sample of American Jazz Musicians Born Since 1950 Who Studied Jazz at the College Level

Musician (Birth Year)	School(s) Attended
Carl Allen (1961)	William Paterson College
Geri Allen (1957)	Howard University; University of Pittsburgh
Ben Allison (1966)	New York University
Jay Anderson (1955)	California State University, Long Beach
Joey Baron (1955)	Berklee College of Music
Bruce Barth (1958)	New England Conservatory of Music
Bob Belden (1956)	North Texas State University
Jeff Berlin (1953)	Berklee College of Music
Tim Berne (1954)	Lewis and Clark College
Peter Bernstein (1967)	William Paterson College; New School for Social Research
Jim Black (1967)	Berklee College of Music
Cindy Blackman (1959)	Berklee College of Music
Brian Blade (1970)	Loyola University New Orleans; University of New Orleans
Terence Blanchard (1962)	Rutgers University

Source: *The New Grove Dictionary of Jazz*, ed. Barry Kernfeld, 2nd ed., vol. 2 (New York: Macmillan, 2002).

Luis Bonilla (1966)	California State University, Los Angeles
Don Byron (1958)	New England Conservatory of Music
Michael Cain (1966)	California Institute of the Arts
Joey Calderazzo (1965)	Berklee College of Music; Manhattan School of Music
Terri Lyne Carrington (1965)	Berklee College of Music
Ndugu Leon Chancellor (1952)	California State University, Dominguez Hills
Cyrus Chestnut (1963)	Berklee College of Music
Billy Childs (1957)	University of Southern California
John Clayton (1952)	Indiana University
Scott Colley (1963)	California Institute of the Arts
Ravi Coltrane (1965)	California Institute of the Arts
Harry Connick Jr (1967)	Loyola University New Orleans; Manhattan School of Music
Adam Cruz (1970)	New School for Social Research
Bill Cunliffe (1956)	Duke University; Eastman School of Music
Anthony Davis (1951)	Yale University
Jesse Davis (1965)	William Paterson College
Al DiMeola (1954)	Berklee College of Music
Dave Douglas (1963)	Berklee College of Music; New England Conservatory of Music
Mark Dresser (1952)	Indiana; University of California, San Diego
Marty Ehrlich (1955)	New England Conservatory of Music
Peter Epstein (1967)	California Institute of the Arts
Peter Erskine (1954)	Indiana University
Ellery Eskelin (1959)	Towson State University
Kevin Eubanks (1957)	Berklee College of Music
Robin Eubanks (1955)	Philadelphia College of Performing Arts
Jon Faddis (1953)	Manhattan School of Music
John Fedchock (1957)	Ohio State University; Eastman School of Music
Russell Ferrante (1952)	California State University, San Jose
Brandon Fields (1957)	California State University, Fullerton
David Fiucynski (1964)	New England Conservatory of Music
Ricky Ford (1954)	New England Conservatory of Music
Michael Formanek (1958)	California State University, Hayward
Curtis Fowlkes (1950)	Manhattan Community College

Rebecca Coupe Franks (1961)	Cabrillo Junior College; New School
Bill Frisell (1951)	Berklee College of Music
Matthew Garrision (1970)	Berklee College of Music
George Garzone (1950)	Berklee College of Music
James Genus (1966)	Virginia Commonwealth University
Greg Gisbert (1966)	Berklee College of Music
Larry Goldings (1968)	New School for Social Research
Wycliffe Gordon (1967)	Florida A & M
Danny Gottlieb (1953)	University of Miami
Larry Grenadier (1966)	San Jose State; Stanford University
Drew Gress (1959)	Towson State University; Manhattan School of Music
Russell Gunn (1971)	Jackson State University
Jamey Haddad (1952)	Berklee College of Music
Craig Handy (1962)	North Texas State University
Roy Hargrove (1969)	Berklee College of Music; New School for Social Research
Winard Harper (1962)	College Conservatory of Music (Cincinnati); Howard University; Hartt School of Music
Stefon Harris (1973)	Manhattan School of Music
Donald Harrison (1960)	Southern University; Berklee College of Music
Antonio Hart (1968)	Berklee College of Music
Graham Haynes (1960)	Queens College
Fred Hersch (1955)	New England Conservatory of Music
Susie Ibarra (1970)	Mannes College of Music; Goddard College
Dennis Irwin (1951)	North Texas State University
Javon Jackson (1965)	Berklee College of Music
Jon Jang (1954)	Oberlin
Marc Johnson (1953)	North Texas State University
Willie Jones III (1968)	California Institute of the Arts
Geoff Keezer (1970)	Berklee College of Music
Dave Kikoski (1961)	Berklee College of Music
Frank Kimbrough (1956)	Appalachian State University; Arizona State University
Kenny Kirkland (1955)	Manhattan School of Music
Larry Koonse (1961)	University of Southern California

Gene Lake (1966)	Berklee College of Music
Will Lee (1952)	University of Miami
Joe Locke (1959)	Eastman School of Music
Joe Lovano (1952)	Berklee College of Music
Carmen Lundy (1954)	University of Miami
Brian Lynch (1956)	Wisconsin Conservatory of Music; New York University
Tony Malaby (1964)	Arizona State University; William Paterson College
Rick Margitza (1961)	Wayne State University; Berklee College of Music; University of Miami; Loyola University New Orleans
Sherrie Maricle (1963)	State University of New York, Binghamton; New York University
Branford Marsalis (1960)	Southern University; Berklee College of Music
Delfeayo Marsalis (1965)	Berklee College of Music
Virginia Mayhew (1959)	New School for Social Research
John Medeski (1965)	New England Conservatory of Music
Myra Melford (1957)	Evergreen State College; Cornish Institute
Pat Metheny (1954)	University of Miami
Ron Miles (1963)	University of Denver; Manhattan School of Music; University of Colorado
Charnett Moffett (1967)	Juilliard
Ben Monder (1962)	University of Miami; Queens College
Jason Moran (1975)	Manhattan School of Music
David Murray (1955)	Pomona College
Lewis Nash (1958)	Arizona State University
Steve Nelson (1954)	Rutgers University
James Newton (1953)	California State University, Los Angeles
Judy Niemack (1954)	Pasadena City College
Adam Nussbaum (1955)	City College of New York
Greg Osby (1960)	Howard University; Berklee College of Music
Jaco Pastorius (1951)	University of Miami
John Patitucci (1959)	San Francisco State University; Long Beach State
Nicholas Payton (1973)	University of New Orleans

Ben Perowsky (1966)	Berklee College of Music; Manhattan School of Music
Chris Potter (1971)	Manhattan School of Music
Marcus Printup (1967)	University of North Florida
Tom Rainey (1957)	Berklee College of Music
Dianne Reeves (1956)	University of Denver
Lee Ritenour (1952)	University of Southern California
Herb Robertson (1951)	Berklee College of Music
Marcus Rojas (1962)	New England Conservatory of Music
Wallace Roney (1960)	Howard University; Berklee College of Music
Michelle Rosewoman (1953)	Laney Junior College
Jim Rotondi (1962)	North Texas State University
Patrice Rushen (1954)	University of Southern California
Michael Sarin (1965)	University of Washington; Cornish Institute
Maria Schneider (1960)	University of Minnesota; University of Miami; Eastman School of Music
Loren Schoenberg (1958)	Manhattan School of Music
John Scofield (1951)	Berklee College of Music
Brad Shepik (1966)	Cornish Institute
Bob Sheppard (1952)	Glassboro State; Eastman School of Music
Matthew Shipp (1960)	University of Delaware; New England Conservatory of Music
Marvin "Smitty" Smith (1961)	Berklee College of Music
Jim Snidero (1958)	North Texas State University
Chris Speed (1967)	New England Conservatory of Music
Mike Stern (1953)	Berklee College of Music
Bill Stewart (1966)	William Paterson College
Craig Taborn (1970)	University of Michigan
Akira Tana (1952)	New England Conservatory of Music
Mark Turner (1965)	California State University, Long Beach; Berklee College of Music
Reginald Veal (1964)	Southern University
Chad Wackerman (1960)	California State University, Long Beach
Nasheet Waits (1971)	Morehouse College; Long Island University
Bobby Watson (1953)	University of Miami
Jeff "Tain" Watts (1960)	Berklee College of Music
Dave Weckl (1960)	University of Bridgeport

Kenny Werner (1951)	Berklee College of Music
James Williams (1951)	Memphis State University
Matt Wilson (1964)	Wichita State University
Kenny Wolleson (1966)	Cabrillo Junior College
Francis Wong (1957)	San Jose State University
Rachel Z (1962)	New England Conservatory of Music
John Zorn (1953)	Webster College

Interview Locations and Dates

Eddie Allen, Paris, July 20, 2002
Steven Bernstein (telephone), November 24, 2007
John Betsch, Paris, June 13, 2002
Larry Browne, Paris, June 25, 2002
Chris Culpo, Paris, July 12, 2002
Mark Dodge, Paris, June 17, 2002
Jerry Edwards, Paris, June 28, 2002
Michael Felberbaum, Paris, July 23, 2002
Glenn Ferris, Paris, July 17, 2002
Danny Fitzgerald, Paris, July 3, 2002
Fred Hersch (telephone), July 15, 2005
Brian Hicks, Paris, June 22, 2002
Tom McClung, Paris, July 1, 2002
Steve McCraven, Paris, June 28, 2002
Dany Michel, Paris, June 24, 2002
David Murray, Paris, June 17, 2002
Katy Roberts, Paris, July 8, 2002
Warren Walker, Reno, June 16, 2005
Andrew White (telephone), May 28, 2008

NOTES

INTRODUCTION

1. Milan Kundera, *Testaments Betrayed: An Essay in Nine Parts* (New York: Perennial, 2001), 15.

2. Ibid.

3. Ibid., 17 (emphasis in original). This was not Kundera's final word on the matter. More recently he wrote, "Art is not a village band marching dutifully along at History's heels. It is there to create its own history" (Milan Kundera, *The Curtain: An Essay in Seven Parts* [New York: Harper Perennial, 2007], 27). My comment about "influences" refers to Harold Bloom, *The Anxiety of Influence: A Theory of Poetry*, 2nd ed. (New York: Oxford University Press, 1997); and John P. Murphy, "Jazz Improvisation: The Joy of Influence," *The Black Perspective in Music* 18, nos. 1–2 (1990): 7–19.

4. See Howard Becker, *Art Worlds* (Berkeley: University of California Press, 1984).

5. Joshua Redman, quoted in Lloyd Peterson, *Music and the Creative Spirit: Innovators in Jazz, Improvisation, and the Avant Garde* (Lanham, MD: Scarecrow Press, 2006), 255.

6. JC Gabel, "Making Knowledge Out of Sound: The *Stop Smiling* Interview with Ornette Coleman," *Stop Smiling* 34 (2008): 44 (emphasis in original).

7. Scott DeVeaux, "Constructing the Jazz Tradition: Jazz Historiography," *Black American Literature Forum* 25, no. 3 (fall 1991): 552. See also DeVeaux's, "Jazz in America: Who's Listening?" *Research Division Report #31, National Endowment for the Arts* (Carson, CA: Seven Locks Press, 1995). Portions of this

document were republished as "Who Listens to Jazz?" in *Keeping Time: Readings in Jazz History,* ed. Robert Walser (New York: Oxford University Press, 1999), 389–95.

8. Wynton Marsalis, "What Jazz Is—and Isn't," *New York Times,* July 31, 1998, 21.

9. It is sad enough that that sloppy and trite performance from this usually brilliant pianist was released posthumously on an album called *Alternate Takes* (Blue Note Records BST-84430); it's downright tragic that Blue Note rereleased it on a compilation called *The Best of Bud Powell* (Blue Note Records CD D 106064, 1989).

10. "[Jazz] is appreciated for its esthetic and intellectual rewards, and it is approached with some effort. . . . Much jazz, especially the post-1930s styles, . . . requires a cultivated taste" (Mark Gridley, *Jazz Styles: History and Analysis,* 10th ed. (Upper Saddle River, NJ: Pearson Prentice Hall, 2009), 12.

11. Notice the lingering Eurocentric attitudes, practices, and policies within many American music schools, for example.

12. For a chilling account of the use of music in the U.S. government's "war on terror" in the early twenty-first century see Suzanne Cusick's "Music as Torture / Music as Weapon," *Transcultural Music Review* 10 (2006): www.sibetrans .com/trans/trans10/cusick_eng.htm (accessed Jan. 31, 2010).

13. For more on the paucity of mid-level jazz gigs see Stuart Nicholson, "Prophets Looking Backward: Jazz at Lincoln Center," in *Is Jazz Dead? (Or Has It Moved to a New Address)* (New York: Routledge, 2005), 52–76. It is worth noting that at the lowest levels no musicians, whatever the genre, make money. Indeed, rock bands in some major markets even face a "pay-to-play" scenario.

14. See, e.g., Ajay Heble, *Landing on the Wrong Note: Jazz, Dissonance, and Critical Practice* (New York: Routledge, 2000); and Peterson, *Music and the Creative Spirit.*

15. Heble, *Landing on the Wrong Note,* 199–228.

16. Ingrid Monson, *Freedom Sounds: Civil Rights Call Out to Jazz and Africa* (New York: Oxford University Press, 2007). See also "Louis Armstrong on Music and Politics," in Walser, *Keeping Time,* 246–50.

17. Eric Drott, "Free Jazz and the French Critic," *Journal of the American Musicological Society* 61, no. 3 (fall 2008): 541–81, 547.

18. Allan Morrison, quoted in Nat Hentoff, "Lester Young," from *A Lester Young Reader,* ed. Lewis Porter (Washington: Smithsonian Institution Press, 1991), 47–73, 72.

19. John Szwed, "The Man," in *Uptown Conversations: The New Jazz Studies,* ed. Robert G. O'Meally, Brent Hayes Edwards, and Farah Jasmine Griffin (New York: Columbia University Press, 2004), 166–86, 166.

20. Joan Jeffri, *Changing the Beat: A Study of the Worklife of Jazz Musicians,* vol. 1, *Executive Summary* (New York: Research Center for Arts and Culture,

National Endowment of the Arts, and the San Francisco Study Center, 2001), 6, 9.

21. Jed Rasula, "The Media of Memory: The Seductive Menace of Records in Jazz History," in *Jazz among the Discourses,* ed. Krin Gabbard (Durham, NC: Duke University Press, 1995), 134–62, 146.

22. The most wide-ranging and thought-provoking study on the interplays of music and time remains Jonathan D. Kramer, *The Time of Music: New Meanings, New Temporalities, New Listening Strategies* (New York: Schirmer, 1988).

23. For example, Court Carney, *Cuttin' Up: How Early Jazz Got America's Ear* (Lawrence: University Press of Kansas, 2009); Charles Hiroshi Garrett, *Struggling to Define a Nation: American Music and the Twentieth Century* (Berkeley: University of California Press, 2008); Charles Hersch, *Subversive Sounds: Race and the Birth of Jazz in New Orleans* (Chicago: University of Chicago Press, 2007); John Howland, *Ellington Uptown: Duke Ellington, James P. Johnson, and the Birth of Concert Jazz* (Ann Arbor: University of Michigan Press, 2009); Jeffrey Magee, *The Uncrowned King of Swing: Fletcher Henderson and Big Band Jazz* (New York: Oxford University Press, 2005); and Bruce Boyd Raeburn, *New Orleans Style and the Writing of American Jazz History* (Ann Arbor: University of Michigan Press, 2009).

24. As a number of writers have shown, squabbles over jazz authenticity stretch back to at least the 1930s. Still, the sheer number of different sounds and styles presented as jazz has seemed to multiply exponentially over the past half century, making this period by far the most challenging in creating a cohesive narrative. See Bernard Gendron, "'Moldy Figs' and Modernists: Jazz at War (1942–1946), in *Jazz Among the Discourses,* ed. Krin Gabbard (Durham, NC: Duke University Press, 1995), 31–56; as well as Raeburn's commentary on Gendron's position in *New Orleans Style,* 179–80. Also see Scott DeVeaux's take on this phenomenon in DeVeaux, "Constructing the Jazz Tradition," 526–27.

25. Others who move freely across the jazz teacher/performer/scholar divide in the United States include Paul Austerlitz, David Borgo, Dana Gooley, Mike Heffley, Vijay Iyer, George Lewis, Lewis Porter, Guthrie Ramsey, Alex Stewart, and Chris Washburne.

26. George Seltzer, *Music Matters: The Performer and the American Federation of Musicians* (Metuchen, NJ: Scarecrow Press, 1989); Doug Ramsey, *Jazz Matters: Reflections on the Music and Some of Its Makers* (Fayetteville: University of Arkansas Press, 1995).

27. Cornel West, *Race Matters* (New York: Vintage, 1994).

CHAPTER ONE

1. Eric Nisenson, *Ascension: John Coltrane and His Quest* (New York: Da Capo, 1995); J. C. Thomas, *Chasin' the Trane: The Music and Mystique of John*

Coltrane (New York: Da Capo Press, 1988). Metaphors of "quest" or "search" can also be found in Madhav Chari, "Pundit Coltrane Shows the Way," *Journal of Asian American Studies* 4 no. 3 (Oct. 2001): 265–83; John Fraim, *Spirit Catcher: The Life and Art of John Coltrane* (West Liberty, OH: Great House, 1996); and Pete Welding, "Spotlight Review: John Coltrane, *Coltrane at the Village Vanguard Again!*" *DownBeat,* Feb. 1967, 26. For more on this see "Jazz 'Training: John Coltrane and the Conservatory," in my *Jazz Cultures* (Berkeley: University of California Press, 2002), 112–45.

2. See, e.g., Gabriel Solis's chapter "A Question of Voice" in his *Monk's Music: Thelonious Monk and Jazz History in the Making* (Berkeley: University of California Press, 2007), 63–80; or Edward T. Cone, *The Composer's Voice* (Berkeley: University of California Press, 1974).

3. Carolyn Abbate, *Unsung Voices: Opera and Musical Narrative in the Nineteenth Century* (Princeton, NJ: Princeton University Press, 1991), xiii.

4. Ingrid Monson, *Freedom Sounds: Civil Rights Call Out to Jazz and Africa* (New York: Oxford University Press, 2007), 304.

5. This practice is not limited to music, of course. People have long ascribed human qualities to any and all inanimate objects, a custom the English art and literary critic John Ruskin (1819–1900) dubbed "the pathetic fallacy." See John Ruskin, *The Modern Painters,* vol. 4, *Of Mountain Beauty* (1856; Boston: Adamant Media Corporation, 2000).

6. It seems that many erstwhile Chet Baker fans, acquaintances, and colleagues were dismayed to find that their idol was oftentimes less sensitive to their feelings than his music led them to believe he would be. See James Gavin, *Deep in a Dream: The Long Night of Chet Baker* (New York: Knopf, 2002).

7. By "formally equivalent portions" I mean that one cannot simply grab random excerpts and paste them together in just any fashion. To return to the "KoKo" example, we couldn't switch bars 1–8 of Parker's solo with bars 33–40 of that solo. The first excerpt would be taken from the first A section of the sixty-four-bar, AABA form, while the second would be taken from the B section (bridge) of that form. Obviously, this would result in serious harmonic discrepancies between the soloist and the rhythm section, and would end up sounding like a mess. Lawrence Gushee addresses this delimiting aspect of song form in his outstanding study, "Lester Young's 'Shoe Shine Boy,'" in *A Lester Young Reader,* ed. Lewis Porter (Washington: Smithsonian Institution Press, 1991), 224–54, 245. That piece originally appeared in the International Musicological Society's *Report of the Twelfth Congress, Berkeley 1977,* ed. Daniel Heartz and Bonnie Wade (Kassel: Bärenreiter, 1981). Also relevant are Solis, *Monk's Music,* esp. 33–46; and Gunther Schuller's "Sonny Rollins and the Challenge of Thematic Improvisation," in *Musings: The Musical Worlds of Gunther Schuller* (New York: Oxford University Press, 1986), 86–97.

8. A handful of jazz musicians tested these boundaries. Some of Duke Ellington's recorded works covered both sides of a 78-rpm record, as did Benny Goodman's megahit "Sing, Sing, Sing." For more on time limitations and performance practices see Mark Katz, "Capturing Jazz," in his *Capturing Sound: How Technology Has Changed Music* (Berkeley: University of California Press, 2004), 74–77.

9. Charles Keil and Steven Feld, *Music Grooves* (Chicago: University of Chicago Press, 1994), 24. See also Ingrid Monson, "Riffs, Repetition, and Theories of Globalization," *Ethnomusicology* 43, no. 1 (winter 1999): 31–65.

10. Paul Berliner's *Thinking in Jazz: The Infinite Art of Improvisation* (Chicago: University of Chicago Press, 1994) offers the most exhaustive study of standard performance practices.

11. Lewis Porter, *John Coltrane: His Life and Music* (Ann Arbor: University of Michigan Press, 1998), 151.

12. Ekkehard Jost, *Free Jazz* (1975; New York: Da Capo, 1994), 25.

13. Bill Cole, *John Coltrane* (New York: Schirmer, 1976), 108. I also discuss this tune in the aforementioned "Jazz 'Traning" (see note 1), esp. 129–33.

14. As these and so many other canonic performances reveal, there are numerous ways to improvise compelling jazz. For this reason improvisation instructors might want to rethink their oft-touted model of the ideal solo as one that starts simply, gradually increases complexity, and trails off at the end.

15. Quoted in Paul Walker, *Theories of Fugue from the Age of Josquin to the Age of Bach* (Rochester, NY: University of Rochester Press, 2000), 117 (the bracketed material is Walker's). Originally published in Michael Praetorius, *Syntagma musicum,* vol. 3 (Wolfenbüttel: Elias Holwein, 1619).

16. Karol Berger, *Bach's Cycle, Mozart's Arrow: An Essay on the Origins of Musical Modernity* (Berkeley: University of California Press, 2007), 95.

17. Ibid., 97.

18. Every musician has to deal with endings in one way or another. Big Joe Turner, a blues/jazz/r & b/rock 'n' roll singer *par excellence,* may have devised the most effective—or at least most emphatic—solution to the problem of signaling closure. On "Roll 'em, Pete" Turner informs pianist Pete Johnson (and the recording engineers and the audience) that he's wrapping things up by singing/shouting "Bye, Bye" three times over the course of the last twelve bars. Joe Turner and Peter Johnson, "Roll 'em, Pete," Vocalion 78-rpm #4607, 1939 [rereleased on *Big Joe Turner, Big, Bad, and Blue: The Big Joe Turner Anthology,* Rhino/Atlantic CD R2 71550, 1994]. For a thought-provoking take on the functions, processes, and philosophical implications of musical endings see John Corbett, "Out of Nowhere: Meditations on Deleuzian Music, Anti-Cadential Strategies, and Endpoints in Improvisation," in *The Other Side of Nowhere: Jazz, Improvisation, and Communities in Dialogue,* ed. Daniel Fischlin and Ajay Heble (Middletown, CT: Wesleyan University Press, 2004), 387–95.

19. One could link the subjectivity configured through this manner of playing to certain notions of jazz masculinity, though that important topic goes beyond the scope of this chapter.

20. This is why studies that offer alternatives to the soloist-centric narrative are so valuable. Examples of a more holistic view include Berliner, *Thinking in Jazz;* David Borgo, *Sync or Swarm: Improvising Music in a Complex Age* (New York: Continuum, 2005); and Ingrid Monson, *Saying Something: Jazz Improvisation and Interaction* (Chicago: University of Chicago Press, 1996).

21. See C. O. Simpkins, *Coltrane: A Biography* (Baltimore: Black Classic Press, 1998), 201–2; Nisenson, *Ascension,* 154; Monson, *Freedom Sounds,* 230–33, 302–4; and Frank Kofsky, *John Coltrane and the Jazz Revolution of the 1960s* (New York: Pathfinder, 1998). Iain Anderson is an exception to this rule, locating a black-nationalist aesthetic in Coltrane's music as early as 1961. See Iain Anderson, "Jazz Outside the Marketplace: Free Improvisation and Nonprofit Sponsorship of the Arts, 1965–1980," *American Music* 20, no. 2 (summer 2004): 131–67.

22. In fact, in an offhand comment to his fellow musicians during the "Giant Steps" recording session, Coltrane mentioned that getting through the chord changes with minimal mistakes was his most realistic goal for that tune (John Coltrane, *The Heavyweight Champion,* Rhino/Atlantic R2 71984, 1995, disc 7, track 1). For an insightful interpretation of this fascinating verbal exchange see Vijay Iyer, "Exploding the Narrative in Jazz Improvisation," in *Uptown Conversations: The New Jazz Studies,* ed. Robert G. O'Meally, Brent Hayes Edwards, and Farah Jasmine Griffin (New York: Columbia University Press, 2004), 394–95. Cornel West eloquently describes the value of discipline and excellence in *Race Matters* (New York: Vintage, 1994), esp. 23–24.

23. For references to "Giant Steps" as bebop's "logical conclusion" see Nisenson, *Ascension,* 72; and Scott Yanow, *Jazz on Record: The First Sixty Years* (San Francisco: Backbeat Books, 2003), 542. For more on the racial politics of bebop see Leroi Jones (now Amiri Baraka), *Blues People: Negro Music in White America* (1963; New York: Quill, 1983); Scott DeVeaux, *The Birth of Bebop: A Social and Musical History* (Berkeley: University of California Press, 1997); Eric Lott, "Double V, Double-Time: Bebop's Politics of Style," in *Jazz among the Discourses,* ed. Krin Gabbard, 243–55; Ingrid Monson, "The Problem with White Hipness: Race, Gender, and Cultural Conceptions in Jazz Historical Discourse," *Journal of the American Musicological Society* 48 (fall 1995): 396–422; and Eric Porter, *What Is This Thing Called Jazz? African American Musicians as Artists, Critics, and Activists* (Berkeley: University of California Press, 2002). I revisit this crucial debate in subsequent chapters.

24. For testimonials of Coltrane's soft-spoken personality see Cole, *John Coltrane,* 171; Miles Davis with Quincy Troupe, *Miles: The Autobiography* (New York: Touchstone, 1989), 287; Simpkins, *Coltrane,* 107; and Nat Hentoff, new

liner notes for John Coltrane, *Giant Steps,* Rhino/Atlantic CD R2 75203, 1998, 4.

25. Nat Hentoff, original liner notes to John Coltrane, *Giant Steps,* Atlantic LP SD-1311, 1959 (reissued on the Rhino/Atlantic disc cited in the previous note).

26. See Monson's *Freedom Sounds* (300) for a discussion of Coltrane's mixed, modal/chordal arrangements, as on his version of "Body and Soul."

27. John Coltrane, *My Favorite Things,* Rhino/Atlantic R2 75204, 1998 [1960].

28. Lawrence Kramer, *Musical Meaning: Toward a Critical History* (Berkeley: University of California Press, 2002), 252.

29. John Coltrane, *Live at Birdland,* MCA Impulse! MCAD 33109, 1984 [1963].

30. Albert Murray, *Stomping the Blues* (New York: Da Capo, 1976), 250–54. Murray includes on his list of blues musicians Lester Young, Charlie Parker, and many others now widely considered to represent jazz. See also Murray's "The Function of the Heroic Image," in *The Jazz Cadence of American Culture,* ed. Robert G. O'Meally (New York: Columbia University Press, 1998), 569–79.

31. Joseph Campbell is the most famous chronicler of this three-part hero cycle. Campbell posthumously became a pop-star scholar of sorts in the 1980s through his conversations with Bill Moyers, which aired after his death in six segments on PBS in 1988 as *The Power of Myth* (now available on Mystic Fire Video DVD, 2001). Many of those dialogues concerned the hero stories that Campbell first outlined in his *The Hero with a Thousand Faces* (1949; Princeton, NJ: Princeton University Press, 1973).

32. John Coltrane, *Coltrane: The Complete 1961 Village Vanguard Recordings,* Impulse! CD IMPD4-232, 1997.

33. Whitney Balliett, "Coltrane," in *Collected Works: A Journal of Jazz, 1954–2000* (New York: St. Martin's, 2000), 291.

34. Martin Williams, *The Jazz Tradition,* rev. ed. (New York: Oxford University Press, 1983), 232.

35. Scott Burnham, *Beethoven Hero* (Princeton, NJ: Princeton University Press, 1995), xiv.

36. Ibid., xv.

37. Ibid., xvi.

38. Monique Guillory, "Black Bodies Swingin': Race, Gender, and Jazz," in *Soul: Black Power, Politics, and Pleasure,* ed. Monique Guillory and Richard C. Green (New York: New York University Press, 1998), 191–215, 192.

39. John Gennari, *Blowin' Hot and Cold: Jazz and Its Critics* (Chicago: University of Chicago Press, 2006), 264.

40. A. B. Spellman, "Trane + 7 = A Wild Night at the Gate," *DownBeat,* Dec. 1965, 15.

41. These comments come from a telephone interview I conducted with White in 2008, but they also reaffirm the position White held when I spoke with him ten years earlier. See my *Jazz Cultures,* 138.

42. Stanley Crouch, *Considering Genius: Writings on Jazz* (New York: Basic Books, 2006), 213–15.

43. David Wild, "Liner Notes: John Coltrane, *The Major Works of John Coltrane,*" Impulse CD GRD-2-113. Both versions of "Ascension" appear on that set. In addition to Coltrane, Garrison, Jones, and Tyner, the *Ascension* session featured Archie Shepp and Pharoah Sanders (tenor saxes), John Tchicai and Marion Brown (alto saxes), Freddie Hubbard and Dewey Johnson (trumpets), and Art Davis (bass).

44. Jost, *Free Jazz,* 94.

45. This phenomenon did not prevent one music theorist from analyzing a portion of Coltrane's playing on "Edition I" to the exclusion of virtually everything else that happens in that performance. See Steven Block, "Pitch-Class Transformation in Free Jazz," *Music Theory Spectrum* 12, no. 2 (autumn 1990): 181–202.

46. I am referring to "Edition II," but either take would work equally well for this analysis.

47. Nat Hentoff, *Jazz Is* (1976; New York: Limelight, 2004), 205.

48. Bill Mathieu, "Record Review: John Coltrane, *Ascension,*" *DownBeat,* May 5, 1966, 25.

49. Bruce Michael McDonald, "Traning the Nineties, or the Present Relevance of John Coltrane's Music of Theophany and Negation," *African American Review* 29, no. 2 (summer 1995): 275–82, 275–76 (emphasis in original).

50. See www.coltranechurch.org (accessed Jan. 31, 2010).

51. Like "Ascension," "Selflessness" appears on *The Major Works* reissue collection (see note 43 above).

52. Frank Kofsky, "John Coltrane: An Interview," repr. in *The John Coltrane Companion: Five Decades of Commentary,* ed. Carl Woideck (New York: Schirmer, 1998), 128–56, 129. Originally published in Kofsky, *Black Nationalism and the Revolution in Music* (New York: Pathfinder, 1970).

53. The Reverend Mark Dukes interviewed in *The Church of Saint Coltrane,* produced by Jeff Swimmer and Gayle Gilman (Tango Films, 1996).

54. McDonald, "Traning the Nineties," 277.

55. Ben Ratliff, *Coltrane: The Story of a Sound* (New York: Farrar, Straus, and Giroux, 2007), x–xi (my emphasis).

56. Ratliff writes, "*Ascension* is not a success in particular. It is hard to get around the tremulous chaos of the group sound, not to mention the many moments of a band whose members are not in synch with one another, reaching points where they might as well stop, but don't" (ibid., 97).

57. This is discussed in Nisenson, *Ascension,* 166–67; and Porter, *John Coltrane,* 265. Perhaps the best-known chronicle of a hallucinogen-induced mystical experience is Aldous Huxley, *The Doors of Perception* (1954; New York: Vintage, 2004). See also Alan Watts, *The Joyous Cosmology: Adventures in the Chemistry of Consciousness* (New York: Vintage, 1965); and R. C. Zaehner, *Mysticism Sacred and Profane: An Inquiry into Some Varieties of Praeternatural Experience* (1957; New York: Oxford University Press, 1980).

CHAPTER TWO

This chapter is a revision and expansion of "Musicology Beyond the Score . . . *and* the Performance: Making Sense of the Creak on Miles Davis's 'Old Folks,'" in *Musicological Identities: Essays in Honor of Susan McClary,* ed. Steven Baur, Raymond Knapp, and Jacqueline Warwick (Burlington, VT: Ashgate, 2008), 219–33.

1. Ian Carr describes *Someday My Prince Will Come* as "uneven in quality" and "lacking in that group identity which always characterizes the best Miles Davis albums" (Ian Carr, *Miles Davis: A Biography* [New York: Quill, 1984], 124). Davis recorded *Someday My Prince Will Come* over three sessions in March 1961. His sidemen for those dates included saxophonists Hank Mobley and John Coltrane, pianist Wynton Kelly, drummer Jimmy Cobb, and bassist Paul Chambers. Davis's "Second Great Quintet" featured pianist Herbie Hancock, bassist Ron Carter, drummer Tony Williams, and saxophonist Wayne Shorter. The "First Great Quintet," with Coltrane, Red Garland, Philly Joe Jones, and Paul Chambers, ran from 1955 to 1957.

2. For more on the cover photo see Carr, *Miles Davis,* 166; see also Miles Davis with Quincy Troupe, *Miles Davis: The Autobiography* (New York: Touchstone, 1989), 252.

3. As the indelible shadow-image on the upper-right corner of *Someday My Prince Will Come* and many of Davis's other Columbia Records album covers suggests, Davis stood while performing in concert. However, videos and photos reveal that he sometimes sat while recording; Nat Hentoff mentions this in *The Jazz Life* (New York: Da Capo, 1975), 132. Also, during the recording of *Kind of Blue* in 1959, Davis called attention to a "squeak" in the floor of 30th Street Studios. This is the same location where Davis recorded "Old Folks." I return to this point below.

4. Davis and Macero had experimented with multiply edited recordings as early as the middle 1950s. See Carl Woideck, "Miles Davis 1955: Performance and Production in the Recording Studio," paper presented at the Annual Meeting of the Society of American Music, Toronto, Nov. 2, 2000. One online discography labels the *Someday My Prince Will Come* version of "Old Folks" as

"take 6" (www.plosin.com/MilesAhead/Disco.aspx?id=Someday-LP [accessed July 4, 2009]). However, I can find no other recordings or discussions of the rejected takes.

5. Jacques Attali, *Noise: The Political Economy of Music* (Minneapolis: University of Minnesota Press, 1985).

6. Richard Leppert, "Paradise, Nature, and Reconciliation, or, a Tentative Conversation with Wagner, Puccini, Adorno, and The Ronettes," *Echo* 4, no. 1 (spring 2002): www.echo.ucla.edu/Volume4-Issue1/leppert/index.html (accessed Jan. 11, 2010).

7. Theodore Gracyk, *Rhythm and Noise: An Aesthetics of Rock* (Durham, NC: Duke University Press, 1996), 56. For another outstanding account of the process of crafting music in the recording studio see Albin Zak, *The Poetics of Rock: Cutting Tracks, Making Records* (Berkeley: University of California Press, 2001).

8. Richard Taruskin, *Text and Act: Essays on Music and Performance* (New York: Oxford University Press, 1995), 59–60.

9. Susan McClary, "1999: Music at the End of the Second Millennium," Keynote Address for Conference, Cross(over) Relations, Eastman School of Music (Sept. 1996), 6.

10. "Old Folks" was written in 1938 by the Tin Pan Alley songsmiths Willard Robison and D.L. Hill and was originally intended for sale as sheet music. Although a number of jazz musicians have covered this song, it has never ranked among the top Tin Pan Alley "standards." It is rarely found in compilations from that era, for example, and recordings of it have charted only once (Larry Clinton's version had a six-week run, peaking at number 4 in 1938). See Joel Whitburn, *Pop Memories, 1890–1954* (Menomonee Falls, WI: Record Research, 1986), 561.

11. Thomas Porcello, "'Tails Out': Social Phenomenology and the Ethnographic Representation of Technology in Music-Making," *Ethnomusicology* 42, no. 3 (autumn 1998): 485–510, 486.

12. John Cage, *Silence: Lectures and Writings by John Cage* (1973; Middletown, CT: Wesleyan University Press, 1979), 8.

13. Ibid., 59.

14. For a pointed critique of Cage's disdain for jazz see George Lewis, "Improvised Music after 1950: Afrological and Eurological Perspectives," *Black Music Research Journal* 16, no. 1 (spring 1996): 91–122.

15. Charles Seeger, *Studies in Musicology, 1935–1975* (Berkeley: University of California Press, 1977); Susan McClary, "Temporality and Ideology: Qualities of Motion in Seventeenth-Century French Music," *Echo* 2, no. 2 (fall 2000): www.echo.ucla.edu/volume2-issue2/mcclary/mcclary-article-part3.html (accessed Feb. 1, 2010).

16. Mark Johnson, *The Body in the Mind: The Bodily Basis of Meaning, Imagination, and Reason* (Chicago: University of Chicago Press, 1987), 202.

17. Joseph N. Straus, "Normalizing the Abnormal: Disability in Music and Music Theory," *Journal of the American Musicological Society* 59, no. 1 (spring 2006), 113–84, 122. See also Robert Walser, "The Body in the Music: Epistemology and Musical Semiotics," *College Music Symposium* 31 (fall 1991): 117–21. For an overview of recent theories of embodiment and cognition as they pertain to jazz see David Borgo, *Sync or Swarm: Improvising Music in a Complex Age* (New York: Continuum, 2005), 36–58.

18. Robert Walser, "Out of Notes: Signification, Interpretation, and the Problem of Miles Davis," *Musical Quarterly* 77, no. 2 (summer 1993): 343–65 (repr. in *Jazz among the Discourses,* ed. Krin Gabbard [Durham, NC: Duke University Press, 1995], 165–88); Krin Gabbard, "Signifyin(g) the Phallus: Mo' Better Blues and Representation of the Jazz Trumpet," in *Representing Jazz,* ed. Krin Gabbard (Durham, NC: Duke University Press, 1995), 104–30.

19. Just as Miles Davis's trumpet playing could sound "fragile" without Davis himself actually *being* fragile, so could he sound "sensitive" without always acting sensitively toward others. In this regard Davis stands alongside a number of other musicians whose prickly or otherwise unsavory dispositions seem to contradict their patently gorgeous music.

20. Lyrics also provide an obvious source of meaning in Tin Pan Alley songs. I had not heard the words to "Old Folks" until quite recently, however, so they could not have contributed to my initial—and persistent—interpretation of that piece.

21. John Gennari, "Jazz Criticism: Its Development and Ideologies," *Black American Literature Forum* 25, no. 3 (autumn 1991): 449–523, 459. For discussions on the central role of recordings in jazz musicians' learning processes see Mark Katz, *Capturing Sound: How Technology Has Changed Music* (Berkeley: University of California Press, 2004), 77–78; and my essay "Learning Jazz, Teaching Jazz," in *The Cambridge Companion to Jazz,* ed. David Horn and Mervyn Cooke (Cambridge, UK: Cambridge University Press, 2002), 255–69. Beyond pedagogy, Evan Eisenberg has argued that "records not only disseminated jazz, but inseminated it," suggesting that the category jazz would not even exist without records' portability, repeatability, and replicability. See Evan Eisenberg, *The Recording Angel: The Experience of Music from Aristotle to Zappa* (New York: Penguin, 1987), 144. Also see John Mowitt, "The Sound of Music in the Age of Electronic Reproducibility," in *Music and Society: The Politics of Composition, Performance, and Reception,* ed. Richard Leppert and Susan McClary (Cambridge, UK: Cambridge University Press, 1987), 173–97.

22. Gabriel Solis, " 'A Unique Chunk of Jazz Reality': Authorship, Musical Work Concepts and Thelonious Monk's Live Recordings from the Five Spot, 1958," *Ethnomusicology* 48, no. 3 (fall 2004): 315–347, 341.

23. Cannonball Adderley, *Inside Straight,* OJC CD B000000YY4, 1995 [1973]. Adderley also used this recording method on *Money in the Pocket* (despite the

recording's subtitle, "Recorded Live at The Club in Chicago in March 1966"). See www.cannonball-adderley.com/2683.htm (accessed July 6, 2008). Charles Mingus, *Mingus Presents Mingus* Candid CD B00004Z3R3, 2000 [1960].

24. *Relaxin' with the Miles Davis Quintet,* Prestige CD 8104, 1991 [1957]. Also check out the beginning of "Trane's Blues" on *Workin' with the Miles Davis Quintet,* Prestige CD OJCCD-296-2, 1987 [1956], or the end of "Circle," from *Miles Smiles,* Columbia Legacy CDCK 65682, 1998 [1967].

25. For an outstanding analysis of how music-industry personnel sometimes control what and how music is played at a recording session see Elijah Wald, *Escaping the Delta: Robert Johnson and the Invention of the Blues* (New York: Amistad, 2005).

26. Mark Gridley, *Jazz Styles,* 9th ed. (Upper Saddle River, NJ: Pearson/Prentice Hall, 2006), 5.

27. Ted Gioia, *The Imperfect Art* (New York: Oxford University Press, 1988), 56.

28. Ibid., 68.

29. Some scholars and musicians (myself included) do disagree, however, with Gridley's assessment that jazz, by definition, *must* contain improvisation (and also a swing feel). See Peter J. Martin, "Spontaneity and Organisation," in *The Cambridge Companion to Jazz,* ed. Mervyn Cooke and David Horn (Cambridge, UK: Cambridge University Press, 2002), 133.

30. Ella Fitzgerald, *Mack the Knife: The Complete Ella in Berlin,* Polygram CD 731451956423, 1993 [originally Verve 1960].

31. Each stanza here equals one chorus, with the words corresponding, more or less, to the original melody.

32. As it turns out, "Mack the Knife" did become one of "Ella's tunes," thanks in no small part to this recording, which earned her a Grammy Award for Best Female Vocal Performance in 1961. She regularly featured "Mack the Knife" in her live sets (and she eventually learned the lyrics).

33. To be sure, the exact definition of "good jazz" can differ widely among the music's various factions. Still, most players, regardless of their preferred style, would agree that standards of jazz excellence are rooted in most if not all of the following parameters: distinctive, yet idiomatically appropriate timbre, phrasing, and note choice; strong rhythmic acuity; consistent "technique" (including, where applicable, intonation) on the instrument; and an ability to blend and interact with other musicians.

34. As a result of both record industry efforts to increase profits and fans' (and scholars') desires to hear everything an artist has recorded, some cuts that were originally—and with good reason—left "in the can" have been subsequently released to the public. For an excellent discussion of the far-reaching implications of such releases see, again, Solis, "A Unique Chunk of Reality."

35. In nonlinear recording all of the sound is converted to digital information and stored directly on a computer hard drive. Because no actual tape runs—that's the "nonlinear" aspect—engineers have virtually free reign over what they can remove or enhance on each track (assuming there is no "bleed through" from other tracks).

36. Miles Davis, "Flamenco Sketches (Studio Sequence 1)," *Kind of Blue,* Legacy Edition, Sony Legacy CD 727105, 2009.

37. Keith Jarrett remains the most well-known jazz musician in this regard. As a quick browse of the Internet will attest, audiences are split on Jarrett's vocalizations (and physical gesticulations) while playing. Some see his demeanor as proof of a ferocious intensity; others find it distracting, egotistical, or comical. Other vocally active jazz musicians include pianists Bud Powell, Oscar Peterson, and Herbie Hancock, as well as drummers Art Blakey and Elvin Jones. In the classical world Glenn Gould represents a similar figure, including the attendant debates. On a related note, legend has it that drummer Rod Morgenstern of the fusion band the Dixie Dregs vocalized so loudly that his bandmates and record producers insisted he seal his mouth with duct tape when performing in the studio so that his "singing" would not spoil the recording. Morgenstern's case may reveal one difference between fusion and some of jazz's other subgenres.

38. David Brackett, *Interpreting Popular Music* (1995; Berkeley: University of California Press, 2000), 125 (emphasis in the original).

39. Suzanne G. Cusick, "Feminist Theory, Music Theory, and the Mind/Body Problem," in *Music/Ideology: Resisting the Aesthetic,* ed. Adam Krims (Canada: G+B Arts, 1998), 37–56, 45–46. For an insightful account of how the structure of concert halls serves to accentuate this "one-way communication" see Christopher Small, "A Place for Hearing," in *Musicking: The Meanings of Performing and Listening* (Hanover, NH: Wesleyan University Press, 1998), 19–29.

40. For more on this fault line's effects on musicology see Susan McClary and Robert Walser, "Theorizing the Body in African-American Music," *Black Music Research Journal* 14, no. 1 (spring 1994): 75–84.

41. As Joseph N. Straus's work exploring perceptions of disability in music and music theory has shown, paying attention to how cultures use bodily centered music metaphors can tell us a great deal about a culture's assumptions and values regarding both its art and its people. And Straus is certainly correct in asserting that "disability should take its place alongside nationality, ethnicity, class, gender, and sexual orientation as a significant category for cultural analysis, including the analysis of music." While a thorough discussion of this crucial topic goes beyond the scope of the present chapter, it is clear that these and other metaphorical descriptors clue us in to the physicality grounding so much of jazz discourse and aesthetics, even as recordings tend to erase the physical presence of the performers. See Straus, "Normalizing the Abnormal," 114. Also

see Rosemarie Garland Thomson, *Extraordinary Bodies: Figuring Disability in American Culture and Literature* (New York: Columbia University Press, 1997). For a more thorough discussion of metaphorical language in jazz see David Such, *Avant-Garde Jazz Musicians Performing "Out There"* (Iowa City: University of Iowa Press, 1993). I take up this topic again in the next chapter.

42. Elisabeth Le Guin, "'Cello-and-Bow Thinking': Boccherini's Cello Sonata in E♭ Major, 'fuori catalogo,'" *Echo* 1, no. 1 (fall 1999): www.echo.ucla.edu/volume1-issue1/leguin/leguin-article.html (accessed Jan. 11, 2010). Also see Susan McClary's previously cited *Echo* article, "Temporality and Ideology" (see note 15 above).

43. Originally released on VIC 27926, 1942, Buster Bailey and His Orchestra's "St. Louis Blues" is now available on *RCA Victor 80th Anniversary: The First Label in Jazz, Vol. 3, 1940–1949* (RCA CD 09026 68779-2, 1997).

44. Rahsaan Roland Kirk, *Bright Moments: Live at Keystone Korner, San Francisco,* Rhino CD 71409 1993 [1974].

45. To be sure, there is also the notion of "play" so crucial to music. I play piano. Jazz musicians not only play "I Got Rhythm" but also play with the melodic, harmonic, and rhythmic structure of that tune, as well as the traditional performance practices established by their forebears. So notions of work and play are not (or should not be, at least) mutually exclusive. The point remains, however, that since we do not always see the musicians whose sounds we hear on our records, we can lose track of the oftentimes very formidable physical challenges these artists face when called on to perform.

CHAPTER THREE

1. William "Billy" Taylor, "Jazz: America's Classical Music," *The Black Perspective in Music* 14, no. 1 (winter 1986): 21–25, 21.

2. Mikhail Bakhtin, *Rabelais and His World,* trans. Hélène Iswolsky (Bloomington: Indiana University Press, 1984).

3. Ibid., 7.

4. I once worked with a drummer who, when a couple got up to dance to one of our slower numbers, suddenly upset the groove by dropping loud and unusually placed accents on the bass drum and snare drum. The confused dancers attempted to carry on through the disjointed rhythm but soon retreated to their seats. After the set I asked the drummer why he'd broken up the time as he had. He responded, "Jazz ain't dance music, man. You gotta make 'em sit down and listen!" Such attitudes are nothing new. See Howard S. Becker, "The Professional Dance Musician and His Audience," *American Journal of Sociology* 57 (1951–52): 136–44; repr. in *Keeping Time: Readings in Jazz History,* ed. Robert Walser (New York: Oxford University Press, 1999), 179–91. There are exceptions

to this rule, of course; audiences in some settings still feel welcome to get up and move. But by and large—and for better or worse—jazz people have traded in the dance floor for chairs.

5. The cultural studies scholar George McKay has also identified a carnival atmosphere, complete with sex, mayhem, and disdain for authority, at some British jazz festivals of the early 1960s. See McKay's *Circular Breathing: The Cultural Politics of Jazz in Britain* (Durham, NC: Duke University Press, 2005), 45–86.

6. Bakhtin, *Rabelais and His World,* 19. For a richly poetic account of the close interactions between "musicianers" and "non-musicians" in early New Orleans jazz see Sidney Bechet, *Treat It Gentle: An Autobiography* (1959; New York: Da Capo, 1978). See also Roger D. Abrahams, with Nick Spitzer, John F. Szwed, and Robert Farris, *Blues for New Orleans: Mardi Gras and America's Creole Soul* (Philadelphia: University of Pennsylvania Press, 2006), 31. For more on the interplay between dancers and musicians during the swing era see Lewis Erenberg, *Swingin' the Dream: Big Band Jazz and the Rebirth of American Culture* (Chicago: University of Chicago Press, 1998).

7. Bakhtin, *Rabelais and His World,* 19. For an outstanding collection of such artworks see Timothy Hyman and Roger Malbert, *Carnivalesque* (London: Hayward Gallery, 2000).

8. Francois Rabelais, *The Five Books of Gargantua and Pantagruel,* trans. Jacques LeClaerq (New York: Modern Library, 1944), 307. Gary Saul Morson and Caryl Emerson note that, in Bakhtin's conception of the carnival, "an individual body is important only as a part of the body of the people. . . . The carnival self can laugh at itself dying because it literally has nothing to lose" (Gary Saul Morson and Caryl Emerson, *Mikhail Bakhtin: Creation of a Prosaics* [Stanford, CA: Stanford University Press, 1990], 226).

9. House, *Congressional Record* 133 (Sept. 23, 1987): H7825–27; repr. as "A Rare National Treasure," in *Keeping Time: Readings in Jazz History,* ed. Robert Walser (New York: Oxford University Press, 1999), 332–33, 333.

10. Duke Ellington was putting this sort of spin on jazz musicians' lifestyles as early as the 1930s. See Edward Kennedy "Duke" Ellington, "Music Is 'Tops' to You and Me . . . and Swing Is a Part of IT," *Tops,* 1938, 14–18; repr. as "Duke Ellington Explains Swing," in *Keeping Time: Readings in Jazz History,* ed. Robert Walser (New York: Oxford University Press, 1999), 106–10.

11. A notable exception to this elitist bent was Sidney Finkelstein, who titled his book *Jazz: A People's Music* (1948; New York: International, 1998).

12. For more on these issues see Nichole T. Rustin and Sherrie Tucker, eds., *Big Ears: Listening for Gender in Jazz Studies* (Durham, NC: Duke University Press, 2008); Alex Stewart, *Making the Scene: Contemporary New York City Big Band Jazz* (Berkeley: University of California Press, 2007), esp. 12–14 and chap.

10; and David Ake, "Regendering Jazz: Ornette Coleman and the New York Scene in the Late 1950s," in *Jazz Cultures* (Berkeley: University of California Press, 2002), 62–82. I return briefly to the topics of gender, sexuality, and sexism in chapter 5.

13. For example, a 2003 collection of some of Miles Davis's work from the early 1970s includes a previously unreleased snippet of Davis praising the guitarist John McLaughlin with the line, "That's some raunchy shit, John." "Duran" (Take 4) on Miles Davis, *The Complete Jack Johnson Sessions,* Columbia Legacy C5K 90926, 2003 (originally recorded March 17, 1970).

14. Charles Mingus, *Beneath the Underdog,* ed. Neil King (New York: Vintage, 1971), 4, 53, 167, 317.

15. See Ajay Heble, "Performing Identity: Jazz Autobiography and the Politics of Literary Improvisation," in *Landing on the Wrong Note: Jazz, Dissonance, and Critical Practice* (New York: Routledge, 2000), 89–116.

16. Along with Bernstein, the full-time members of Sex Mob are Kenny Wolleson (drums), Tony Scherr (bass), and Briggan Krauss (saxophone).

17. See, e.g., Archie Shepp:

> You don't have to accept the term 'jazz.' Jazz used to mean fucking, pussy. Sidney Bechet and people like that told you that very clearly. Why are we still supporting names that degrade our music, except for the fact that white people like those names? . . . It is a black art music. It's not a dance music. It's not a popular music. . . . The white man called it jazz. In fact, you didn't call it jazz, you called [it] j-a-s-s. And it referred to the activities that took place in the places where this music was played. Not the music. In the original jass emporiums, the music was played on piano. And it was played behind a screen by people like Jelly Roll Morton and Tony Jackson, while light-skinned black women danced for white men. And when the white men wanted to see these women, they said they were looking for jass. And today we treasure that word jazz as though we created it. It's absurd. (Interviewed in Ollie Bivens, "Archie Shepp: The Cries of My People," *All about Jazz* [Feb. 24, 2005], www.allaboutjazz.com/php/article.php?id=16663 [accessed Feb. 1, 2010])

See also Max Roach, "What 'Jazz' Means to Me," *Black Scholar,* summer 1972, 3–6; or note the scare quotes in the title of Karlton Hester's *Bigotry and the Afrocentric "Jazz" Evolution,* 3rd ed. (Binghamton, NY: Global Academic Publishing, 2004). For an excellent study of the ambivalence some black musicians have toward "jazz" as a label see Eric Porter, *What Is This Thing Called Jazz? African American Musicians as Artists, Critics, and Activists* (Berkeley: University of California Press, 2002). A recent twist in this saga involves a generation of white musicians who resist or are at least uncomfortable with the "jazz" designation because they feel it has come to be equated with the neotraditionalist aesthetic based at Lincoln Center. These performers maintain this stance even while their records are reviewed in publications such as *DownBeat, JazzTimes,* and *Jazziz* and generally perform in venues and settings billed as jazz clubs or jazz festivals, or as guest artists of university jazz programs.

18. See, e.g., www.kennedy-center.org/programs/millennium/artist_detail .cfm?artist_id=sexsexmobs; and www.ink19.com/issues_F/98_10/wet_ink/ music_sz/093_sex_mob_nf.html (both accessed Feb. 1, 2010).

19. Amiri Baraka, "The 'Blues Aesthetic' and the 'Black Aesthetic': Aesthetics as the Continuing Political History of a Culture," *Black Music Research Journal* 11, no. 2 (autumn 1991): 101–9, 104; repr. in Amiri Baraka, *Digging: The Afro-American Soul of American Classical Music* (Berkeley: University of California Press, 2009), 19–27, 22. Decades earlier, the white writer Norman Mailer had contributed his own two cents to this discussion when he declared that "jazz is orgasm" (Norman Mailer, "The White Negro: Superficial Reflections on the Hipster," *Dissent* 4, no. 3 [summer 1957]: 276–93, 279).

20. In his liner notes to the CD, Roswell Rudd spells it "Wiener" rather than "Weiner." Given the various ways the term is deployed on Sex Mob's disc, it's pretty clear the group is using the name playfully (some might say sophomorically, . . . but that's part of the carnivalesque, too). For the record, Norbert Weiner (1894–1964) was an award-winning mathematician and the founder of cybernetics.

21. *Din of Inequity,* Columbia/Knitting Factory CK 69432, 1998; *Dime Grind Palace,* Rope a Dope 0–7567–93187–2, 2003; *Sexotica,* Thirsty Ear THi 57171.2, 2006; *Solid Sender,* Knitting Factory KFW-244, 1999.

22. I am not the only scholar to connect certain jazz timbres to the lower strata. In the late 1950s one Dr. Miles D. Miller published an article titled "Jazz and Aggression" in which he wrote of jazz trombone techniques: "It is striking how closely some of the musical sounds resemble the normal noises produced by the human body such as belching, intestinal rumbling and flatus." In a decidedly Freudian reading, Dr. Miller posits that the pleasure people experience by playing or listening to the trombone derive from a "transgression of cultural codes" associated with "the pleasurable sense of mastery and power first felt in childhood after attaining control over the anal musculature. . . . The low pitch of the trombone is especially well suited for expression of these anal sounds and this may be a contributing factor to its enjoyment." I cannot abide Dr. Miller's study—he never specifies which players or styles of jazz he bases his research on, and his conclusions connecting musical techniques, digestion, and emotional development in humans suggest pathology rather than vitality—yet I find them worth mentioning because they do remind us how some listeners in the past have equated certain sounds with grotesque elements and apparently enjoyed the messiness there (if not necessarily for the reasons Dr. Miller outlines). See Miles D. Miller, "Jazz and Aggression," *Psychiatric Communications* (1958): 7–10; repr. as "Psychoanalyzing Jazz," in *Keeping Time: Readings in Jazz History,* ed. Robert Walser (New York: Oxford University Press, 1999), 234–38.

23. For an insightful discussion of Monk's veiled humor see Gabriel Solis, *Monk's Music: Thelonious Monk and Jazz History* (Berkeley: University of California Press, 2008), 52–56.

24. Sigmund Freud, "Humor," in *The Philosophy of Laughter and Humor,* ed. John Morreall (Albany: State University of New York Press, 1987), 113. This piece was originally published as "Humour," *International Journal of Psychoanalysis* 9 (1928): 1–6.

25. For more on the uses of and reasons behind irony and satire in jazz see Ingrid Monson, "Doubleness and Jazz Improvisation: Irony, Parody, and Ethnomusicology," *Critical Inquiry* 20, no. 2 (winter 1994): 283–313.

26. See Jure Gantar, *The Pleasure of Fools: Essays in the Ethics of Laughter* (Montreal: McGill-Queen's University Press, 2005), 32. Or, as Bakhtin put it, "This is one of the essential differences of the people's festive laughter from the pure satire of modern times. The satirist whose laughter is negative places himself above the object of his mockery, he is opposed to it" (Bakhtin, *Rabelais and His World,* 12).

27. F. H. Buckley, *The Morality of Laughter* (Ann Arbor: University of Michigan Press, 2003), 36.

28. Bill Lamb, "Month of Guilty Pleasures—Los del Rio Featuring the Bayside Boys—Macarena," *About.com: Top 40/Pop,* http://top40.about.com/b/a/208672.htm (accessed April 28, 2008).

29. For a rare opposing view to this bias see Richard Dyer, "In Defense of Disco," in *Only Entertainment* (London: Routledge, 1992), 149–58. For an overview of qualities that have typically marked a recording, performer, or genre as "bad" see Simon Frith, "What Is Bad Music?" in *Bad Music: The Music We Love to Hate,* ed. Christopher J. Washburne and Maiken Derno (New York: Routledge, 2004), 15–36.

30. Bakhtin, *Rabelais and His World,* 246. The group's "Entrance Music," the opening track of *Dime Grind Palace,* is an even clearer example of this "just start it" philosophy.

31. ProTools, by Digidesign, is the industry standard in nonlinear digital recording hardware and software.

32. This instrument is sometimes known as a soprano trombone; it has the same range as a typical B-flat trumpet (or one octave higher than a typical B-flat trombone).

33. Robert Walser, review of *Bad Music: The Music We Love to Hate,* ed. Christopher J. Washburne and Maiken Derno, *Journal of the Society for American Music* 1, no. 4 (Nov. 2007): 511–16, 515.

34. Bakhtin, *Rabelais and His World,* 9.

35. The Burns CD compilation is somewhat more inclusive than the documentary, containing works associated with fusion and even hip-hop. Nonetheless, it feels to me as if the CD's editors purposely chose selections that fell

most cleanly into the "pop-jazz" category—and so easily are dismissed as "not really jazz"—rather than those that might complicate or nuance notions of jazz history. For instance, they used the "single version" of Miles Davis's "Spanish Key," not the album version. Such a choice supports perceptions that Davis "sold out." And why not include something from Herbie Hancock's *Thrust* or *Headhunters,* instead of "Rockit," which was never really understood as "jazz" in the first place? In the end the lines between "authentic" and "inauthentic" are still all-too-clearly drawn.

36. Ralph Ellison, "The Golden Age, Time Past," *Esquire,* Jan. 1959; repr. in *Living with Music: Ralph Ellison's Jazz Writings,* ed. by Robert G. O'Meally (New York: Modern Library, 2001), 50–64.

37. Gary Giddins, *Weather Bird: Jazz at the Dawn of Its Second Century* (New York: Oxford University Press, 2004), 542. Marsalis has displayed a degree of sensuality, oftentimes less than refined, in both his music and his personal life. In contrast to the egalitarian looseness that mark's Bernstein's group, however, Marsalis takes firm control over the Lincoln Center Jazz Orchestra, while the trumpeter's reputation as a "ladies man" seems to be as much about "conquest" as "romance." See "*Blood on the Fields:* Wynton Marsalis and the Transformation of the Lincoln Center Jazz Orchestra," in Stewart, *Making the Scene,* 278–307.

38. Alan Nahigian, "Trading Fours: Bandstand Anarchy," *DownBeat,* Feb. 1999, 46.

39. Ross Russell, "Bebop," in *The Art of Jazz,* ed. Martin Williams (New York: Oxford University Press, 1959), 202.

40. John Janowiack, "Reviews: Sex Mob, *Din of Inequity,*" *DownBeat,* Dec. 1998, 77–78.

41. Quoted in Solis, *Monk's Music,* 51.

42. Hyman and Malbert, *Carnivalesque,* 15.

43. Milan Kundera, *Testaments Betrayed: An Essay in Nine Parts* (New York: Perennial, 2001), 32.

44. Mikhail Bakhtin, "From Notes Made in 1970–71," in *Speech Genres and Other Late Essays,* trans. Vern W. McGee, Caryl Emerson, and Michael Holquist (Austin: University of Texas Press, 1986), 45–46.

CHAPTER FOUR

This chapter is a revision and expansion of "The Emergence of the Rural American Ideal in Jazz: Keith Jarrett and Pat Metheny on ECM Records," *Jazz Perspectives* 1, no. 1 (May 2007): 29–59, available at www.informaworld.com.

1. Mona Hadler, quoted in David Brown, *Noise Orders: Jazz, Improvisation, and Architecture* (Minneapolis: University of Minnesota Press, 2006), xxvii, originally in Mona Hadler, "Jazz and the Visual Arts," *Arts Magazine,* June 1983, 92. Similarly, Leroy Ostransky called jazz "a musical reflection of the growth of

our cities" (Leroy Ostransky, *Jazz City: The Impact of Our Cities on the Development of Jazz* [Englewood Cliffs, NJ: Prentice Hall, 1978], back cover).

2. Richard Leppert, "Paradise, Nature, and Reconciliation, or a Tentative Conversation with Wagner, Puccini, Adorno, and the Ronettes," *Echo* 4, no. 1 (spring 2002): www.echo.ucla.edu/Volume4-Issue1/leppert/leppert3.html (accessed Aug. 10, 2006).

3. Each of these singers has played with genre boundaries and stereotypes at one time or another. Wilson has explored the terrain of Delta blues. Monheit and Krall have traversed the more familiar (and sometimes also more blurry) lines separating jazz from cabaret and Broadway.

4. Richard Peterson has shown that city dwellers as far back as the early decades of the twentieth century generally considered country (then known as "hillbilly") music "the antithesis of their own aesthetic and worldview because it evoked the image of rural poverty and small-town morality that so many in the rapidly urbanizing American society were trying to escape" (Richard Peterson, *Creating Country Music* [Chicago: University of Chicago Press, 1997], 6).

5. Thanks to Lewis Porter for reminding me of Buddy Rich's sarcastic line. Despite Rich and the many other ardent antagonists, it is important to note that a handful of jazz musicians from all eras have at least toyed with country idioms. Perhaps the most intriguing early instance of jazz-country collaboration was the July 1930 recording of "Blue Yodel No. 9," which grouped Jimmie Rodgers, the "Father of Country Music," with Louis Armstrong on trumpet and (most likely) Lil Armstrong on piano. Other examples include guitarist Lenny Breau, who performed as Lone Pine Junior at twelve years of age with his parents' country band and later played alongside Chet Atkins (Atkins himself earned respect for his jazz skills). Perhaps the most relevant figure for this study is vibraphonist Gary Burton, who made records as a young man alongside country musicians Hank Garland (also a fine jazz player), Boots Randolph, and (again) Chet Atkins. Burton's name will surface again in this chapter. One might also be tempted to cite Ray Charles's 1962 landmark *Modern Sounds in Country and Western,* but by the time that record was released, Charles was widely recognized as an r&b singer. Hence, while *Modern Sounds in Country and Western* certainly pushed against racial and musical stereotypes, the geographic and ethnic loci of jazz were not really in play.

6. William Claxton, photographer of the Rollins disc, claims that this image inspired Mel Brooks to make his film *Blazing Saddles* (1974), which starred Cleavon Little as a black sheriff in an otherwise all-white western town. See www.greatyarmouthlive.com/news/t_section_info.php?page=William_Claxton_-_Legendary_Jazz_Photographer (accessed Aug. 10, 2006). *Blazing Saddles* also features the incongruous scene in which the Count Basie Orchestra plays "April in Paris" in the midst of the western plains. That said, black audiences in the South were neither unfamiliar with nor necessarily averse to the sounds of

white country music stars. Elijah Wald has written on the popularity of country songs on the jukeboxes of black clubs in the Mississippi Delta during the 1930s, as well as the Hollywood career of Herb Jeffries, Duke Ellington's longtime singer, as a cowboy—"the Bronze Buckaroo"—in a pair of films. See Elijah Wald, *Escaping the Delta: Robert Johnson and the Invention of the Blues* (New York: Amistad, 2004), 97–98.

7. Geoffrey Himes, "A New Intersection at the Crossroads: Bill Frisell, Robin Holcomb, Wayne Horvitz, and Danny Barnes Cultivate a Common Ground between Country and Jazz in Seattle," *No Depression* 43 (Jan./Feb. 2003), 72–83, 83.

8. Frisell's sidemen on *Nashville* included Viktor Krauss (bass), Pat Bergeson (harmonica), Adam Steffey (mandolin), Ron Block (banjo and acoustic guitar), and Jerry Douglas (dobro). The album peaked at #21 on *Billboard's* Contemporary Jazz Chart in 1997. For more on *Have a Little Faith* see the chapter "Jazz Traditioning: Setting Standards at Century's Close," in my *Jazz Cultures* (Berkeley: University of California Press, 2002).

9. Quoted in Himes, "A New Intersection at the Crossroads." Frisell had, in fact, gestured toward country, or at least some of the sounds, textures, and images associated with rural America, for a number of years prior to *Nashville.* Listen to the two-part "Jimmy Carter" from his 1994 release *This Land* (Elektra/Nonesuch CD 79316–2, 1994), and note, too, the Walker Evans photograph used for the CD cover.

10. Geoffrey Himes, "Hybrid Harmony: Bill Frisell Pitches His Tent at the Intersection of Country and Jazz," *Chicago Tribune,* April 20, 2001, 3. Republished online with the new title "Pastoral Jazz and the Unspoken Code," www .jazzhouse.org/library/index.php3?read=himes1 (accessed Aug. 8, 2006).

11. John R. Gold, "From 'Dust Storm Disaster' to 'Pastures of Plenty': Woody Guthrie and Landscapes of the American Depression," in *The Place of Music,* ed. Andrew Leyshon, David Matless, and George Revill (New York: Guilford Press, 1998), 249–68, 263. For more on the nature-inspired music of the art-music composers cited see Brooks Tolliver, "Eco-ing in the Canyon: Ferde Grofé's *Grand Canyon Suite* and the Transformation of Wilderness," *Journal of the American Musicological Society* 57 (summer 2004): 325–67; Denise von Glahn, *The Sounds of Place: Music and the American Cultural Landscape* (Boston: Northeastern University Press, 2003); and Beth Levy, "'The White Hope of American Music,' or How Roy Harris Became Western," *American Music* 19, no. 2 (summer 2001): 131–67.

12. The so-called counterculture was never a single, monolithic community. Participants in the Free Speech Movement, Black Panthers, Weathermen, Students for a Democratic Society, the Youth International Party, and other groups each followed their own agendas and codes of conduct. Still, members of these various organizations shared the belief that *something* needed to change and

that young people were the most qualified to effect that change. For evocative accounts of both the factionalism that characterized the late 1960s, and the disillusion (and dissolution) of these and other groups, see Todd Gitlin, *The Sixties: Years of Hope, Days of Rage* (New York: Bantam, 1987); as well as Peter Braunstein and Michael William Doyle, "Introduction: Historicizing the American Counterculture of the 1960s and '70s," in *Imagine Nation: The American Counterculture of the 1960s and '70s,* ed. Peter Braunstein and Michael William Doyle (New York: Routledge, 2002), 5–14.

13. Thoreau hovers as ghost or chorus or guide over Raymond Mungo's *Total Loss Farm: A Year in the Life* (New York: Dutton: 1970), perhaps the most widely read firsthand description of communal living in the 1960s. For an overview of cooperative communities during that period see Timothy Miller, "The Sixties-Era Communes," in Braunstein and Doyle, *Imagine Nation*, 327–51.

14. Compare the Grateful Dead's *Workingman's Dead* (1970) and *American Beauty* (1971) with the group's earlier, more rock-, blues-, and psychedelic-tinged releases *Anthem of the Sun* (1968) and *Aoxomoxoa* (1969). Similarly, after shocking the folk-revivalist movement by "going electric" at the Newport Folk Festival in 1965, Bob Dylan turned around and released a string of country-inflected recordings, beginning with the 1968 album *John Wesley Harding* and running through *Nashville Skyline* (1969) and *New Morning* (1970). Some of Dylan's sidemen from this period also began composing and recording their own material as the Band, perhaps the quintessential North American-pastoral group.

15. From the mid-1950s through the 1970s some African American jazz musicians referenced the rural South via harmonies, melodic shapes, and song titles associated with black gospel traditions. Such performers include Art Blakey ("Moanin'"), Horace Silver ("Home Cookin'"), Charles Mingus, ("Wednesday Night Prayer Meeting"), and Cannonball Adderley ("Work Song"). The musicologist Guthrie Ramsey makes a strong case to view this tension in black cultures between a contemporary northern cosmopolitanism and southern agrarian past as a "powerfully rich and complicated dialectic" (Guthrie Ramsey, *Race Music: Black Cultures from Bebop to Hip-Hop* [Berkeley: University of California Press, 2003], 47). Further complicating how we understand the intersections of sound, ethnicity, and location, Adderley's two biggest gospel-inflected tunes, "Mercy, Mercy, Mercy" and "Country Preacher," were composed by the white, Austrian-born pianist Joe Zawinul. These occasional celebrations of southern cultural heritage aside, however, black musicians of this period tended to extol the virtues of the city (including, increasingly, those of Europe and Japan) over rural areas. Dizzy Gillespie and his bandmates made their preferences quite clear when they chanted, "Never Going Back to Georgia," during many of Gillespie's live performances.

16. Olivia Mather, "'Cosmic American Music': Place and the Country Rock Movement, 1965–1974" (PhD diss., UCLA, 2006), 234–35.

17. Ian Carr, *Keith Jarrett: The Man and His Music* (New York: Da Capo, 1992), 32.

18. San Francisco's Fillmore Auditorium (1965–89) and New York's Fillmore East (1968–71), founded by entrepreneur Bill Graham, served as important venues for counterculture music in the 1960s, hosting the Byrds, Buffalo Springfield, and the Grateful Dead, alongside jazz acts including the Charles Lloyd Quartet and Miles Davis. The Jarrett interview originally aired on the National Public Radio series *Sidran on Record*. It was subsequently transcribed and published in Ben Sidran, *Talking Jazz: An Oral History,* exp. ed. (New York: Da Capo, 1995), 284.

19. Tom Wolfe, "The 'Me' Decade and the Third Great Awakening," *New York,* Aug. 23, 1976, 26–40.

20. For more on the rise of country rock see Mather "'Cosmic American Music.'" For more on folk-infused "prog" rock see Mitchell Morris, "Kansas and the Prophetic Tone," *American Music* 18, no. 1 (spring 2000): 1–38. Great Britain nurtured its own version of this trend through the sounds of Pentangle, Fairport Convention, and (at times) even heavy-metal gods Led Zeppelin.

21. Andrew G. Kirk, *Counterculture Green:* The Whole Earth Catalog *and American Environmentalism* (Lawrence: University Press of Kansas, 2007), 11.

22. ECM stands for Edition of Contemporary Music.

23. Sales figures quoted from Nate Chinen, "One Extraordinary Night, Annotated by Its Architect," *New York Times,* Sept. 24, 2006.

24. "Part IIc" of *The Köln Concert* is an exception. Although the official notated transcription of that recording maintains the "Part IIc" designation, this segment clearly follows a regular song form. A lead sheet of it appears in *The Real Book* compilation as "Memories of Tomorrow." Keith Jarrett, *The Köln Concert: Original Transcription* (New York: Schott, 1991), 82; *The Real Book,* vol. 1, 6th ed. (New York: Hal Leonard, 2004), 267.

25. See, e.g., Gunther Schuller, "Sonny Rollins and the Challenge of Thematic Improvisation," in *Musings: The Musical Worlds of Gunther Schuller* (New York: Oxford University Press, 1986), 86–97; repr. from the *Jazz Review,* Nov. 1958.

26. Quoted in Eric Porter, *What Is This Thing Called Jazz? African American Musicians as Artists, Critics, and Activists* (Berkeley: University of California Press, 2002), 90. Originally published as L. D. Reddick, "Dizzy Gillespie in Atlanta," *Phylon* 10 (first quarter, 1949), 45–48. See chapter 1 for more on the racial and political debates surrounding early bebop.

27. *Belonging* won the Deutscher Schallplattenpreis and *Jazz Forum*'s Record of the Year. Ian Carr heralded both discs as "masterpieces" in *Jazz: The Rough Guide,* 2nd ed. (New York: Penguin, 2005), 385.

28. Carr, *Keith Jarrett,* 78.

29. "Country" resurfaced in 2001 as a theme song of sorts in the German film *Bella Martha* (English title: "Mostly Martha"; Bavaria Film et al., 2001). One American film reviewer singled out the tune's use in the soundtrack, describing "Country" as "Keith Jarrett's c & w-inflected ballad . . . a sprightly, lilting, slightly melancholy piece for a jazz quartet." Given the critic's mention of "c & w"—country and western—it is clear, and more than a little remarkable, that the song retains a rural-American flavor, even in a German-language film set in Hamburg about a widowed chef. Michael Wilmington, review of *Mostly Martha,* http://chicago.metromix.com/movies/review/movie-review-mostly-martha/158442/content (accessed Feb. 1, 2010).

30. *Keith Jarrett: The Art of Improvisation,* produced by Danny Nissim and Mike Dibb (EuroArts DVD, 2005). See also Art Lange, "The Keith Jarrett Interview," *DownBeat,* June 1984, 19. Alongside Jarrett in the American Quartet were bassist Charlie Haden, drummer Paul Motian, and saxophonist Dewey Redman.

31. Jarrett did suggest Native American lore at times with tunes like "Yaqui Indian Song," "Great Bird," and "Sundance." However, he recorded those with other musicians (the American Quartet) for other labels, and they never achieved the commercial success or artistic influence of the ECM discs. Ironically, one ECM musician who did record a Native American–inspired tune was Jarrett's Norwegian colleague Jan Garbarek, with "Witchi-Tai-To," composed by the saxophonist Jim Pepper, a member of the Kaw Indian nation.

32. For a discussion of "glocalization" see Stuart Nicholson, *Is Jazz Dead? (Or Has It Moved to a New Address)* (New York: Routledge, 2005). Elsewhere in that book Nicholson interviews the British saxophonist Iain Ballamy, who said:

> My first few years as a player were spent learning and absorbing the music of the American jazz masters, but the biggest personal revelation for me was the discovery of the music typified by the ECM label, especially albums like *My Song* with Jan Garbarek and Keith Jarrett. . . . This music—non-blues based, lyrical, and occasionally folky—seemed to resonate more strongly with me, being a European. It came to me at the time I was beginning to write my own material and [I] very quickly discovered that playing one's own tunes in a way that felt right as an "Englishman," rather than in an appropriated genre from another place and time, felt natural and right for me. (174)

See also the mention of Jarrett by Swedish pianist Esbjörn Svensson in Christopher Porter, "Taking Five with . . . E.S.T.," *JazzTimes* 36 (Feb. 2006): 36.

33. Metheny first recorded as a sideman for the label on *Ring,* led by Gary Burton and Eberhard Weber.

34. Neil Tesser, "Pat Metheny: Fresh Face of Fusion," *DownBeat,* March 22, 1979, 12.

35. Considered one of the earliest instances of "adult education" in the United States, the movement's name derives from the location of the group's headquarters at Lake Chautauqua, New York. The center there served as the home to an annual eight-week series of courses and lectures. The program eventually became mobile, as tent-show Chautauquas brought speakers to communities throughout the nation. Lecturers included Mark Twain, William Jennings Bryan, and both Theodore and Franklin Roosevelt.

36. For a discussion of Jarrett's sartorial choices see Carr, *Keith Jarrett*, 32.

37. *New Chautauqua* was released before ECM began its New Series label featuring classical composers, new and old. Much the same question about genre could be posed regarding Frisell's *Nashville* release. Although scholars including Scott DeVeaux, Krin Gabbard, and Gary Tomlinson have produced important work on this topic, the area remains open for more research. See Scott DeVeaux, "Constructing the Jazz Tradition: Jazz Historiography," *Black American Literature Forum* 25 (fall 1991): 525–60; Krin Gabbard, "Introduction: The Jazz Canon and Its Consequences," in *Jazz among the Discourses,* ed. Krin Gabbard (Durham, NC: Duke University Press, 1995), 1–28; and Gary Tomlinson, "Cultural Dialogics and Jazz: A White Historian Signifies," *Black Music Research Journal* 11, no. 2 (Aug. 1991): 229–64. Also relevant are my essays "Jazz Historiography and the Problem of Louis Jordan" and the previously cited "Jazz Traditioning," both in *Jazz Cultures.*

38. Larry Birnbaum, "Record Reviews: Pat Metheny, *New Chautauqua,*" *DownBeat,* Sept. 6, 1979, 36.

39. Metheny did return to the solo-acoustic pastoral format with *One Quiet Night,* released by Warner Brothers in 2003. Fittingly, the album features covers of Norah Jones's "Don't Know Why" and Jarrett's "My Song."

40. Rafi Zabor, "Charlie Haden, Liberation and Revelation: The Probing Essence of the Bass," *Musician* 66 (April 1984): 42–52, 44.

41. For more on Coleman and responses to his music see John Litweiler, *Ornette Coleman: A Harmolodic Life* (New York: Morrow, 1992); and Peter Niklas Wilson, *Ornette Coleman: His Life and Music* (Berkeley, CA: Berkeley Hills Books, 1999).

42. *Pat Metheny Songbook* (Milwaukee: Hal Leonard, n. d. but ca. 2000).

43. Tim Schneckloth, "Pat Metheny: A Step beyond Tradition," *DownBeat,* Nov. 1982, 16.

44. Gary Giddins has described Metheny's music from the *80/81* era as a "syncretism" of Keith Jarrett and Ornette Coleman. See Gary Giddins, *Rhythm-a-ning: Jazz Tradition and Innovation in the '80s* (New York: Oxford University Press, 1985), 56. The implied connection among Coleman, Haden, Metheny, and DeJohnette became literal in 1986 when they all recorded *Song X.* At the time of those later sessions, however, the musicians seemed less interested in

reexamining their shared attraction to rural traditions than in exploring the sonic possibilities afforded by the emerging digital technology, featuring as it did both Metheny's Synclavier and the electric drums played by the record's other percussionist, Denardo Coleman. As a new kind of dense, angular, and loud "electric jazz," *Song X* represents in many ways the antithesis to *80/81*'s bucolic vision. Although *Song X* marks the only time that Metheny recorded with Ornette Coleman, the guitarist has continued to play with both DeJohnette and, more frequently, with Haden. Of particular relevance to this chapter is Metheny's and Haden's 1997 collaboration, *Beyond the Missouri Sky (Short Stories)*, the cover photo for which depicts a farmhouse draped in the pastel hues of twilight. Metheny also guests on Haden's 2008 release, *Rambling Boy*, which includes a variety of country, rock, and bluegrass musicians performing rural fare such as the Carter Family's "Wildwood Flower" and, once again, "Old Joe Clark." In the liner notes to that disc Haden states, "Since continuing my career in contemporary music and in the world of jazz, the music that I sang and heard during these early experiences in the Ozark Mountains of Missouri has stayed inside my soul, my heart, my being and I continue to draw on it whenever I play" (Charlie Haden, liner notes to Charlie Haden Family and Friends, *Rambling Boy* [Decca, 2008] [no page numbers]).

45. Note that I have written "rural = white," not "white = rural." White TV characters in the 1960s and 1970s were free to roam both the country and the city. Thus, audiences could watch Sheriff Andy Taylor (Andy Griffith) keep safe the streets of Mayberry while *Dragnet*'s Sergeant Joe Friday (Jack Webb) did the same for Los Angeles. African American characters were rarely afforded that degree of mobility. (The same goes for Asian or Latino/a characters, in the few times they appeared at all). Consider, too, that the radio industry's "urban" format designation referred almost exclusively to black artists.

46. Greil Marcus, "The Old, Weird America," in *Invisible Republic: Bob Dylan's Basement Tapes* (New York: Henry Holt, 1997), 87–126. On a related note Harry Smith (editor of the folk revivalists' bible, *The Anthology of American Folk Music*), recalled, "It took years before anybody discovered that [African American guitarist] Mississippi John Hurt wasn't a hillbilly" (Quoted in Marcus, *Invisible Republic*, 104).

47. Further cementing the connection to Keith Jarrett, Mays and Metheny regularly performed Jarrett's "The Wind Up" in their group's live sets into the 1980s.

48. John Alan Simon, "Pat Metheny: Ready to Tackle Tomorrow," *DownBeat* 45, July 13, 1978, 23.

49. Bassist Jaco Pastorius, Metheny's friend and former colleague, adopted that very term to describe his own sound. See Bill Milkowski, *Jaco: The Extraordinary and Tragic Life of Jaco Pastorius, "The World's Greatest Bass Player"* (San Francisco: Backbeat Books, 1995).

50. Not all jazz critics appreciated *American Garage*'s reassuring musical topography. Elaine Guregian lamented that "by relieving their audience of effort, Metheny and Mays also deprive us of the pleasure of surprise and the possibility of inspiration." She concludes, "Metheny fans may be satisfied with this sleek effort but I don't think they should be. It is a shame for Metheny and the rest of the group to waste so much talent on artifice" ("Record Reviews: Pat Metheny Group, *American Garage*," *DownBeat*, April 1980, 42).

51. Svetlana Boym, *The Future of Nostalgia* (New York: Basic Books, 2001), xiii.

52. With New York City facing possible bankruptcy in the middle 1970s, Mayor Abraham Beame requested "bail-out" funds from the federal government. The headline in the *Daily News* summed up President Gerald Ford's response. Singer/songwriter Randy Newman satirized the combustibility of the Cuyahoga River in "Burn On," from *Sail Away* (1972).

53. Metheny settled in Woodstock, New York, as did Dave Holland, Jack De-Johnette, Anthony Braxton, and a host of others. Keith Jarrett moved to rural New Jersey. To this day Steve Coleman, Fred Hersch, Dave Liebman, and Phil Woods each maintain at least a part-time residence in eastern Pennsylvania.

54. Bill Milkowski, "Evolution of Jazz Education," *Jazz Education Guide: Special Supplement to JazzTimes* (2001/2002): 34–40, 40.

55. Iain Anderson, "Jazz Outside the Marketplace: Free Improvisation and Nonprofit Sponsorship of the Arts, 1965–1980," *American Music* 20, no. 2 (summer 2004): 131–67.

56. Neil Tesser and Fred Bourque, "Pat Metheny: Musings on Neo Fusion," *DownBeat*, March 12, 1979, 12 (emphasis in the original).

57. Ibid. Dave Brubeck's lineage reaches back not only to England and Germany but also to Modoc Indian peoples. Despite this ancestry Brubeck is typically understood as a "white musician." For a discussion of the Native American lineage of Brubeck and other jazz musicians, including the "white" guitarist Jim Hall and the "black" bassist Oscar Pettiford, see "The Man on the Buffalo Nickel: Dave Brubeck," in Gene Lees, *Cats of Any Color: Jazz, Black and White* (New York: Oxford University Press, 1995).

CHAPTER FIVE

1. "Jazz 'Traning: John Coltrane and the Conservatory," in David Ake, *Jazz Cultures* (Berkeley: University of California Press, 2002), 112–45; and David Ake, "Learning Jazz/Teaching Jazz," in *The Cambridge Companion to Jazz*, ed. Mervyn Cooke and David Horn (Cambridge, UK: Cambridge University Press, 2002), 255–69. Other recent scholarship on jazz pedagogy includes David Borgo, "Free Jazz in the Classroom: An Ecological Approach to Music Education," *Jazz Perspectives* 1, no. 1 (May 2007): 61–88; John P. Murphy. "Beyond

the Improvisation Class: Learning to Improvise in a University Jazz Studies Program," in *Musical Improvisation: Sound, Education, Society*, ed. Gabriel Solis and Bruno Nettle (Urbana: University of Illinois Press, 2009); Kenneth Prouty, "Orality, Literacy, and Mediating Musical Experience: Rethinking Oral Tradition in the Learning of Jazz Improvisation," *Popular Music and Society* 29, no. 3 (July 2006): 317–34; and Ken Prouty, "The 'Finite' Art of Improvisation: Pedagogy and Power in Jazz Education," *Critical Studies in Improvisation* 4, no. 1 (2008): www.criticalimprov.com/index.php/csieci/article/view/346/966 (accessed Nov. 28, 2008).

2. Nate Chinen, "Jazz Is Alive and Well in the Classroom, Anyway," *New York Times*, Jan. 7, 2007, sec. 2, p. 1.

3. To give music scholars a sense of the IAJE conference's scope, the 2000 Musical Intersections convention in Toronto, which brought together the meetings of fifteen professional organizations, including the American Musicological Society, the Society for Ethnomusicology, the Society for American Music, the Society for Music Theory, and the International Association for the Study of Popular Music, drew fewer than four thousand attendees. Ann Besser Scott, "Toronto, 2000," *AMS Newsletter* 31, no. 1 (Feb. 2001): 1.

4. Chinen, "Jazz Is Alive and Well," 1, 19. This would turn out to be the IAJE's final conference. The association declared bankruptcy in April 2008. By all accounts it folded as a result of administrative incompetence, not from a decline in membership. In fact, the organization continued to grow at an impressive rate even as it lost large sums of money. See "IAJE R.I.P.," *JazzTimes* 38 (July/August 2008): 82–86, 130–31.

5. Bill Pierce, email correspondence with author, March 27, 2007.

6. Quoted in Brian Priestly, *Mingus: A Critical Biography* (New York: Da Capo, 1982), 174. Original interview with Nat Hentoff, BBC Radio, Nov. 2, 1964.

7. John Coltrane, for instance, based much of his practice regimen and even part of his composition "Giant Steps" on Nicolas Slonimsky's *Thesaurus of Scales and Patterns* (1945; New York: Amsco, 1975). And yet I have heard (though can find no hard evidence to substantiate) that word of Coltrane's famous *Thesaurus* studies amused Slonimsky, who reputedly dashed off his compendium merely as a kind of nerdy musical joke. For descriptions of Coltrane's use of Slonimsky's book see Lewis Porter, *John Coltrane: His Life and Music* (Ann Arbor: University of Michigan Press, 1998), 149–50; Carl Woideck, *The John Coltrane Companion: Five Decades of Commentary* (New York: Schirmer, 1998), 172; and Ashley Kahn's interview with Joe Zawinul, in Ashley Kahn, *A Love Supreme* (New York: Viking, 2002), 28–29.

8. Christopher Small, *Music, Society, Education* (Hanover, NH: Wesleyan University Press, 1996), 198.

9. Hal Galper, "Rants and Raves: Jazz Pedagogy," http://halgalper.com (accessed Jan. 16, 2009). See also Galper's "Articles: Jazz in Academia" at that same Web site.

10. Mark Gridley, *Jazz Styles: History and Analysis,* 9th ed. (Upper Saddle River, NJ: Pearson Prentice Hall, 2006), 349 (my emphasis).

11. Ibid, 380–86.

12. Henry Martin and Keith Waters, *Jazz: The First 100 Years,* 2nd ed. (Belmont, CA: Thomson Schirmer, 2006), 360, 376–77.

13. Ted Gioia, *The History of Jazz* (New York: Oxford University Press, 1997); Ken Burns, *Jazz: A Film by Ken Burns* (PBS Paramount DVD, 2004); Gary Giddins, *Weather Bird: Jazz at the Dawn of Its Second Century* (New York: Oxford University Press, 2004).

14. Charles Beale, "Jazz Education," in *The Oxford Companion to Jazz,* ed. Bill Kirchner (New York: Oxford University Press, 2000), 745–55.

15. Robert G. O'Meally, Brent Hayes Edwards, and Farah Jasmine Griffin, "Introductory Notes," in *Uptown Conversations: The New Jazz Studies,* ed. Robert G. O'Meally, Brent Hayes Edwards, and Farah Jasmine Griffin (New York: Columbia University Press, 2004), 1.

16. Stuart Nicholson, *Is Jazz Dead? (Or Has It Moved to a New Address)* (New York: Routledge, 2005), 99–100.

17. Ibid., 110.

18. Ibid., 120.

19. Ibid.

20. See also Nicholson's "The Way It Is," *Jazzwise,* Feb. 2007, 15; "Europeans Cut in with a New Sound and Beat," *New York Times* June 3, 2001, Arts sec.; and "Crossing the Atlantic: Overseas Jazz Education," *JazzTimes,* Jazz Education Guide Special Issue (2003–4): 46–50.

21. Gary Kennedy, "Jazz Education," in *The New Grove Dictionary of Jazz,* ed. Barry Kernfeld, 2nd ed., 3 vols. (New York: Macmillan, 2002), 2:396–98 (my emphasis).

22. For more on these important figures see Andrew Goodrich, "Jazz in Historically Black Colleges," *Jazz Educators Journal* 34, no. 3 (Nov. 2001): 54–58; and Al Kennedy, *Chord Changes on the Chalkboard: How Public School Teachers Shaped Jazz and the Music of New Orleans* (Lanham, MD: Scarecrow Press, 2002).

23. I chose 1950 as a cut-off date for this list because those born in that year would have been eighteen years old (i.e., college age) in 1968, the year the National Association of Jazz Education was founded.

24. Now-prominent school-trained figures not mentioned in the *Grove Dictionary* include Ralph Alessi (California Institute of the Arts), Shane Endsley (Eastman), Briggan Krauss (Cornish College of the Arts), Donny McCaslin

(Berklee), Cuong Vu (New England Conservatory), and Miguel Zénon (Berklee).

25. Dennis Ford, *The Search for Meaning: A Short History* (Berkeley: University of California Press, 2007), 43.

26. Bruce Johnson et al., "Nightclubs and Other Venues," in Kernfeld, *The New Grove Dictionary of Jazz*, 2:1.

27. See http://steinhardt.nyu.edu/music/jazz/ (accessed Feb.2, 2010).

28. Ibid.

29. Development efforts at the University of Nevada, Reno (UNR) include meet-and-greet functions between donors and visiting jazz artists; free distribution to donors and potential donors of CD recordings by the Collective (UNR's resident faculty jazz group); and even using recordings by the Collective as "on-hold" music for the university's phone system.

30. Howard S. Becker, "The Professional Dance Musician and His Audience," *American Journal of Sociology* 57 (1951–52): 136–44; repr. in *Keeping Time: Readings in Jazz History*, ed. Robert Walser (New York: Oxford University Press, 1999), 179–91.

31. For more on the preference for big bands in colleges see Bruno Nettl, *Heartland Excursions: Ethnomusicological Reflections on Schools of Music* (Urbana: University of Illinois Press, 1995), 107; and Ake, "Jazz 'Traning," 113–14. Exceptions to the small-group bias among today's hip contingent include the Mingus Big Band and the larger groups led by Carla Bley, Charlie Haden, Dave Holland, and Maria Schneider. For an informed and insightful overview of practices and aesthetics in big bands today (including a critique of my work) see Alex Stewart, *Making the Scene: Contemporary New York City Big Band Jazz* (Berkeley: University of California Press, 2007).

32. Jessica Bissett, " 'Too Close for Comfort': Negotiating Identity and Institutionalized Space for Pacific Northwest Vocal Jazz Ensembles," paper delivered to the annual meeting of the Society for American Music, Eugene, OR, Feb. 2005.

33. Ingrid Monson, "The Problem with White Hipness: Race, Gender, and Cultural Conceptions in Jazz Historical Discourse," *Journal of the American Musicological Society* 48 (fall 1995): 396–422. See also Phil Ford, "Somewhere/Nowhere: Hipness as an Aesthetic," *Musical Quarterly* 86, no. 1 (spring 2002): 49–81; and Phil Ford, "Hip Sensibility in an Age of Mass Counterculture," *Jazz Perspectives* 2, no. 2 (Nov. 2008), 121–63.

34. Monson, "The Problem with White Hipness," 422.

35. Ann Douglas, *The Feminization of American Culture* (1977; New York: Noonday, 1998), 76.

36. James White, "Male Teacher Shortage Hits Home," http://www.men teach.org/news/male_teacher_shortage_hits_home (accessed Feb. 2, 2010).

37. All of this also helps to explain the lingering homophobia in jazz, which genre, as Monique Guillory has noted, has remained "a hermetically sealed boys' club for nearly a century" (Monique Guillory, "Black Bodies Swingin': Race, Gender, and Jazz," in *Soul: Black Power, Politics, and Pleasure*, ed. Monique Guillory and Richard C. Green [New York: New York University Press, 1998], 191–215, 193). Taking on the mantle of what he jokingly described as the self-professed "poster boy for gay jazz musicians," Fred Hersch told me that "a lot of this masculinity stuff, if you let it get to you, it can." And while Hersch also noted that the situation for homosexual musicians has "changed a lot for the better over the [last] 20 or 30 years," strong biases remain. See Giovanni Petranicht, "Gays in Jazz," *JazzTimes* 32 (May 2002): 28; and Ajay Heble's discussion of Charles Gayle, "Up for Grabs: The Ethicopolitical Authority of Jazz," in *Landing on the Wrong Note: Jazz, Dissonance, and Critical Practice* (New York: Routledge, 2000), 199–228.

38. To be fair to the larger magazines, they have sometimes featured "borderline" jazz acts, such as Yellowjackets and Chuck Mangione. *DownBeat* has long sponsored the DB awards for student groups while providing advice columns from educators, and *JazzTimes* publishes its annual *Jazz Education Guide*. Still, these publications focus overwhelmingly on the people and places I have noted. One recent exception to this rule is *JazzEd*. First published in 2006, that periodical explicitly seeks to highlight both jazz stars and jazz educators. The September 2008 issue even featured a cover story on Kenny G.

39. Ake, "Jazz 'Traning" (see note 1 above).

40. One small step toward that end: Because the stereotypical jazz-education identities just outlined blithely forgo those qualities that have come to be understood as hip (or, in the case of the berets and sunglasses, work from an anachronistic approach to hipness), I offer that scholars and others might begin hearing, seeing, and describing such groups as "nonhip," rather than "unhip," a distinction that marks these musical presentations as alternatives to, rather than absences of, certain understandings of jazz identity and behavior.

41. James Lincoln Collier explored and explained this "problem" in jazz education as early as 1993. See his *Jazz: The American Theme Song* (New York: Oxford University Press, 1993), 153–54. Stanley Crouch expressed his very different take on the innovation aesthetic very clearly. See his article "Jazz Tradition Is Not Innovation," *JazzTimes* 32 (Jan./Feb. 2002): 26.

42. Bill Shoemaker, "Waxing On: Self-Produced Artists," *DownBeat,* Aug. 1984, 42.

43. Thanks to Ken Prouty for reminding me of this tendency.

44. John McDonough, "Pro and Con: Failed Experiment," *DownBeat,* Jan. 1992, 31. McDonough was writing on what he saw as evidence of the "failure" of free jazz as a viable subgenre because of the support its proponents have received from arts organizations.

45. The notion that jazz musicians should play solely "for the love of the music" without any thought of financial considerations has deep roots. See Scott DeVeaux, "The Emergence of the Jazz Concert, 1935–1945," *American Music* 7, no. 1, Special Jazz Issue (spring 1989): 11–12.

46. Mark Kross, "Letters: Jazz Education, in Service of the Music," *New York Times,* Jan. 21, 2007, sec. 2, p. 6.

47. The director of the Jazz Studies program at the Manhattan School of Music approximated that between 60 and 70 percent of the jazz students at that school play professional gigs in New York. See Ben Ratliff, "A New Generation Knocks at the Gates of Jazz," *New York Times,* March 18, 1997, C14.

48. Statistics from Bill Milkowski, "Evolution of Jazz Education," *JazzTimes: Jazz Education Guide* (2001/2002): 40.

49. KneeBody surely ranks among the most impressive examples of on-the-fly group decision-making ever developed by a jazz ensemble. For any who may have the opportunity to see this group, it is well worth the time to talk to the musicians about how they devise arrangements and structure sets during *and through* their performances.

50. Or consider the "backwards" career path of keyboardist (and Eastman grad) Gary Versace. While many jazz musicians opt to leave the road for the more stable college environment, Versace went the opposite direction, relinquishing a tenured Jazz Studies position at the University of Oregon in 2002 to focus on playing. He now works alongside major artists, including Lee Konitz, John Scofield, and Maria Schneider and gives numerous concerts, workshops, and master classes at schools across the country.

51. Richard Taruskin, *Text & Act: Essays on Music and Performance* (New York: Oxford University Press, 1995), 18.

52. The 2002 figures from the International Association of Jazz Education showed that men outnumbered women in the association by a four-to-one ratio (4800/1200).

53. It remains to be seen whether that organization is as accurate with the second half of its tagline: ". . . and the IASJ is the chain" (www.iasj.com [accessed Jan. 17, 2009]).

CHAPTER SIX

This chapter is a revision and expansion of "Negotiating Style, Nation, and Identity among American Jazz Musicians in Paris," *Journal for Musicological Research* 23, no. 2 (April–June 2004): 159–86.

1. For the purposes of this study *American* generally denotes natural-born citizens of the United States.

2. Bruce Johnson, "The Jazz Diaspora," in *The Cambridge Companion to Jazz*, ed. Mervyn Cooke and David Horn (New York: Cambridge University Press, 2002), 39.

3. The IAJE was called the *National* (that is to say, "American") Association of Jazz Educators from its founding in 1968 to 1989, when it changed its name in order to "more accurately reflect its membership base and global commitment to jazz education" (www.iaje.org/about.asp [accessed June 2007]).

4. James Lincoln Collier, *Jazz: The American Theme Song* (New York: Oxford University Press, 1993); William "Billy" Taylor, "Jazz: America's Classical Music," *The Black Perspective in Music* 14, no. 1 (winter 1986): 21–25; Grover Sales, *Jazz: America's Classical Music* (1984; New York: Da Capo, 1992); and the 5-CD set *Ken Burns Jazz: The Story of America's Music*, Columbia Legacy 61432.

5. E. Taylor Atkins, *Blue Nippon: Authenticating Jazz in Japan* (Durham, NC: Duke University Press, 2001). Cultural historian George McKay has identified a similar lack of confidence among some British jazz musicians. See George McKay, *Circular Breathing: The Cultural Politics of Jazz in Britain* (Durham, NC: Duke University Press, 2005), ix.

6. Stuart Hall, "Ethnicity: Identity and Difference," *Radical America* 23, no. 4 (1989): 9–20. Quoted in Ajay Heble, *Landing on the Wrong Note: Jazz, Dissonance, and Critical Practice* (New York: Routledge, 2000), 95.

7. See, e.g., Bernard Gendron, *Between Montmartre and the Mudd Club: Popular Music and the Avant-Garde* (Chicago: University of Chicago Press, 2002); Chris Goddard, *Jazz Away from Home* (London: Paddington Press, 1979); A. B. Bill Moody, *The Jazz Exiles* (Reno: University of Nevada Press, 1993); William A. Shack, *Harlem in Montmartre: A Paris Story between the Great Wars* (Berkeley: University of California Press, 2001); Tyler Stovall, *Paris Noir: African Americans in the City of Light* (New York: Houghton Mifflin), 1996; as well as other studies cited below.

8. Unless otherwise noted, all direct quotes are taken from these interviews. Dates and locations of the interviews can be found in Appendix 2.

9. Jeffrey H. Jackson, *Making Jazz French: Music and Modern Life in Interwar Paris* (Durham, NC: Duke University Press, 2003), 26. Charley Gerard has observed a similar "mystique of black creativity," as he calls it, in the United States: "Many jazz musicians, both white and African-American, have a nagging suspicion that there is a strong correlation between artistic success in jazz and being African American" (Charley Gerard, *Jazz in Black and White: Race, Culture, and Identity in the Jazz Community* [Westport, CT: Praeger, 1998], 105, xiv). See also Monique Guillory, "Black Bodies Swingin': Race, Gender, and Jazz," in *Soul: Black Power, Politics, and Pleasure*, ed. Monique Guillory and Richard C. Green (New York: New York University Press, 1998), 191–215, esp. 194–95; and Ingrid Monson, *Saying Something: Jazz Improvisation and Interaction* (Chicago: University of Chicago Press, 1996).

10. Lester Bowie, quoted in George E. Lewis, "Experimental Music in Black and White: The AACM in New York, 1970–1985," *Current Musicology* 71–73 (spring 2001–spring 2002): 100–157, 115. Originally published in *Art Ensemble of Chicago: Great Black Music; Ancient to the Future*, ed. Lincoln T. Beauchamp Jr. (Chicago: Art Ensemble of Chicago, 1998), 43.

11. Eric Porter, *What Is This Thing Called Jazz? African American Musicians as Artists, Critics, and Activists* (Berkeley: University of California Press, 2002), xv. See also Paul Austerlitz, *Jazz Consciousness: Music, Race, and Humanity* (Middletown, CT: Wesleyan University Press, 2005), ix.

12. While scholars and journalists frequently use the term *expatriate* to describe the many American painters, composers, performers, and, especially, writers who have relocated to France, Bill Moody argues against employing that term for jazz musicians. Moody contends that most jazz players would have preferred to stay in the United States and moved to Europe only because of the improved professional opportunities. For this reason he designates American jazz musicians abroad as "exiles," cast off from their homeland. Moody's point is well taken. Still, we should recognize that a number of prominent musicians, including Chet Baker and Josephine Baker, clearly preferred their adopted land to the country of their birth. Hence, I suggest we use both terms: *exile* for those living abroad only for professional survival and *expatriate* for those who feel more at home in their new country.

13. Ernest Ansermet, "Sur un Orchestre Negre," *Revue Romande*, Oct. 1919. That piece was later translated by Walter Schapp and published in *Jazz Hot*, Nov./Dec. 1938, 4–9. It has since been reprinted in numerous compilations.

14. See James Reese Europe's account of his successes in Grenville Vernon, "That Mysterious 'Jazz,'" *New York Tribune*, March 30, 1919, sec. 4, p. 5. Reprinted as "A Negro Explains 'Jazz,'" in *Keeping Time: Readings in Jazz History*, ed. Robert Walser (New York: Oxford University Press, 1999), 12–14.

15. For more on the Parisian scene during the Nazi occupation see Michael H. Kater, *Different Drummers: Jazz in the Culture of Nazi Germany* (New York: Oxford University Press, 1992); and the chapter "*Le Jazz-Cold:* The Silent Forties," in Shack, *Harlem in Montmartre*.

16. Illustrating the degree to which France reigned as the most common destination for American jazz performers, Bill Moody compiled a list of one hundred performers who had (have) logged significant time abroad. Of those musicians, forty-nine of them spent at least a portion of their time in France. The five other most common destinations were Germany (sixteen), Sweden (twelve), Denmark (nine), England (eight), and Holland (five) (Moody, *Jazz Exiles*, 173–76). Kevin Whitehead and John Edward Hasse composed a similar register. Of the thirty-one Americans they cited, seventeen had lived in France for at least a part of their time overseas. Whitehead's and Hasse's next most commonly listed countries are Germany (seven), Denmark (six), England (six),

Holland (five) (*Jazz: The First Century*, ed. John Edward Hasse [New York: Morrow, 2000], 180).

17. Quoted in Leonard Feather, "Riffing from Paris to Pinsk," *Rogue,* Jan. 1964, 62 (ellipsis in original).

18. Mike Zwerin, "Django Reinhardt: The King of European Jazz," *International Herald Tribune,* Nov. 10, 2000. There were exceptions to this rule, most notably French bassist Pierre Michelot, who, as early as 1948 (and for decades afterward), provided a solid, swinging foundation for a number of bop-based musicians, including Dexter Gordon, Bud Powell, Kenny Clarke, and Miles Davis.

19. For more on France's Afrophilia during the first half of the twentieth century see Jody Blake, *Le Tumulte Noir: Modernist Art and Popular Entertainment in Jazz-Age Paris, 1900–1930* (University Park: Pennsylvania State University Press, 1999); and Sieglinde Lemke, *Primitivist Modernism: Black Culture and the Origins of Transatlantic Modernism* (New York: Oxford University Press, 1998).

20. George E. Lewis, *A Power Stronger Than Itself: The AACM and American Experimental Music* (Chicago: University of Chicago Press, 2008), 220, 222.

21. Eric Drott, "Free Jazz and the French Critic," *Journal of the American Musicological Society* 61, no. 3 (fall 2008): 541–82, 541–42.

22. Lewis, *A Power Stronger Than Itself,* 247. George McKay uses similar terms, describing the attitude of many European players toward the tradition of a swing feel as "at best an obstacle, at worst a tyranny" (McKay, *Circular Breathing,* 13). E. Taylor Atkins describes the same situation in Japan, where some local jazz musicians found their "liberation" from American dominance through free jazz-inspired models (Atkins, *Blue Nippon,* 225). See also the saxophonist Dave Liebman's comments in Nicholson, *Is Jazz Dead?* 118.

23. Mike Heffley, *Northern Sun, Southern Moon: Europe's Reinvention of Jazz* (New Haven, CT: Yale University Press, 2005), 3–4. Heffley's study stands as the most insightful and comprehensive history of European jazz.

24. See Mike Zwerin, "Jazz in Europe," in *The Oxford Companion to Jazz,* ed. Bill Kirchner (New York: Oxford University Press, 2000), 547.

25. Alexander Gelfand, "No Nostalgia," *Jazziz* 22, no. 12 (Dec. 2005): 28. See also Stuart Nicholson, "Europeans Cut in with a New Jazz Sound and Beat," *New York Times,* June 3, 2001, Arts sec.

26. Michael Felberbaum represents a somewhat unique case. Born in Italy to American parents, Felberbaum attended American schools in Rome before moving to Boston to study guitar at the Berklee College of Music. In many ways he considers Rome "home," but he also recognizes a strong connection to New York, where much of his extended family resides.

27. Government support for the arts in France was codified as early as the Revolution, when composer François-Josef Gossec successfully pushed for a state-sponsored patronage system. Gossec argued, "Who then will encourage

the useful sciences, if not the government, which owes them an existence that in times past was procured for them by the rich and powerful, amateurs in taste and tone?" ("Argumentaire de Gossec et autres," Archives Nationales, A XVIIIe, 384, quoted in Jacques Attali, *Noise: The Political Economy of Music*, trans. Brian Massumi [Minneapolis: University of Minnesota Press, 1985], 56).

28. The Art Ensemble drummer Don Moye recalled a similar interaction when he moved to France in the late 1960s. Moye told George Lewis, "You know the Paris scene, it was people from all over the world. I was playing a lot with the drummers from Guinea, Senegal, and Ivory Coast" (Lewis, *A Power Stronger Than Itself*, 246).

29. Peter Margasak, "Return of a Continental Drifter: SCOTT ROSEN-BERG, Jazzed Again," *Chicago Reader*, Aug. 30, 2002, www.chicagoreader.com/chicago (accessed Jan. 14, 2010).

30. Roberts refers here to the widely used thirty-two-bar, AABA song form of George Gershwin's "I Got Rhythm." Incidentally, Katy Roberts is the only woman I was able to interview in Paris and, indeed, seemed to be one of the few female jazz instrumentalists working regularly in the city at that time. It appears that no matter how one marks jazz's nationality, men continue to dominate the jazz world.

31. These openly pro-American feelings had largely subsided by the time I arrived in Paris eight months after 9/11, and I am told they faded much more as the United States pushed toward war with Iraq in 2003.

32. Monson, *Saying Something*, 203.

33. David Murray quoted in Lloyd Peterson, *Music and the Creative Spirit: Innovators in Jazz, Improvisation, and the Avant Garde* (Lanham, MD: Scarecrow Press, 2006), 212. See also Murray's comments in Dan Ouellette, "The Question Is . . . Where in Europe Is the Best Jazz Being Made?" *DownBeat*, May 2003, 22.

34. This strategy is not exclusive to Paris-based musicians, by the way. The singer Nnenna Freelon limits herself to one performance per year in her hometown of Durham, North Carolina, and saxophonist Jane Bunnett takes a similar approach in Toronto. Both have expressed concerns that appearing more frequently in their respective cities would diminish public perceptions of them as "special" (from talks presented at the Conference of the International Association for Jazz Education, Toronto, Jan. 8–11, 2003). At that same conference the Toronto-based saxophonist Jim Galloway recounted a European tour on which he was billed as "American," because, he said, the concert promoters believed that "Canadian" didn't sell.

INDEX

Note: *Italicized page numbers indicate illustrations.*

Abbate, Carolyn, 18, 154n3
Abrahams, Roger D., 165n6
Adderley, Cannonball, 45, 49, 161–62n23, 172n15
African Americans: African Americanist Paris-based American-born musicians and, 123–24, 126, 135–36, 138, 183n9; black-male authority and, 45–46; black music label for jazz and, 60, 123–24, 131, 166–67n17, 183n9; country music and, 79–80, 170–71n6, 172n15; education and, 108, 113–14; as exiles and expatriates, 126; place and, 94–95, 176nn45–46; Saint John Coltrane African Orthodox Church and, 33–34. *See also* race
"Afro-Blue" (Coltrane), 26–27, 28–30, 32, 36
Ake, David, 180n31, 181n39; *Jazz Cultures*, 12, 153–54n1, 158n41, 165–66n12, 171n8, 175n37, 177–78n1; "Jazz 'Traning'", 153–54n1, 155n13

Alessi, Ralph, 116, 179–80n24
Allen, Eddie, 126, 130, 138–39
alternate takes, and studio recordings, 49, 162n34
America: Americanist Paris-based musicians born in, 123–24, 126, 135–38; "America's classical music" premise and, 4–6, 54, 57–58, 64, 121–22, 165nn10–11; attitudes toward, 134, 186n31; Canadian musicians and, 6, 186n34; musicians' perspectives on, 138–39; white Americans and, 94–95, 100–101, 113, 124, 126, 132–36, 138, 176n45. *See also* African Americans; Paris-based American-born musicians
American Garage (Pat Metheny Group), 95–98, 176n47
American Musicological Society, 178n3
Anderson, Iain, 156n21, 177n55
Ansermet, Ernest, 125, 184n13
Armstrong, Lil, 170n5
Armstrong, Louis, 4, 8, 47–48, 71, 170n5
Art Ensemble of Chicago, 124, 127, 185n28
arts/artists: artist-equals-the-art phenomenon and, 18, 29, 44, 161n19; context

arts/artists: (continued)
for, 1–2, 151n3; "New Thing" artists,
93, 115, 127; Paris-based American-
born musicians and, 130, 185–86n27;
work as art and, 52–53, 164n45
Ascension (Coltrane), 32–35, 158n56
"Ascension" (Coltrane), 32–33, 35, 36,
158n43, 158n45
assimilationist Paris-based American-born
musicians, 124, 132–35, 138
Atkins, Chet, 89, 170n5
Atkins, E. Taylor, 122, 183n5, 185n22
Attali, Jacques, 38, 160n5, 185–86n27
Austerlitz, Paul, 153n25, 184n11
Ayler, Albert, 63, 127

Bach, J. S., 5, 21–22
Bailey, Buster, 52–53, 164n43
Baker, Chet, 18, 44, 63, 154n6, 184n12
Baker, Josephine, 125–26, 184n12
Bakhtin, Mikhail: carnivalesque aesthetic
and, 54–58, 67, 69–70, 73, 165n8,
168n26; publications of, 164n2,
165n6, 165n7, 168n26, 168n30, 168n34,
169n44
Ballamy, Ian, 174n32
Balliett, Whitney, 29, 30, 157n33
Band (group), 172n14
bands and band directors, 112–13, 180n31
Baraka, Amiri (Leroi Jones), 60, 156n23,
167n19
Basie, Count, 8, 47, 50, 69, 70, 170–71n6
Beale, Charles, 107, 179n14
Beame, Abraham, 177n52
Beauchamp, Lincoln T., Jr., 184n10
bebop aesthetic: about, 11, 19–20, 106, 112;
Coltrane's performances informed
by, 20–24, 26; education and, 107–8;
Paris jazz performances informed
by, 126–29, 132–33, 136–37, 185n18;
pastoral style jazz performances and,
83, 86, 92; as urban, 86
Bechet, Sidney, 165n6
Becker, Howard S., 2, 112, 151n4, 164n1,
180n30
becoming subjectivities, 24–26, 31
Beethoven, Ludwig van, 5, 29–30, 53

being subjectivities, 18–24, 31, 36, 154n7,
155n8, 155n14
Belamy, Ian, 174n32
Bella Martha (Mostly Martha; film),
174n29
Belonging (Jarrett), 86, 173n27
Beneath the Underdog (Mingus), 59, 166n14
Benjamin, Adam, 118
Berger, Karol, 21–22, 155n16
Bergeson, Pat, 171n8
Berklee College of Music, 89, 104–5, 106,
115–16
Berliner, Paul, 155n10, 156n20
Bernstein, Steven, 59–61, 63–64, 67–68,
70–72
Birdland, 27–30, 110
Birnbaum, Larry, 91, 175n38
Bissett, Jessica, 113, 141, 180n32
Bivens, Ollie, 166–67n17
black Americans. *See* African Americans
black music label for jazz, 60, 123–24, 131,
166–67n17, 183n9
Blake, Jody, 185n19
Blakey, Art, 163n37, 172n15
Blazing Saddles (film), 170–71n6
Bley, Carla, 63, 72, 180n31
Block, Ron, 171n8
Block, Steven, 158n45
Bloom, Harold, 151n3
body, performance of musical, 43, 50–53,
163–64n41
bop aesthetic. *See* bebop aesthetic
Borgo, David, 153n25, 156n20, 161n17,
177–78n1
Bourque, Fred, 177n56
Bowie, Lester, 63, 71, 124, 184n10
Boyd, Bruce, 153n23
Boym, Svetlana, 99, 177n51
Brackett, David, 163n38
Braunstein, Peter, 171–72n12
Breau, Lenny, 170n5
Brecker, Michael, 93
Brown, David, 169–70n1
Brown, Marion, 158n43
Browne, Larry, 130
Brubeck, Dave, 8, 100, 177n57
Bryan, William Jennings, 175n35

improvisation aesthetic, 46, 81, 100, 104, 107, 115, 155n14, 162n29

income, and economic success: for musicians, 7, 9, 117–18, 152n13, 182n45; for Paris-based American-born musicians, 123, 126, 129–30, 137

innovation myth, 115–16, 181n41

International Association for the Study of Popular Music, 178n3

Iyer, Vijay, 153n25, 156n22

Jackson, Jeffrey H., 123–24, 183n9

Jamal, Ahmad, 10

Janowiack, John, 71–72, 169n40

Jarrett, Keith: *Belonging*, 86, 173n27; biographical information about, 83; "Country," 86–87, 174nn29; European-born musicians and, 128; "Great Bird," 174n31; innovation and, 115; *Keith Jarrett*, 174n30; *Köln Concert*, 173n24; "Memories of Tomorrow," 173n24; *My Song*, 86, 87, 174n32, 175n39; "My Song," 175n39; Native American lore and, 174n31; pastoral style in America and stylistic shifts played by, 83, 85–88, 95, 176n47; "Sundance," 174n31; vocalizations during studio recordings of, 163n37; "The Wind Up," 176n47; "Yaqui Indian Song," 174n31

Jazz (documentary), 70, 72, 91, 101, 106, 168–69n35, 179n13, 183n4

Jazz Cultures (Ake), 12, 153–54n1, 158n41, 165–66n12, 171n8, 175n37, 177–78n1

Jazz Forum's Record of the Year Award, 173n27

Jazz Styles (Gridley), 105–6

"Jazz 'Traning" (Ake), 153–54n1, 155n13

Jefferson, Thomas, 82

Jeffri, Joan, 152–53n20

Jeffries, Herb, 170–71n6

Johnson, Bruce, 121, 180n26, 183n2

Johnson, Dewey, 158n43

Johnson, Mark, 43, 160n16

Johnson, Peter, 155n18

Jones, Elvin, 27, 31, 35–36, 158n43, 163n37

Jones, Leroi (Amiri Baraka), 60, 156n23, 167n19

Jones, Norah, 78, 80, 88, 175n39

Jones, Philly Joe, 159n1

Jost, Ekkehard, 20, 32, 155n12, 158n44

Kahn, Ashley, 178n7

Kater, Michael H., 184n15

Katz, Mark, 155n8, 161n21

Keil, Charles, 19, 155n9

Keith Jarrett: The Art of Improvisation (documentary), 174n30

Kelly, Wynton, 37, 44, 159n1

Kennedy, Al, 179n22

Kennedy, Gary, 108–9, 115, 116, 179n21

Kenny G., 181n38

Kenton, Stan, 59, 100, 115

Kind of Blue (Davis), 49, 159–60n4, 163n36

King, Bishop Franzo, 34–35

Kirchner, Bill, 107

Kirk, Andrew G., 173n21

Kirk, Rahsaan Roland, 53, 72, 164n44

KneeBody, 118, 119, 182n49

Knitting Factory, 59, 60, 64, 72, 110

Kofsky, Frank, 34, 156n21, 158n52

"KoKo" (Parker), 19, 21, 154n7

Köln Concert (Jarrett), 173n24

Konitz, Lee, 182n50

Krall, Diana, 78, 170n3

Kramer, Jonathan D., 153n22

Kramer, Lawrence, 25, 157n28

Krauss, Briggan, 63, 67, 166n16, 171n8, 179–80n24

Krims, Adam, 163n39

Kross, Mark, 182n46

Kundera, Milan, 1–2, 73, 151n1, 151n3, 169n43

Lacy, Steve, 133

Lamb, Bill, 168n28

Lange, Art, 174n30

language choice, and identity, 133–34

laughter, 55–56, 64–66, 71–73, 164n45, 168n26

Led Zeppelin, 173n20

Le Guin, Elisabeth, 52, 164n42

Lemke, Sieglinde, 185n19

Leppert, Richard, 39, 77, 160n6, 161n21, 170n2

"Lester Leaps In" (Bassie and Young), 47, 50

levels of gigs, 7, 152n13

Levy, Beth, 171n11

Lewis, George E., 127, 128, 153n25, 160n14, 184n10, 185n20, 185n22, 186n28

Lewis, John, 4, 64, 73

Leyshon, Andrew, 171n11

Liebman, David, 119, 177n53, 185n22

Litweiler, John, 175n41

Live at Birdland (Coltrane), 26, 27–30, 32, 36, 157n29

Lloyd, Charles, 83, 99, 173n18

Lott, Eric, 156n23

lower strata, and carnivalesque aesthetic, 59–64, *61, 62,* 167n20, 167n22

"Macarena" (Sex Mob), 66–68

Macero, Teo, 38, 159–60n4

"Mack the Knife" (Fitzgerald), 47–48, 50, 162nn31–32

Mack the Knife (Fitzgerald), 162n30

Magee, Jeffrey, 153n23

Mailer, Norman, 167n19

Malbert, Roger, 73, 165n7, 169n42

Mangione, Chuck, 181n38

Marcus, Greil, 95, 176n46

Margasak, Peter, 131, 186n29

market forces myth, 116–19, 181n44, 182n45, 182n50

Marsalis, Wynton, 4, 5, 49, 69–70, 71, 152n8, 169n37

Martin, Henry, 106, 179n12

Martin, Peter J., 162n29

Mather, Olivia, 83, 172n16, 173n20

Mathieu, Bill, 33, 158n48

Matless, David, 171n11

Mays, Lyle, 92, 95–96, 176n47, 177n50

McCaslin Donny, 179–80n24

McClary, Susan, 40–42, 160n9, 160n15, 161n21, 163n40, 164n42, 165n5

McClung, Tom, 130

McCraven, Steven, 130, 131, 134

McDonald, Michael Bruce, 33–35, 158n49, 158n54

McDonough, John, 181n44

McKay, George, 165n5, 183n5, 185n22

media, 3, 7, 41–42, 57, 114, 181n38

"Memories of Tomorrow" (Jarrett), 173n24

men: black-male authority and, 45–46; jazz masculinity and, 22, 114, 156n20, 169n37, 181n37. *See also* African Americans; white Americans

Metheny, Pat: *American Garage* (Pat Metheny Group), 95–98, *97, 98,* 176n47; biographical information about, 88–89, 174n33, 175n39; Coleman, Ornette and, 175–76n44; digital recording technology and, 175–76n44; *80/81,* 92–95; European-born musicians and, 128; guitar heroes and, 88–89; *New Chautauqua,* 89–92, *90, 94,* 175n35, 175n37; pastoral style in America and, 88, 89–91, 92–95, 175–76n44; Pat Metheny Group and, 95–98, 100, 176n47; *Pat Metheny Songbook,* 175n42; race and, 100; as sideman, 174n33; *Song X* (Coleman) and, 175–76n44; stylistic shifts and, 88; "Two Folk Songs," 92–94; "The Wind Up" (Jarrett), 176n47

Michelot, Pierre, 185n18

Milkowski, Bill, 176n49, 177n54, 182n48

Miller, Miles D., 167n22

Miller, Timothy, 172n13

Milne, Andy, 116

Mingus, Charles: *Beneath the Underdog,* 59, 166n14; black-male authority and, 45; country music and, 172n15; humor and, 65–66, 68; jazz discourses and, 59; Mingus Big Band, 180n31; *Mingus Presents Mingus,* 45, 161–62n23; pedagogy discourse and, 104–5; politics and, 23; styles of, 30

Mobley, Hank, 44, 159n1

Monder, Ben, 116, 147

Monheit, Jane, 78, 170n3

Monk, Thelonious, 7, 65

Monson, Ingrid: being subjectivities and, 18; on hipness aesthetic, 113–14; on politics, 8; publications by, 152n16, 154n4, 155n9, 156nn20–21, 156n23, 157n26, 168n25, 180nn33–34, 183n9, 186n32; on "universalist" position, 135

Moody, Bill, 183n7, 184n12, 184–85n16

Moore, Brew, 126

Twain, Mark, 175n35
"Two Folk Songs" (Metheny), 92–94
Tyner, McCoy, 25–26, 28, 31, 35–36, 158n43

unintended sounds: aesthetic of imperfections and, 46–50; audio media phenomena and, 41–42; "the creak" in "Old Folks" (Davis) and, 37–39, 41–42, 46, 49–50, 159–60n4; *Kind of Blue* (Davis), 49, 159–60n4; "Mack the Knife" (Fitzgerald) and, 47–48, 50, 162nn31–32; musical values and practices and, 45–46; performance of musical body and, 43, 50–53, 163–64n41; prestige and, 50; rock music recordings with, 39; scholarship and, 39–40, 53; studio recordings and, 41; vocalizations during studio recordings and, 50, 163n37
United States. *See* America
"universalist" position, 135
UNR (University of Nevada), 11, 118–19, 180n29
urban place, 77–78, 86, 110–11

value judgments, about jazz, 5–7, 152n9, 152n11
Vernon, Grenville, 184n14
Versace, Gary, 182n50
Village Vanguard, 28, 29, 53, 110
vocalizations during studio recordings, 50, 163n37
Von Glahn, Denise, 171n11
Vu, Cuong, 179–80n24

Wade, Bonnie, 154n7
Wald, Elijah, 162n25, 170–71n6
Walker, Paul, 155n15
Walser, Robert: carnivalesque aesthetic and, 69; publications of, 151–52n7, 152n16, 161nn17–18, 163n40, 164–65n4, 165nn9–10, 167n22, 168n33, 180n30, 184n14
Washburne, Christopher J., 153n25, 168n29, 168n33
Waters, Keith, 106, 179n12
Watts, Alan, 159n57

Way Out West (Rollins), *79,* 79–80, 170–71n6
Webb, Jack, 175–76n45
Weber, Eberhard, 128, 174n33
Weiner, Norbert, 167n20
Welding, Pete, 153–54n1
The Well-Tempered Clavier (Bach), 21–22
West, Cornel, 12, 153n27, 156n22
Whitburn, Joel, 160n10
White, Andrew, 31–32, 34, 158n41
White, James, 180n36
white Americans, 94–95, 100–101, 113, 124, 126, 132–36, 138, 176n45. *See also* race
Whitehead, Kevin, 184–85n16
Wild, David, 158n43
Williams, Martin, 29–30, 157n34
Williams, Tony, 159n1
Wilmington, Michael, 174n29
Wilson, Cassandra, 78, 170n3
Wilson, Peter Niklas, 175n41
"The Wind Up" (Jarrett), 176n47
Woideck, Carl, 158n52, 159–60n4, 178n7
Wolfe, Tom, 84, 173n19
Wolleson, Kenny, 67–68, 149, 166n16
women, and jazz, 78, 114, 170n3. See also *specific female singers*
Wood, Nate, 118
Woodstock, New York, 84, 177n53
work, as art, 52–53, 164n45

Yanow, Scott, 156n23
"Yaqui Indian Song" (Jarrett), 174n31
Yellowjackets, 181n38
Young, Lester, 47, 50, 65, 112, 127, 157n30

Zabor, Rafi, 82, 175n40
Zaehner, R. C., 159n57
Zak, Albin, 160n7
Zawinul, Joe, 172n15, 178n7
Zénon, Miguel, 179–80n24
Zwerin, Mike, 185n18, 185n24

Text: 11.25/13.5 Adobe Garamond
Display: Adobe Garamond and Perpetua
Compositor: BookComp, Inc.
Printer and binder: Maple-Vail Book Manufacturing Group